Essentials
of Psychological Assessment Series

W9-BZY-699

Everything you need to know to administer, score, and interpret the major psychological tests.

I'd like to order the following *Essentials of Psychological Assessment:*

- [ ] WAIS®-IV Assessment (w/CD-ROM) / 978-0-471-73846-6 • $48.95
- [ ] WJ III™ Cognitive Abilities Assessment, Second Edition / 978-0-470-56664-0 • $38.95
- [ ] Cross-Battery Assessment, Second Edition (w/CD-ROM) / 978-0-471-75771-9 • $48.95
- [ ] Nonverbal Assessment / 978-0-471-38318-5 • $38.95
- [ ] PAI® Assessment / 978-0-471-08463-1 • $38.95
- [ ] CAS Assessment / 978-0-471-29015-5 • $38.95
- [ ] MMPI®-2 Assessment, Second Edition / 978-0-470-92323-8 • $38.95
- [ ] Myers-Briggs Type Indicator® Assessment, Second Edition / 978-0-470-34390-6 • $38.95
- [ ] Rorschach® Assessment / 978-0-471-33146-9 • $38.95
- [ ] Millon™ Inventories Assessment, Third Edition / 978-0-470-16862-2 • $38.95
- [ ] TAT and Other Storytelling Assessments, Second Edition / 978-0-470-28192-5 • $38.95
- [ ] MMPI-A™ Assessment / 978-0-471-39815-8 • $38.95
- [ ] NEPSY®-II Assessment / 978-0-470-43691-2 • $38.95
- [ ] Neuropsychological Assessment, Second Edition / 978-0-470-43747-6 • $38.95
- [ ] WJ III™ Tests of Achievement Assessment / 978-0-471-33059-2 • $38.95
- [ ] Evidence-Based Academic Interventions / 978-0-470-20632-4 • $38.95
- [ ] WRAML2 and TOMAL-2 Assessment / 978-0-470-17911-6 • $38.95
- [ ] WMS®-IV Assessment / 978-0-470-62196-7 • $38.95
- [ ] Behavioral Assessment / 978-0-471-35367-6 • $38.95
- [ ] Forensic Psychological Assessment, Second Edition / 978-0-470-55168-4 • $38.95
- [ ] Bayley Scales of Infant Development II Assessment / 978-0-471-32651-9 • $38.95
- [ ] Career Interest Assessment / 978-0-471-35365-2 • $38.95
- [ ] WPPSI™-III Assessment / 978-0-471-28895-4 • $38.95
- [ ] 16PF® Assessment / 978-0-471-23424-1 • $38.95
- [ ] Assessment Report Writing / 978-0-471-39487-7 • $38.95
- [ ] Stanford-Binet Intelligence Scales (SB5) Assessment / 978-0-471-22404-4 • $38.95
- [ ] WISC®-IV Assessment, Second Edition (w/CD-ROM) / 978-0-470-18915-3 • $48.95
- [ ] KABC-II Assessment / 978-0-471-66733-9 • $38.95
- [ ] WIAT®-III and KTEA-II Assessment (w/CD-ROM) / 978-0-470-55169-1 • $48.95
- [ ] Processing Assessment / 978-0 471-71925-0 • $38.95
- [ ] School Neuropsychological Assessment / 978-0-471-78372-5 • $38.95
- [ ] Cognitive Assessment with KAIT & Other Kaufman Measures / 978-0-471-38317-8 • $38.95
- [ ] Assessment with Brief Intelligence Tests / 978-0-471-26412-5 • $38.95
- [ ] Creativity Assessment / 978-0-470-13742-0 • $38.95
- [ ] WNV™ Assessment / 978-0-470-28467-4 • $38.95
- [ ] DAS-II® Assessment (w/CD-ROM) / 978-0-470-22520-2 • $48.95
- [ ] Executive Function Assessment (w/CD-ROM) / 978-0-470-42202-1 • $48.95
- [ ] Conners Behavior Assessments™ / 978-0-470-34633-4 • $38.95
- [ ] Temperament Assessment / 978-0-470-44447-4 • $38.95
- [ ] Response to Intervention / 978-0-470-56663-3 • $38.95
- [ ] Specific Learning Disability Identification / 978-0-470-58760-7 • $38.95
- [ ] IDEA for Assessment Professionals (w/CD-ROM) / 978-0-470-87392-2 • $48.95
- [ ] Dyslexia Assessment and Intervention / 978-0-470-92760-1 • $38.95
- [ ] Autism Spectrum Disorders Evaluation and Assessment / 978-0-470-62194-3 • $38.95

Please complete the order form on the back.
To order by phone, call toll free 1-877-762-2974
To order online: www.wiley.com/essentials
To order by mail: refer to order form on next page

of **Psychological Assessment** Series

ORDER FORM

Please send this order form with your payment (credit card or check) to:
John Wiley & Sons, Attn: J. Knott, 111 River Street, Hoboken, NJ 07030-5774

QUANTITY	TITLE	ISBN	PRICE
_____	_____	_____	_____
_____	_____	_____	_____
_____	_____	_____	_____
_____	_____	_____	_____
_____	_____	_____	_____

Shipping Charges:	Surface	2-Day	1-Day
First item	$5.00	$10.50	$17.50
Each additional item	$3.00	$3.00	$4.00

For orders greater than 15 items,
please contact Customer Care at 1-877-762-2974.

ORDER AMOUNT _____

SHIPPING CHARGES _____

SALES TAX _____

TOTAL ENCLOSED _____

NAME_____

AFFILIATION_____

ADDRESS_____

CITY/STATE/ZIP _____

TELEPHONE _____

EMAIL_____

❏ Please add me to your e-mailing list

PAYMENT METHOD:

❏ Check/Money Order   ❏ Visa   ❏ Mastercard   ❏ AmEx

Card Number _____ Exp. Date _____

Cardholder Name *(Please print)* _____

Signature _____

*Make checks payable to **John Wiley & Sons**. Credit card orders invalid if not signed.*
All orders subject to credit approval. • Prices subject to change.

To order by phone, call toll free 1-877-762-2974
To order online: www.wiley.com/essentials

Essentials of Research Design and Methodology

Essentials of Behavioral Science Series

Founding Editors, Alan S. Kaufman and Nadeen L. Kaufman

Essentials

of Research Design

and Methodology

Geoffrey Marczyk

David DeMatteo

David Festinger

 John Wiley & Sons, Inc.

Published by John Wiley & Sons, Inc., Hoboken, New Jersey.
Published simultaneously in Canada.

Limit of Liability/Disclaimer of Warranty: While the publisher and author have used their best efforts in preparing this book, they make no representations or warranties with respect to the accuracy or completeness of the contents of this book and specifically disclaim any implied warranties of merchantability or fitness for a particular purpose. No warranty may be created or extended by sales representatives or written sales materials. The advice and strategies contained herein may not be suitable for your situation. You should consult with a professional where appropriate. Neither the publisher nor author shall be liable for any loss of profit or any other commercial damages, including but not limited to special, incidental, consequential, or other damages.

This publication is designed to provide accurate and authoritative information in regard to the subject matter covered. It is sold with the understanding that the publisher is not engaged in rendering professional services. If legal, accounting, medical, psychological or any other expert assistance is required, the services of a competent professional person should be sought.

Designations used by companies to distinguish their products are often claimed as trademarks. In all instances where John Wiley & Sons, Inc. is aware of a claim, the product names appear in initial capital or all capital letters. Readers, however, should contact the appropriate companies for more complete information regarding trademarks and registration.

For general information on our other products and services please contact our Customer Care Department within the United States at (800) 762-2974, outside the United States at (317) 572-3993 or fax (317) 572-4002.

Wiley also publishes its books in a variety of electronic formats. Some content that appears in print may not be available in electronic books. For more information about Wiley products, visit our website at www.wiley.com.

Library of Congress Cataloging-in-Publication Data:

Marczyk, Geoffrey R., 1964–
    Essentials of research design and methodology/Geoffrey Marczyk, David DeMatteo,
    David Festinger.
        p. cm.—(Essentials of behavioral science series)
    Includes bibliographical references and index.
    ISBN 978-0-471-47053-3 (pbk.)
        1. Psychology—Research—Methodology. I. DeMatteo, David, 1972– II. Festinger, David.
    III. Title. IV. Series.
BF76.5.M317 2005
150′.72—dc22   2004058384

10   9   8

To Helene and my family

G.M.

To Christina and Emma

D.D.

To Tracy, Ashley, and Elijah

D.F.

CONTENTS

I n the *Essentials of Behavioral Science* series, our goal is to provide readers with books that will deliver key practical information in an efficient, accessible style. The series features books on a variety of topics, such as statistics, psychological testing, and research design and methodology, to name just a few. For the experienced professional, books in the series offer a concise yet thorough review of a specific area of expertise, including numerous tips for best practices. Students can turn to series books for a clear and concise overview of the important topics in which they must become proficient to practice skillfully, efficiently, and ethically in their chosen fields.

Wherever feasible, visual cues highlighting key points are utilized alongside systematic, step-by-step guidelines. Chapters are focused and succinct. Topics are organized for an easy understanding of the essential material related to a particular topic. Theory and research are continually woven into the fabric of each book, but always to enhance the practical application of the material, rather than to sidetrack or overwhelm readers. With this series, we aim to challenge and assist readers in the behavioral sciences to aspire to the highest level of competency by arming them with the tools they need for knowledgeable, informed practice.

The purposes of *Essentials of Research Design and Methodology* are to discuss the various types of research designs that are commonly used, the basic process by which research studies are conducted, the research-related considerations of which researchers should be aware, the manner in which the results of research can be interpreted and disseminated, and the typical pitfalls faced by researchers when designing and conducting a research study. This book is ideal for those readers with minimal knowledge of research as well as for those readers with intermediate knowledge who need a quick refresher regarding particular aspects of research design and methodology. For those readers with an advanced knowledge of research design and methodology, this book can be used as a concise summary of basic research techniques and principles, or as an adjunct to a more advanced research methodology and design textbook. Finally, even for those readers who do not conduct research, this book will become a valuable addition to your bookcase because it will assist you in becoming a more educated consumer of research. Being able to evaluate the appropriateness of a research design or the conclusions drawn from a particular research study will become increasingly more important as research becomes more accessible to nonscientists. In that regard, this book will improve your ability to efficiently and effectively digest and understand the results of a research study.

Alan S. Kaufman, PhD, and Nadeen L. Kaufman, EdD, Founding Editors
Yale University School of Medicine

ACKNOWLEDGMENTS

We would like to thank Karen Dugosh and Audrey Cleary for their helpful comments on earlier drafts of this book. We would also like to thank Susan Matties for her research assistance. Additional thanks go to Dr. Virginia Brabender for introducing us to John Wiley and Sons. Finally we'd like to thank Tracey Belmont, our editor, for her support and sense of humor.

Essentials of Research Design and Methodology

One

INTRODUCTION AND OVERVIEW

Progress in almost every field of science depends on the contributions made by systematic research; thus research is often viewed as the cornerstone of scientific progress. Broadly defined, the purpose of research is to answer questions and acquire new knowledge. Research is the primary tool used in virtually all areas of science to expand the frontiers of knowledge. For example, research is used in such diverse scientific fields as psychology, biology, medicine, physics, and botany, to name just a few of the areas in which research makes valuable contributions to what we know and how we think about things. Among other things, by conducting research, researchers attempt to reduce the complexity of problems, discover the relationship between seemingly unrelated events, and ultimately improve the way we live.

Although research studies are conducted in many diverse fields of science, the general goals and defining characteristics of research are typically the same across disciplines. For example, across all types of science, research is frequently used for describing a thing or event, discovering the relationship between phenomena, or making predictions about future events. In short, research can be used for the purposes of description, explanation, and prediction, all of which make important and valuable contributions to the expansion of what we know and how we live our lives. In addition to sharing similar broad goals, scientific research in virtually all fields of study shares certain defining characteristics, including testing hypotheses, careful observation and measurement, systematic evaluation of data, and drawing valid conclusions.

In recent years, the results of various research studies have taken center stage in the popular media. No longer is research the private domain of research professors and scientists wearing white lab coats. To the contrary, the results of research studies are frequently reported on the local evening news, CNN, the Internet, and various other media outlets that are accessible to both scientists and nonscientists alike. For example, in recent years, we have all become familiar with research regarding the effects of stress on our psychological well-being, the health benefits of a low-cholesterol diet, the effects of exercise in preventing certain forms of cancer, which automobiles are safest to drive, and the deleterious effects of pollution on global warming. We may have even become familiar with research studies regarding the human genome, the Mars Land Rover, the use of stem cells, and genetic cloning. Not too long ago, it was unlikely that the results of such highly scientific research studies would have been shared with the general public to such a great extent.

Despite the accessibility and prevalence of research in today's society, many people share common misperceptions about exactly what research is, how research can be used, what research can tell us, and the limitations of research. For some people, the term "research" conjures up images of scientists in laboratories watching rats run through mazes or mixing chemicals in test tubes. For other people, the term "research" is associated with telemarketer surveys, or people approaching them at the local shopping mall to "just ask you a few questions about your shopping habits." In actuality, these stereotypical examples of research are only a small part of what research comprises. It is therefore not surprising that many people are unfamiliar with the various types of research designs, the basics of how research is conducted, what research can be used for, and the limits of using research to answer questions and acquire new knowledge. Rapid Reference 1.1 discusses what we mean by "research" from a scientific perspective.

Before addressing these important issues, however, we should first briefly review what science is and how it goes about telling us what we know.

≣ Rapid Reference 1.1

What Exactly is Research?

Research studies come in many different forms, and we will discuss several of these forms in more detail in Chapter 5. For now, however, we will focus on two of the most common types of research—*correlational* research and *experimental* research.

Correlational research: In *correlational research,* the goal is to determine whether two or more variables are related. (By the way, "variables" is a term with which you should be familiar. A *variable* is anything that can take on different values, such as weight, time, and height.) For example, a researcher may be interested in determining whether age is related to weight. In this example, a researcher may discover that age is indeed related to weight because as age increases, weight also increases. If a correlation between two variables is strong enough, knowing about one variable allows a researcher to make a prediction about the other variable. There are several different types of correlations, which will be discussed in more detail in Chapter 5. It is important to point out, however, that a correlation—or relationship—between two things does not necessarily mean that one thing caused the other. To draw a cause-and-effect conclusion, researchers must use experimental research. This point will be emphasized throughout this book.

Experimental research: In its simplest form, *experimental research* involves comparing two groups on one outcome measure to test some hypothesis regarding causation. For example, if a researcher is interested in the effects of a new medication on headaches, the researcher would randomly divide a group of people with headaches into two groups. One of the groups, the *experimental group,* would receive the new medication being tested. The other group, the *control group,* would receive a placebo medication (i.e., a medication containing a harmless substance, such as sugar, that has no physiological effects). Besides receiving the different medications, the groups would be treated exactly the same so that the research could isolate the effects of the medications. After receiving the medications, both groups would be compared to see whether people in the experimental group had fewer headaches than people in the control group. Assuming this study was properly designed (and properly designed studies will be discussed in detail in later chapters), if people in the experimental group had fewer headaches than people in the control group, the researcher could conclude that the new medication reduces headaches.

OVERVIEW OF SCIENCE AND THE SCIENTIFIC METHOD

In simple terms, *science* can be defined as a methodological and systematic approach to the acquisition of new knowledge. This definition of science highlights some of the key differences between how scientists and non-scientists go about acquiring new knowledge. Specifically, rather than relying on mere casual observations and an informal approach to learn about the world, scientists attempt to gain new knowledge by making careful observations and using systematic, controlled, and methodical approaches (Shaughnessy & Zechmeister, 1997). By doing so, scientists are able to draw valid and reliable conclusions about what they are studying. In addition, scientific knowledge is not based on the opinions, feelings, or intuition of the scientist. Instead, scientific knowledge is based on objective data that were reliably obtained in the context of a carefully designed research study. In short, scientific knowledge is based on the accumulation of empirical evidence (Kazdin, 2003a), which will be the topic of a great deal of discussion in later chapters of this book.

The defining characteristic of scientific research is the scientific method (summarized in Rapid Reference 1.2). First described by the English philosopher and scientist Roger Bacon in the 13th century, it is still generally agreed that the scientific method is the basis for all scientific investigation. The *scientific method* is best thought of as an approach to the acquisition of new knowledge, and this approach effectively distinguishes science from nonscience. To be clear, the scientific method is not actually a single method, as the name would erroneously lead one to believe, but rather an overarching perspective on how scientific investigations should proceed. It is a set of research principles and methods that helps researchers obtain valid results from their research studies. Because the scientific method deals with the general *approach* to research rather than the *content* of specific research studies, it is used by researchers in all different scientific disciplines. As will be seen in the following sections, the biggest benefit of the scientific method is that it provides a set of clear and agreed-upon guidelines for gathering, evaluating, and reporting information in the context of a research study (Cozby, 1993).

≋ Rapid Reference 1.2

The Scientific Method

The development of the scientific method is usually credited to Roger Bacon, a philosopher and scientist from 13th-century England, although some argue that the Italian scientist Galileo Galilei played an important role in formulating the scientific method. Later contributions to the scientific method were made by the philosophers Francis Bacon and René Descartes. Although some disagreement exists regarding the exact characteristics of the scientific method, most agree that it is characterized by the following elements:

• Empirical approach
• Observations
• Questions
• Hypotheses
• Experiments
• Analyses
• Conclusions
• Replication

There has been some disagreement among researchers over the years regarding the elements that compose the scientific method. In fact, some researchers have even argued that it is impossible to define a universal approach to scientific investigation. Nevertheless, for over 100 years, the scientific method has been the defining feature of scientific research. Researchers generally agree that the scientific method is composed of the following key elements (which will be the focus of the remainder of this chapter): an empirical approach, observations, questions, hypotheses, experiments, analyses, conclusions, and replication.

Before proceeding any further, one word of caution is necessary. In the brief discussion of the scientific method that follows, we will be introducing several new terms and concepts that are related to research design and methodology. Do not be intimidated if you are unfamiliar with some of the content contained in this discussion. The purpose of the following is simply to set the stage for the chapters that follow, and we will be elaborating on each of the terms and concepts throughout the remainder of the book.

Empirical Approach

The scientific method is firmly based on the empirical approach. The *empirical approach* is an evidence-based approach that relies on direct observation and experimentation in the acquisition of new knowledge (see Kazdin, 2003a). In the empirical approach, scientific decisions are made based on the data derived from direct observation and experimentation. Contrast this approach to decision making with the way that most nonscientific decisions are made in our daily lives. For example, we have all made decisions based on feelings, hunches, or "gut" instinct. Additionally, we may often reach conclusions or make decisions that are not necessarily based on data, but rather on opinions, speculation, and a hope for the best. The empirical approach, with its emphasis on direct, systematic, and careful observation, is best thought of as the guiding principle behind all research conducted in accordance with the scientific method.

Observations

An important component in any scientific investigation is observation. In this sense, *observation* refers to two distinct concepts—being aware of the world around us and making careful measurements. Observations of the world around us often give rise to the questions that are addressed through scientific research. For example, the Newtonian observation that apples fall from trees stimulated much research into the effects of gravity. Therefore, a keen eye to your surroundings can often provide you with many ideas for research studies. We will discuss the generation of research ideas in more detail in Chapter 2.

In the context of science, observation means more than just observing the world around us to get ideas for research. *Observation* also refers to the process of making careful and accurate measurements, which is a distinguishing feature of well-conducted scientific investigations. When making measurements in the context of research, scientists typically take great precautions to avoid making biased observations. For example, if a researcher is observing the amount of time that passes between two events, such as the length of time that elapses between lightning and thunder, it would certainly be advisable for the researcher to use a measurement device that has a high degree of accuracy and reliability. Rather than simply trying to "guesstimate" the amount of time that elapsed between those two events, the researcher would be advised to use a stopwatch or similar measurement device. By doing so, the researcher ensures that the measurement is accurate and not biased by extraneous factors. Most people would likely agree that the observations that we make in our daily lives are rarely made so carefully or systematically.

An important aspect of measurement is an *operational definition*. Researchers define key concepts and terms in the context of their research studies by using operational definitions. By using operational definitions, researchers ensure that everyone is talking about the same phenomenon. For example, if a researcher wants to study the effects of exercise on stress levels, it would be necessary for the researcher to define what "exercise" is. Does exercise refer to jogging, weight lifting, swimming, jumping rope, or all of the above? By defining "exercise" for the purposes of the study, the researcher makes sure that everyone is referring to the same thing. Clearly, the definition of "exercise" can differ from one study to another, so it is crucial that the researcher define "exercise" in a precise manner in the context of his or her study. Having a clear definition of terms also ensures that the researcher's study can be replicated by other researchers. The importance of operational definitions will be discussed further in Chapter 2.

Questions

After getting a research idea, perhaps from making observations of the world around us, the next step in the research process involves translating that research idea into an answerable question. The term "answerable" is particularly important in this respect, and it should not be overlooked. It would obviously be a frustrating and ultimately unrewarding endeavor to attempt to answer an unanswerable research question through scientific investigation. An example of an unanswerable research question is the following: "Is there an exact replica of me in another universe?" Although this is certainly an intriguing question that would likely yield important information, the current state of science cannot provide an answer to that question. It is therefore important to formulate a research question that can be answered through available scientific methods and procedures. One might ask, for example, whether exercising (i.e., perhaps operationally defined as running three times per week for 30 minutes each time) reduces cholesterol levels. This question could be researched and answered using established scientific methods.

Hypotheses

The next step in the scientific method is coming up with a *hypothesis,* which is simply an educated—and testable—guess about the answer to your research question. A hypothesis is often described as an attempt by the researcher to explain the phenomenon of interest. Hypotheses can take various forms, depending on the question being asked and the type of study being conducted (see Rapid Reference 1.3).

A key feature of all hypotheses is that each must make a *prediction.* Remember that hypotheses are the researcher's attempt to explain the phenomenon being studied, and that explanation should involve a prediction about the variables being studied. These predictions are then tested by gathering and analyzing data, and the hypotheses can either be supported or refuted (falsified; see Rapid Reference 1.4) on the basis of the data.

In their simplest forms, hypotheses are typically phrased as "if-then" statements. For example, a researcher may hypothesize that "*if* people exercise for 30 minutes per day at least three days per week, *then* their cholesterol levels will be reduced." This hypothesis makes a prediction about the effects of exercising on levels of cholesterol, and the prediction can be tested by gathering and analyzing data.

Two types of hypotheses with which you should be familiar are the null

≋Rapid Reference 1.3

Relationship Between Hypotheses and Research Design

Hypotheses can take many different forms depending on the type of research design being used. Some hypotheses may simply describe how two things may be related. For example, in correlational research (which will be discussed in Chapter 5), a researcher might hypothesize that alcohol intoxication is related to poor decision making. In other words, the researcher is hypothesizing that there is a relationship between using alcohol and decision making ability (but not necessarily a causal relationship). However, in a study using a randomized controlled design (which will also be discussed in Chapter 5), the researcher might hypothesize that using alcohol *causes* poor decision making. Therefore, as may be evident, the hypothesis being tested by a researcher is largely dependent on the type of research design being used. The relationship between hypotheses and research design will be discussed in more detail in later chapters.

≋Rapid Reference 1.4

Falsifiability of Hypotheses

According to the 20th-century philosopher Karl Popper, hypotheses must be *falsifiable* (Popper, 1963). In other words, the researcher must be able to demonstrate that the hypothesis is wrong. If a hypothesis is not falsifiable, then science cannot be used to test the hypothesis. For example, hypotheses based on religious beliefs are not falsifiable. Therefore, because we can never prove that faith-based hypotheses are wrong, there would be no point in conducting research to test them. Another way of saying this is that the researcher must be able to reject the proposed explanation (i.e., hypothesis) of the phenomenon being studied.

hypothesis and the alternate (or experimental) hypothesis. The *null hypothesis* always predicts that there will be no differences between the groups being studied. By contrast, the *alternate hypothesis* predicts that there will be a difference between the groups. In our example, the null hypothesis would predict that the exercise group and the no-exercise group will not differ significantly on levels of cholesterol. The alternate hypothesis would predict that the two groups will differ significantly on cholesterol levels. Hypotheses will be discussed in more detail in Chapter 2.

Experiments

After articulating the hypothesis, the next step involves actually conducting the experiment (or research study). For example, if the study involves investigating the effects of exercise on levels of cholesterol, the researcher would design and conduct a study that would attempt to address that question. As previously mentioned, a key aspect of conducting a research study is measuring the phenomenon of interest in an *accurate* and *reliable* manner (see Rapid Reference 1.5). In this example, the researcher would collect data on the cholesterol levels of the study participants by using an accurate and reliable measurement device. Then, the researcher would compare the cholesterol levels of the two groups to see if exercise had any effects.

≋ Rapid Reference 1.5

Accuracy vs. Reliability

When talking about measurement in the context of research, there is an important distinction between being accurate and being reliable. *Accuracy* refers to whether the measurement is correct, whereas *reliability* refers to whether the measurement is consistent. An example may help to clarify the distinction. When throwing darts at a dart board, "accuracy" refers to whether the darts are hitting the bull's eye (an *accurate* dart thrower will throw darts that hit the bull's eye). "Reliability," on the other hand, refers to whether the darts are hitting the same spot (a *reliable* dart thrower will throw darts that hit the same spot). Therefore, an accurate and reliable dart thrower will consistently throw the darts in the bull's eye. As may be evident, however, it is possible for the dart thrower to be reliable, but not accurate. For example, the dart thrower may throw all of the darts in the same spot (which demonstrates high reliability), but that spot may not be the bull's eye (which demonstrates low accuracy). In the context of measurement, both accuracy and reliability are equally important.

Analyses

After conducting the study and gathering the data, the next step involves analyzing the data, which generally calls for the use of statistical techniques. The type of statistical techniques used by a researcher depends on the design of the study, the type of data being gathered, and the questions being asked. Although a detailed discussion of statistics is beyond the scope of this text, it is important to be aware of the role of statistics in conducting a research study. In short, statistics help researchers minimize the likelihood of reaching an erroneous conclusion about the relationship between the variables being studied.

A key decision that researchers must make with the assistance of statistics is whether the null hypothesis should be rejected. Remember that the null hypothesis always predicts that there will be no difference between the groups. Therefore, rejecting the null hypothesis means that there *is* a difference between the groups. In general, most researchers seek to reject the null hypothesis because rejection means the phenomenon being studied (e.g., exercise, medication) had some effect.

It is important to note that there are only two choices with respect to the null hypothesis. Specifically, the null hypothesis can be either rejected or not rejected, but it can never be accepted. If we reject the null hypothesis, we are concluding that there is a significant difference between the groups. If, however, we do not reject the null hypothesis, then we are concluding that we were unable to detect a difference between the groups. To be clear, it does not mean that there is no difference between the two groups. There may in actuality have been a significant difference between the two groups, but we were unable to detect that difference in our study. We will talk more about this important distinction in later chapters.

The decision of whether to reject the null hypothesis is based on the results of statistical analyses, and there are two types of errors that researchers must be careful to avoid when making this decision—Type I errors and Type II errors. A *Type I error* occurs when a researcher concludes that there is a difference between the groups being studied when, in fact, there is no difference. This is sometimes referred to as a "false positive."

By contrast, a *Type II error* occurs when the researcher concludes that there is *not* a difference between the two groups being studied when, in fact, there is a difference. This is sometimes referred to as a "false negative." As previously noted, the conclusion regarding whether there is a difference between the groups is based on the results of statistical analyses. Specifically, with a Type I error, although there is a statistically significant result, it occurred by chance (or error) and there is not actually a difference between the two groups (Wampold, Davis, & Good, 2003). With a Type II error, there is a nonsignificant statistical result when, in fact, there actually is a difference between the two groups (Wampold et al.).

The typical convention in most fields of science allows for a 5% chance of erroneously rejecting the null hypothesis (i.e., of making a Type I error). In other words, a researcher will conclude that there is a significant difference between the groups being studied (i.e., will reject the null hypothesis) only if the chance of being incorrect is less than 5%. For obvious reasons, researchers want to reduce the likelihood of concluding that there is a significant difference between the groups being studied when, in fact, there is not a difference.

The distinction between Type I and Type II errors is very important, although somewhat complicated. An example may help to clarify these terms. In our example, a researcher conducts a study to determine whether a new medication is effective in treating depression. The new medication is given to Group 1, while a placebo medication is given to Group 2. If, at the conclusion of the study, the researcher concludes that there is a significant difference in levels of depression between Groups 1 and 2 when, in fact, there is no difference, the researcher has made a Type I error. In simpler terms, the researcher has detected a difference between the groups that in actuality does not exist; the difference between the groups occurred by chance (or error). By contrast, if the researcher concludes that there is *no* significant difference in levels of depression between Groups 1 and 2 when, in fact, there is a difference, the researcher has made a Type II error. In simpler terms, the researcher has failed to detect a difference that actually exists between the groups.

Which type of error is more serious—Type I or Type II? The answer to this question often depends on the context in which the errors are made. Let's use the medical context as an example. If a doctor diagnoses a patient with cancer when, in fact, the patient does not have cancer (i.e., a false positive), the doctor has committed a Type I error. In this situation, it is likely that the erroneous diagnosis will be discovered (perhaps through a second opinion) and the patient will undoubtedly be relieved. If, however, the doctor gives the patient a clean bill of health when, in fact, the patient actually has cancer (i.e., a false negative), the doctor has committed a Type II error. Most people would likely agree that a Type II error would be more serious in this example because it would prevent the patient from getting necessary medical treatment.

You may be wondering why researchers do not simply set up their research studies so that there is even less chance of making a Type I error. For example, wouldn't it make sense for researchers to set up their research studies so that the chance of making a Type I error is less than 1% or, better yet, 0%? The reason that researchers do not set up their studies in this manner has to do with the relationship between making Type I errors and making Type II errors. Specifically, there is an inverse relationship

CAUTION

Type I Errors vs. Type II Errors

Type I Error (false positive): Concluding there is a difference between the groups being studied when, in fact, there is no difference.

Type II Error (false negative): Concluding there is no difference between the groups being studied when, in fact, there is a difference.

Type I and Type II errors can be illustrated using the following table:

	Actual Results	
Researcher's Conclusion	**Difference**	**No Difference**
Difference	Correct decision	Type I error
No difference	Type II error	Correct decision

between Type I errors and Type II errors, which means that by decreasing the probability of making a Type I error, the researcher is increasing the probability of making a Type II error. In other words, if a researcher reduces the probability of making a Type I error from 5% to 1%, there is now an increased probability that the researcher will make a Type II error by failing to detect a difference that actually exists. The 5% level is a standard convention in most fields of research and represents a compromise between making Type I and Type II errors.

Conclusions

After analyzing the data and determining whether to reject the null hypothesis, the researcher is now in a position to draw some conclusions about the results of the study. For example, if the researcher rejected the null hypothesis, the researcher can conclude that the phenomenon being studied had an effect—a *statistically significant* effect, to be more precise. If the researcher rejects the null hypothesis in our exercise-cholesterol example, the researcher is concluding that exercise had an effect on levels of cholesterol.

It is important that researchers make only those conclusions that can be supported by the data analyses. Going beyond the data is a cardinal sin that researchers must be careful to avoid. For example, if a researcher conducted a correlational study and the results indicated that the two things being studied were strongly related, the researcher could not conclude that one thing caused the other. An oft-repeated statement that will be explained in later chapters is that correlation (i.e., a relationship between two things) does not equal causation. In other words, the fact that two things are related does not mean that one caused the other.

Replication

One of the most important elements of the scientific method is replication. *Replication* essentially means conducting the same research study a second time with another group of participants to see whether the same

DON'T FORGET

Correlation Does Not Equal Causation

Before looking at an example of why correlation does not equal causation, let's make sure that we understand what a correlation is. A *correlation* is simply a relationship between two things. For example, size and weight are often correlated because there is a relationship between the size of something and its weight. Specifically, bigger things tend to weigh more. The results of correlational studies simply provide researchers with information regarding the relationship between two or more variables, which may serve as the basis for future studies. It is important, however, that researchers interpret this relationship cautiously.

For example, if a researcher finds that eating ice cream is correlated with (i.e., related to) higher rates of drowning, the researcher cannot conclude that eating ice cream *causes* drowning. It may be that another variable is responsible for the higher rates of drowning. For example, most ice cream is eaten in the summer and most swimming occurs in the summer. Therefore, the higher rates of drowning are not caused by eating ice cream, but rather by the increased number of people who swim during the summer.

results are obtained (see Kazdin, 1992; Shaughnessy & Zechmeister, 1997). The same researcher may attempt to replicate previously obtained results, or perhaps other researchers may undertake that task. Replication illustrates an important point about scientific research—namely, that researchers should avoid drawing broad conclusions based on the results of a single research study because it is always possible that the results of that particular study were an aberration. In other words, it is possible that the results of the research study were obtained by chance or error and, therefore, that the results may not accurately represent the actual state of things. However, if the results of a research study are obtained a second time (i.e., replicated), the likelihood that the original study's findings were obtained by chance or error is greatly reduced.

The importance of replication in research cannot be overstated. Replication serves several integral purposes, including establishing the reliability (i.e., consistency) of the research study's findings and determining whether the same results can be obtained with a different group of participants. This last point refers to whether the results of the original study are *generalizable* to other groups of research participants. If the results of a study are replicated, the researchers—and the field in which the researchers work—can have greater confidence in the reliability and generalizability of the original findings.

GOALS OF SCIENTIFIC RESEARCH

As stated previously, the goals of scientific research, in broad terms, are to answer questions and acquire new knowledge. This is typically accomplished by conducting research that permits drawing valid inferences about the relationship between two or more variables (Kazdin, 1992). In later chapters, we discuss the specific techniques that researchers use to ensure that valid inferences can be drawn from their research, and in Rapid References 1.6 and 1.7 we present some research-related terms you should become familiar with. For now, however, our main discussion will focus on the goals of scientific research in more general terms. Most researchers agree that the three general goals of scientific research are description, prediction, and understanding/explanation (Cozby, 1993; Shaughnessy & Zechmeister, 1997).

Description

Perhaps the most basic and easily understood goal of scientific research is description. In short, *description* refers to the process of defining, classifying, or categorizing phenomena of interest. For example, a researcher may wish to conduct a research study that has the goal of describing the relationship between two things or events, such as the relationship between cardiovascular exercise and levels of cholesterol. Alternatively, a researcher may be interested in describing a single phenomenon, such as the effects of stress on decision making.

Descriptive research is useful because it can provide important information regarding the average member of a group. Specifically, by gather-

≡Rapid Reference 1.6

Categories of Research

There are two broad categories of research with which researchers must be familiar.

Quantitative vs. Qualitative

* *Quantitative research* involves studies that make use of statistical analyses to obtain their findings. Key features include formal and systematic measurement and the use of statistics.
* *Qualitative research* involves studies that do not attempt to quantify their results through statistical summary or analysis. Qualitative studies typically involve interviews and observations without formal measurement. A *case study*, which is an in-depth examination of one person, is a form of qualitative research. Qualitative research is often used as a source of hypotheses for later testing in quantitative research.

Nomothetic vs. Idiographic

* The *nomothetic approach* uses the study of groups to identify general laws that apply to a large group of people. The goal is often to identify the average member of the group being studied or the average performance of a group member.
* The *idiographic approach* is the study of an individual. An example of the idiographic approach is the aforementioned case study.

The choice of which research approaches to use largely depends on the types of questions being asked in the research study, and different fields of research typically rely on different categories of research to achieve their goals. Social science research, for example, typically relies on quantitative research and the nomothetic approach. In other words, social scientists study large groups of people and rely on statistical analyses to obtain their findings. These two broad categories of research will be the primary focus of this book.

ing data on a large enough group of people, a researcher can describe the average member, or the average performance of a member, of the particular group being studied. Perhaps a brief example will help clarify what we mean by this. Let's say a researcher gathers Scholastic Aptitude Test (SAT) scores from the current freshman class at a prestigious university. By

Rapid Reference 1.7

Sample vs. Population

Two key terms that you must be familiar with are "sample" and "population." The *population* is all individuals of interest to the researcher. For example, a researcher may be interested in studying anxiety among lawyers; in this example, the population is all lawyers. For obvious reasons, researchers are typically unable to study the entire population. In this case it would be difficult, if not impossible, to study anxiety among *all* lawyers. Therefore, researchers typically study a subset of the population, and that subset is called a *sample*.

Because researchers may not be able to study the entire population of interest, it is important that the sample be *representative* of the population from which it was selected. For example, the sample of lawyers the researcher studies should be similar to the population of lawyers. If the population of lawyers is composed mainly of White men over the age of 35, studying a sample of lawyers composed mainly of Black women under the age of 30 would obviously be problematic because the sample is not representative of the population. Studying a representative sample permits the researcher to draw valid inferences about the population. In other words, when a researcher uses a representative sample, if something is true of the sample, it is likely also true of the population.

---

using some simple statistical techniques, the researcher would be able to calculate the average SAT score for the current college freshman at the university. This information would likely be informative for high school students who are considering applying for admittance at the university.

One example of descriptive research is correlational research. In *correlational research* (as mentioned earlier), the researcher attempts to determine whether there is a relationship—that is, a correlation—between two or more variables (see Rapid Reference 1.8 for two types of correlation). For example, a researcher may wish to determine whether there is a relationship between SAT scores and grade-point averages (GPAs) among a sample of college freshmen. The many uses of correlational research will be discussed in later chapters.

≡Rapid Reference 1.8

Two Types of Correlation

Positive correlation: A *positive correlation* between two variables means that both variables change in the same direction (either both increase or both decrease). For example, if GPAs increase as SAT scores increase, there is a positive correlation between SAT scores and GPAs.

Negative (inverse) correlation: A *negative correlation* between two variables means that as one variable increases, the other variable decreases. In other words, the variables change in opposite directions. So, if GPAs decrease as SAT scores increase, there is a negative correlation between SAT scores and GPAs.

Prediction

Another broad goal of research is prediction. Prediction-based research often stems from previously conducted descriptive research. If a researcher finds that there is a relationship (i.e., correlation) between two variables, then it may be possible to predict one variable from knowledge of the other variable. For example, if a researcher found that there is a relationship between SAT scores and GPAs, knowledge of the SAT scores alone would allow the researcher to predict the associated GPAs.

Many important questions in both science and the so-called real world involve predicting one thing based on knowledge of something else. For example, college admissions boards may attempt to predict success in college based on the GPAs and SAT scores of the applicants. Employers may attempt to predict job success based on work samples, test scores, and candidate interviews. Psychologists may attempt to predict whether a traumatic life event leads to depression. Medical doctors may attempt to predict what levels of obesity and high blood pressure are associated with cardiovascular disease and stroke. Meteorologists may attempt to predict the amount of rain based on the temperature, barometric pressure, humidity, and weather patterns. In each of these examples, a prediction is being made based on existing knowledge of something else.

Understanding/Explanation

Being able to describe something and having the ability to predict one thing based on knowledge of another are important goals of scientific research, but they do not provide researchers with a true understanding of a phenomenon. One could argue that true understanding of a phenomenon is achieved only when researchers successfully identify the cause or causes of the phenomenon. For example, being able to predict a student's GPA in college based on his or her SAT scores is important and very practical, but there is a limit to that knowledge. The most important limitation is that a relationship between two things does not permit an inference of causality. In other words, the fact that two things are related and knowledge of one thing (e.g., SAT scores) leads to an accurate prediction of the other thing (e.g., GPA) does not mean that one thing caused the other. For example, a relationship between SAT scores and freshman GPAs does not mean that the SAT scores *caused* the freshman-year GPAs. More than likely, the SAT scores are indicative of other things that may be more directly responsible for the GPAs. For example, the students who score high on the SAT may also be the students who spend a lot of time studying, and it is likely the amount of time studying that is the cause of a high GPA.

The ability of researchers to make valid causal inferences is determined by the type of research designs they use. Correlational research, as previously noted, does not permit researchers to make causal inferences regarding the relationship between the two things that are correlated. By contrast, a randomized controlled study, which will be discussed in detail in Chapter 5, permits researchers to make valid cause-and-effect inferences.

There are three prerequisites for drawing an inference of causality between two events (see Shaughnessy & Zechmeister, 1997). First, there must be a relationship (i.e., a correlation) between the two events. In other words, the events must *covary*—as one changes, the other must also change. If two events do not covary, then a researcher cannot conclude that one event caused the other event. For example, if there is no relationship between television viewing and deterioration of eyesight, then one cannot reasonably conclude that television viewing causes a deterioration of eyesight.

Second, one event (the cause) must precede the other event (the effect). This is sometimes referred to as a *time-order relationship*. This should make intuitive sense. Obviously, if two events occur simultaneously, it cannot be concluded that one event caused the other. Similarly, if the observed effect comes before the presumed cause, it would make little sense to conclude that the cause *caused* the effect.

Third, alternative explanations for the observed relationship must be ruled out. This is where it gets tricky. Stated another way, a causal explanation between two events can be accepted only when other possible causes of the observed relationship have been ruled out. An example may help to clarify this last required condition for causality. Let's say that a researcher is attempting to study the effects of two different psychotherapies on levels of depression. The researcher first obtains a representative sample of people with the same level of depression (as measured by a valid and reliable measure) and then randomly assigns them to one of two groups. Group 1 will get Therapy A and Group 2 will get Therapy B. The obvious goal is to compare levels of depression in both groups after providing the therapy. It would be unwise in this situation for the researcher to assign all of the participants under age 30 to Group 1 and all of the participants over age 30 to Group 2: If, at the conclusion of the study, Group 1 and Group 2 differed significantly in levels of depression, the researcher would be unable to determine which variable—type of therapy or age—was responsible for the reduced depression. We would say that this research has been *confounded*, which means that two variables (in this case, the type of therapy and age) were allowed to vary (or be different) at the same time. Ideally, only the vari-

DON'T FORGET

Prerequisites for Inferences of Causality

- There must be an existing relationship between two events.
- The cause must precede the effect.
- Alternative explanations for the relationship must be ruled out.

able being studied (e.g., the type of therapy) will differ between the two groups.

OVERVIEW OF THE BOOK

The focus of this book is, obviously, research design and methodology. Although these terms are sometimes incorrectly used interchangeably, they are distinct concepts with well-defined and circumscribed meanings. Therefore, before proceeding any further, it would behoove us to define these terms, at least temporarily. As defined by Kazdin (1992, 2003a), a recognized leader in the field of research, *methodology* refers to the principles, procedures, and practices that govern research, whereas *research design* refers to the plan used to examine the question of interest. "Methodology" should be thought of as encompassing the entire process of conducting research (i.e., planning and conducting the research study, drawing conclusions, and disseminating the findings). By contrast, "research design" refers to the many ways in which research can be conducted to answer the question being asked. These concepts will become clearer throughout this book, but it is important that you understand the focus of this book before reading any further.

Essentials of Research Design and Methodology succinctly covers all of the major topic areas within research design and methodology. Each chapter in this book covers a specific research-related topic using easy-to-understand language and illustrative examples. The book is not meant, however, to replace the very extensive and comprehensive coverage of research issues that can be found in other publications. For those readers who would like a more in-depth understanding of the specific topic areas covered in this book, we would suggest looking to the publications included in the reference list at the end of this book. Finally, although each chapter builds upon the knowledge obtained from the previous chapters, each chapter can also be used as a stand-alone summary of the important points within that topic area. For this reason, we occasionally cover some of the same material in more than one chapter.

The chapters in *Essentials of Research Design and Methodology* are organized in a manner that accurately reflects the logical flow of a research project from development to conclusion. The first three chapters lay the foundation for conducting a research project. This chapter introduced you to some of the key concepts relating to science, research design, and methodology. As will be discussed, at a basic level, the first step in conducting research involves coming up with an idea and translating that idea into a testable question or statement. Chapter 2 discusses these preliminary stages of research, including choosing a research idea, formulating a research problem, choosing appropriate independent and dependent variables, and selecting a sample of participants for your study. As every researcher knows, coming up with a well-designed research study can be a challenging process, but the importance of that task cannot be overstated. Chapter 3 discusses some of the more common pitfalls faced by researchers when thinking about the design of a research study.

After a research question has been formulated, researchers must choose a research design, collect and analyze the data, and draw some conclusions. Chapter 4 will introduce you to the common measurement issues and strategies that must be considered when designing a research study. Chapter 5 will present a concise summary of the most common types of research designs that are available to researchers; as will be discussed, the type of research design chosen for a particular study depends largely on the question being asked. Chapter 6 will focus on one of the most important considerations in all of research—validity. Put simply, *validity* refers to the soundness of the research design being used, with high validity typically producing more accurate and meaningful results. Validity comes in many forms, and Chapter 6 will discuss each one and how to maximize it in the course of research. Chapter 7 will introduce you to many of the issues faced by researchers when analyzing data and attempting to draw conclusions based on the data.

Most research is subject to oversight by one or more ethical review committees, such as a university-based institutional review board. These committees are charged with the important task of reviewing all proposed research studies to ensure that they comply with applicable regulations governing research, which may be established by the university, the city, the state, or the federal government, depending on the nature of the research being conducted. Knowledge of the commonly encountered ethical issues will assist researchers in avoiding ethical violations and resolving ethical dilemmas. To this end, Chapter 8 will focus on the most commonly encountered ethical issues faced by researchers when designing and conducting a research study. Among other things, Chapter 8 will focus on the important topic of informed consent to research.

Finally, Chapter 9 will present a brief section on the dissemination of research results, including publication in peer-reviewed journals and presentations at professional conferences. Chapter 9 will include a distillation of major principles of research design and methodology that are applicable for those conducting research in a variety of capacities and settings. Chapter 9 will conclude by presenting a checklist of the major research-related concepts and considerations covered throughout this book.

Before concluding this chapter, one word of caution is necessary regarding the focus of this book. As stated previously, research studies come in many different forms, depending on the scientific discipline within which the research is being conducted. For example, most research studies in the field of quantum physics take place in a laboratory and do not involve human participants. Contrast this with the research studies that are conducted by social scientists, which may often take place in real-world settings and involve human participants. For the sake of clarity, consistency, and ease of reading, we thought that it was necessary to narrow the focus of this book to one broad type of research. Therefore, throughout this book, we will focus primarily on empirical research involving human participants, which is most commonly found in the social and behavioral sciences. Focusing on this type of research permits us to explore a wider range of research-related considerations that must be addressed by researchers across many scientific disciplines.

🖋 TEST YOURSELF 🖋

1. _____ can be defined as a methodological and systematic approach to the acquisition of new knowledge.

2. The defining characteristic of scientific research is the _____ _____.

3. The _____ approach relies on direct observation and experimentation in the acquisition of new knowledge.

4. Scientists define key concepts and terms in the context of their research studies by using _____ definitions.

5. What are the three general goals of scientific research?

Answers: 1. Science; 2. scientific method; 3. empirical; 4. operational; 5. description, prediction, and understanding/explaining

Two

PLANNING AND DESIGNING A RESEARCH STUDY

As discussed in Chapter 1, engaging in research can be an exciting and rewarding endeavor. Through research, scientists attempt to answer age-old questions, acquire new knowledge, describe how things work, and ultimately improve the way we all live. Despite the exciting and rewarding nature of research, deciding to conduct a research study can be intimidating for both inexperienced and experienced researchers alike. Novice researchers are frequently surprised—and often overwhelmed—by the sheer number of decisions that need to be made in the context of a research study. Depending on the scope and complexity of the research study being considered, there are typically dozens of research-related issues that need to be addressed in the planning stage alone. As a result, the early stages of planning a research study can often seem overwhelming for novice researchers with little experience (and even for seasoned researchers with considerable experience, although they may not always freely admit it).

As will become clear throughout this chapter, much of the work involved in conducting a research study actually takes place prior to conducting the study itself. All too often, novice researchers underestimate the amount of preparatory groundwork that needs to be accomplished prior to collecting any data. Although the preliminary work of getting a research study started differs depending on the type of research being conducted, there are some research-related issues that are common to most types of research. For example, prior to collecting any data at all, researchers must typically identify a topic area of interest, conduct a literature review, formulate a researchable question, articulate hypotheses, determine who or what will be studied, identify the independent and dependent variables that will be examined in the study, and choose an appropriate research methodology. And these are just a few of the more common research-related issues encountered by researchers. Furthermore, depending on the context in which the research is taking place, there may be a push to get the research study started sooner rather than later, which may further contribute to the researcher's feeling overwhelmed during the planning stage of a research study.

In addition to these research-related issues, researchers may also need to consider several logistical and administrative issues. Administrative and logistical issues include things such as who is paying for the research, whether research staff need to be hired, where and when the research study will be conducted, and what approvals need to be obtained (and from whom) to conduct the research study. And this is just a small sampling of the preliminary issues that researchers need to address during the planning stage of a research study.

The purpose of this chapter is to introduce you to this planning stage. Because research studies differ greatly, both in terms of scope and content, this chapter cannot possibly address all of the issues that need to be considered when planning and designing a research study. Instead, this chapter will focus on the research-related issues that are most commonly encountered by researchers in all scientific fields (particularly those that involve human participants) when planning and designing a research study. In some ways, you can think of this chapter as a checklist of the major research-related issues that need to be considered during the planning stage. Although some of the topics discussed in this chapter may not be applicable in the context of your particular research, it is important for you to be aware of these issues. After discussing how researchers typically select the topics that they study, this chapter will discuss literature reviews, the formulation of research problems, the development of testable hypotheses, the identification and operationalization of independent and dependent variables, and the selection and assignment of research participants. Finally, this chapter will conclude with a discussion of the impact of multicultural issues on research.

CHOOSING A RESEARCH TOPIC

The first step in designing any research study is deciding what to study. Researchers choose the topics that they study in a variety of ways, and their decisions are necessarily influenced by several factors. For example, choosing a research topic will obviously be largely influenced by the scientific field within which the researcher works. As you know, "science" is a broad term that encompasses numerous specialized and diverse areas of study, such as biology, physics, psychology, anthropology, medicine, and economics, just to name a few. Researchers achieve competence in their particular fields of study through a combination of training and experience, and it typically takes many years to develop an area of expertise.

As you can probably imagine, it would be quite difficult for a researcher in one scientific field to undertake a research study involving a topic in an entirely different scientific field. For example, it is highly unlikely that a botanist would choose to study quantum physics or macroeconomics. In addition to his or her lacking the training and experience necessary for studying quantum physics or macroeconomics, it is probably reasonable to conclude that the botanist does not have an interest in conducting research studies in those areas. So, assuming that researchers have the proper training and experience to conduct research studies in their respective fields, let's turn our attention to how researchers choose the topics that they study (see Christensen, 2001; Kazdin, 1992).

Interest

First and foremost, researchers typically choose research topics that are of interest to them. Although this may seem like common sense, it is important to occasionally remind ourselves that researchers engage in research presumably because they have a genuine interest in the topics that they study. A good question to ask at this point is how research interests develop in the first place. There are several answers to this question.

Many researchers entered their chosen fields of study with long-standing interests in those particular fields. For example, a psychologist may have decided to become a researcher because of a long-standing interest in how childhood psychopathology develops or how anxiety disorders can be effectively treated with psychotropic medications. For other researchers, they may have entered their chosen fields of study with specific interests, and then perhaps refined those interests over the course of their careers. Further, as many researchers will attest, it is certainly not uncommon for researchers to develop new interests throughout their careers. Through the process of conducting research, as well as the long hours that are spent reviewing other people's research, researchers can often stumble onto new and often unanticipated research ideas.

Regardless of whether researchers enter their chosen fields with specific interests or develop new interests as they go along, many researchers become interested in particular research ideas simply by observing the world around them (as discussed in Chapter 1). Merely taking an interest in a specific observed phenomenon is the impetus for a great amount of research in all fields of study. In summary, a researcher's basic curiosity about an observed phenomenon typically provides sufficient motivation for choosing a research topic.

Problem Solving

Some research ideas may also stem from a researcher's motivation to solve a particular problem. In both our private and professional lives, we have probably all come across some situation or thing that has caught our attention as being in need of change or improvement. For example, a great deal of research is currently being conducted to make work environments less stressful, diets healthier, and automobiles safer. In each of these research studies, researchers are attempting to solve some specific problem, such as work-related stress, obesity, or dangerous automobiles. This type of problem-solving research is often conducted in corporate and professional settings, primarily because the results of these types of research studies typically have the added benefit of possessing practical utility. For example, finding ways for employers to reduce the work-related stress of employees could potentially result in increased levels of employee productivity and satisfaction, which in turn could result in increased economic growth for the organization. These types of benefits are likely to be of great interest to most corporations and businesses.

Previous Research

Researchers also choose research topics based on the results of prior research, whether conducted by them or by someone else. Researchers will likely attest that previously conducted research is a rich and plentiful source of research ideas. Through exposure to the results of research studies, which are typically published in peer-reviewed journals (see Chapter 9 for a discussion of publishing the results of research studies), a researcher may develop a research interest in a particular area. For example, a sociologist who primarily studies the socialization of adolescents may take an interest in studying the related phenomenon of adolescent gang behavior after being exposed to research studies on that topic. In these instances, researchers may attempt to replicate the results obtained by the other researchers or perhaps extend the findings of the previous research to different populations or settings. As noted by Kazdin (1992), a large portion of research stems from researchers' efforts to build upon, expand, or reexplain the results of previously conducted research studies. In fact, it is often quipped that "research begets research," primarily because research tends to raise more questions than it answers, and those newly raised questions often become the focus of future research studies.

Theory

Finally, theories (see Rapid Reference 2.1 for a definition) often serve as a good source for research ideas. Theories can serve several purposes, but in the research context, they typically function as a rich source of hypotheses that can be examined empirically. This brings us to an important point that should not be glossed over—specifically, that research ideas (and the hypotheses and research designs that follow from those ideas) should be based on some theory (Serlin, 1987). For example, a researcher may have a theory regarding the development of depression among elderly males. In this example, the researcher may theorize that elderly males become depressed due to their reduced ability to engage in enjoyable physical activities. This hypothetical theory, like most other theories, makes a prediction. In this instance, the theory makes a specific prediction about what causes depression among elderly males. The predictions suggested by theories can often be transformed into testable hypotheses that can then be examined empirically in the context of a research study.

Rapid Reference 2.1

Theory

A *theory* is a conceptualization, or description, of a phenomenon that attempts to integrate all that we know about the phenomenon into a concise statement or question.

In the preceding paragraphs, we have only briefly touched upon several possible sources for research ideas. There are obviously many more sources we could have discussed, but space limitations preclude us from entering into a full discourse on this topic. The important point to remember from this discussion is that research ideas can—and do—come from a variety of different sources, many of which we commonly encounter in our daily lives.

Throughout this discussion, you may have noticed that we have not commented on the *quality* of the research idea. Instead, we have limited our discussion thus far to how researchers choose research ideas, and not to whether those ideas are good ideas. There are many situations, however, in which the quality of the research idea is of paramount importance. For example, when submitting a research proposal as part of a grant application, the quality of the research idea is an important consideration in the funding decision. Although judging whether a research idea is good may appear to be somewhat subjective, there are some generally accepted criteria that can help in this determination. Is the research idea creative? Will the results of the research study make a valuable and significant contribution to the literature or practice in a particular field? Does the research study address a question that is considered important in the field? Questions like these can often be answered by looking through the existing literature to see how the particular research study fits into the bigger picture. So, let's turn our attention to the logical next step in the planning phase of a research study: the literature review.

LITERATURE REVIEW

Once a researcher has chosen a specific topic, the next step in the planning phase of a research study is reviewing the existing literature in that topic area. If you are not yet familiar with the process of conducting a literature review, it simply means becoming familiar with the existing literature (e.g., books, journal articles) on a particular topic. Obviously, the amount of available literature can differ significantly depending on the topic area being studied, and it can certainly be a time-consuming, arduous, and difficult process if there has been a great deal of research conducted in a particular area. Ask any researcher (or research assistant) about conducting literature reviews and you will likely encounter similar comments about the length of time that is spent looking for literature on a particular topic.

Fortunately, the development of comprehensive electronic databases has facilitated the process of conducting literature reviews. In the past few years, individual electronic databases have been developed for several specific fields of study. For example, medical researchers can access existing medical literature through Medline; social scientists can use PsychINFO (see Rapid Reference 2.2) or PsychLIT; and legal researchers can use Westlaw or Lexis. Access to most of these electronic database services is restricted to individuals with subscriptions or to those who are affiliated with university-based library systems. Although gaining access to these services can be expensive, the advent of these electronic databases has made the process of conducting thorough literature reviews much easier and more efficient. No longer are researchers (or their student assistants!) forced to look through shelf after shelf of dusty scientific journals.

The importance and value of a well-conducted and thorough literature review cannot be overstated in the context of planning a research study (see Christensen, 2001). The primary purpose of a literature review is to help researchers become familiar with the work that has already been conducted in their selected topic areas. For example, if a researcher decides to investigate the onset of diabetes among the elderly, it would be important for him or her to have an understanding of the current state of the knowledge in that area.

Literature reviews are absolutely indispensable when planning a research study because they can help guide the researcher in an appropriate direction by answering several questions related to the topic area. Have other researchers done any work in this topic area? What do the results of their studies suggest? Did previous researchers encounter any unforeseen methodological difficulties of which future researchers should be aware when planning or conducting studies? Does more research need to be conducted on this topic, and if so, in what specific areas? A thorough literature review should answer these and related questions, thereby helping to set the stage for the research being planned.

Often, the results of a well-conducted literature review will reveal that the study being planned has, in fact, already been conducted. This would obviously be important to know during the planning phase of a study, and it would certainly be beneficial to be aware of this fact sooner rather than later. Other times, researchers may change the focus or methodology of their studies based on the types of studies that have already been con-

DON'T FORGET

Literature Reviews

Scouring the existing literature to get ideas for future research is a technique used by most researchers. It is important to note, however, that being familiar with the literature in a particular topic area also serves another purpose. Specifically, it is crucial for researchers to know what types of studies have been conducted in particular areas so they can determine whether their specific research questions have already been answered. To be clear, it is certainly a legitimate goal of research to replicate the results of other studies—but there is a difference between replicating a study for purposes of establishing the robustness or generalizability of the original findings and simply duplicating a study without having any knowledge that the same study has already been conducted. You can often save yourself a good deal of time and money by simply looking to the literature to see whether the study you are planning has already been conducted.

ducted. Literature reviews can often be intimidating for novice researchers, but like most other things relating to research, they become easier as you gain experience.

FORMULATING A RESEARCH PROBLEM

After selecting a specific research topic and conducting a thorough literature review, you are ready to take the next step in planning a research study: clearly articulating the research problem. The *research problem* (see Rapid Reference 2.3) typically takes the form of a concise question regarding the relationship between two or more variables. Examples of research problems include the following: (1) Is the onset of depression among elderly males related to the development of physical limitations? (2) What effect does a sudden dip in the Dow Jones Industrial Average have on the economy of small businesses? (3) Will a high-fiber, low-fat diet be effective in reducing cholesterol levels among middle-aged females? (4) Can a memory enhancement class improve the memory functioning of patients with progressive dementia?

When articulating a research question, it is critically important to make sure that the question is specific enough to avoid confusion and to indicate clearly what is being studied. In other words, the research problem should be composed of a precisely stated research question that clearly identifies the variables being studied. A vague research question often results in methodological confusion, because the research question does not clearly indicate what or who is being studied. The following are some examples of

Rapid Reference 2.3

Criteria for Research Problems

Good research problems must meet three criteria (see Kerlinger, 1973). First, the research problem should describe the relationship between two or more variables. Second, the research problem should take the form of a question. Third, the research problem must be capable of being tested empirically (i.e., with data derived from direct observation and experimentation).

vague and nonspecific research questions: (1) What effect does weather have on memory? (2) Does exercise improve physical and mental health? (3) Does taking street drugs result in criminal behavior? As you can see, each of these questions is rather vague, and it is impossible to determine exactly what is being studied. For example, in the first question, what type of *weather* is being studied, and *memory* for what? In the second question, is the researcher studying all types of *exercise,* and the effects of exercise on the physical and mental *health* of all people or a specific subgroup of people? Finally, in the third question, which *street drugs* are being studied, and what specific types of *criminal behavior?*

An effective way to avoid confusion in formulating research questions is by using operational definitions. Through the use of operational definitions, researchers can specifically and clearly identify what (or who) is being studied (see Kazdin, 1992). As briefly discussed in Chapter 1, researchers use operational definitions to define key concepts and terms in the specific contexts of their research studies. The benefit of using operational definitions is that they help to ensure that everyone is talking about the same phenomenon. Among other things, this will greatly assist future researchers who attempt to replicate a given study's results. Obviously, if researchers cannot determine what or whom is being studied, they will certainly not be able to replicate the study. Let's look at an example of how operational definitions can be effectively used when formulating a research question.

Let's say that a researcher is interested in studying the effects of large class sizes on the academic performance of gifted children in high-population schools. The research question may be phrased in the following manner: "What effects do large class sizes have on the academic performance of gifted children in high-population schools?" This may seem to be a fairly straightforward research question, but upon closer examination, it should become evident that there are several important terms and concepts that need to be defined. For example, what constitutes a "large class"; what does "academic performance" refer to; which kids are considered "gifted"; and what is meant by "high-population schools"?

To reduce confusion, the terms and concepts included in the research question need to be clarified through the use of operational definitions. For example, "large classes" may be defined as classes with 30 or more students; "academic performance" may be limited to scores received on standardized achievement tests; "gifted" children may include only those chil-

DON'T FORGET

Operational Definitions

An important point to keep in mind is that an operational definition is specific to the particular study in which it is used. Although researchers can certainly use the same operational definitions in different studies (which facilitates replication of the study results), different studies can operationally define the same terms and concepts in different ways. For example, in one study, a researcher may define "gifted children" as those children who are in advanced classes. In another study, however, "gifted children" may be defined as children with IQs of 130 or higher. There is no one correct definition of "gifted children," but providing an operational definition reduces confusion by specifying what is being studied.

dren who are in advanced classes; and "high-population schools" may be defined as schools with more than 1,000 students. Without operationally defining these key terms and concepts, it would be difficult to determine what exactly is being studied. Further, the specificity of the operational definitions will allow future researchers to replicate the research study.

ARTICULATING HYPOTHESES

The next step in planning a research study is articulating the hypotheses that will be tested. This is yet another step in the planning phase of a research study that can be somewhat intimidating for inexperienced researchers. Articulating hypotheses is truly one of the most important steps in the research planning process, because poorly articulated hypotheses can ruin what may have been an otherwise good study. The following discussion regarding hypotheses can get rather complicated, so we will attempt to keep the discussion relatively short and to the point.

As briefly discussed in Chapter 1, *hypotheses* attempt to explain, predict, and explore the phenomenon of interest. In many types of studies, this means that hypotheses attempt to explain, predict, and explore the relationship between two or more variables (Kazdin, 1992; see Christensen, 2001). To this end, hypotheses can be thought of as the researcher's educated guess about how the study will turn out. As such, the hypotheses articulated in a particular study should logically stem from the research problem being investigated.

Before we discuss specific types of hypotheses, there are two important points that you should keep in mind. First, all hypotheses must be *falsifiable*. That is, hypotheses must be capable of being refuted based on the results of the study (Christensen, 2001). This point cannot be emphasized enough. Put simply, if a researcher's hypothesis cannot be refuted, then the researcher is not conducting a scientific investigation. Articulating hypotheses that are not falsifiable is one sure way to ruin what could have otherwise been a well-conducted and important research study. Second, as briefly discussed in Chapter 1, a hypothesis must make a *prediction* (usually about the relationship between two or more variables). The predictions embodied in hypotheses are subsequently tested empirically by gathering and analyzing data, and the hypotheses can then be either supported or refuted.

Now that you have been introduced to the topic of hypotheses, we should turn our attention to specific types of hypotheses. There are two broad categories of hypotheses with which you should be familiar.

Null Hypotheses and Alternate Hypotheses

The first category of research hypotheses, which was briefly discussed in Chapter 1, includes the *null hypothesis* and the *alternate* (or *experimental*) *hypothesis*. In research studies involving two groups of participants (e.g., experimental group vs. control group), the null hypothesis always predicts that there will be no differences between the groups being studied (Kazdin, 1992). If, however, a particular research study does not involve groups of study participants, but instead involves only an examination of selected variables, the null hypothesis predicts that there will be no relationship between the variables being studied. By contrast, the alternate hypothesis always predicts that there will be a difference between the groups being studied (or a relationship between the variables being studied).

Let's look at an example to clarify the distinction between null hypotheses and alternate hypotheses. In a research study investigating the effects of a newly developed medication on blood pressure levels, the null hypothesis would predict that there will be no difference in terms of blood pressure levels between the group that receives the medication (i.e., the experimental group) and the group that does not receive the medication (i.e., the control group). By contrast, the alternate hypothesis would predict that there will be a difference between the two groups with respect to blood pressure levels. So, for example, the alternate hypothesis may predict that the group that receives the new medication will experience a greater reduction in blood pressure levels than the group that does not receive the new medication.

It is not uncommon for research studies to include several null and alternate hypotheses. The number of null and alternate hypotheses included in a particular research study depends on the scope and complexity of the study and the specific questions being asked by the researcher. It is important to keep in mind that the number of hypotheses being tested has implications for the number of research participants that will be needed to conduct the study. This last point rests on rather complex statistical concepts that we will not discuss in this section. For our purposes, it is sufficient to remember that as the number of hypotheses increases, the number of required participants also typically increases.

In scientific research, keep in mind that it is the null hypothesis that is tested, and then the null hypothesis is either *confirmed* or *refuted* (sometimes phrased as *rejected* or *not rejected*). Remember, if the null hypothesis is rejected (and that decision is based on the results of statistical analyses, which will be discussed in later chapters), the researcher can reasonably conclude that there is a difference between the groups being studied (or a relationship between the variables being studied). Rejecting the null hypothesis allows a researcher to *not* reject the alternate hypothesis, and not rejecting a hypothesis is the most we can do in scientific research. To be clear, we can never *accept* a hypothesis; we can only *fail to reject* a hypothesis (as was briefly discussed in Chapter 1). Accordingly, researchers typically seek to reject the null hypothesis, which empirically demonstrates that the groups being studied differ on the variables being examined in the study. This last point may seem counterintuitive, but it is an extremely important concept that you should keep in mind.

Directional Hypotheses and Nondirectional Hypotheses

The second category of research hypotheses includes directional hypotheses and nondirectional hypotheses. In research studies involving groups of study participants, the decision regarding whether to use a directional or a nondirectional hypothesis is based on whether the researcher has some idea about how the groups being studied will differ. Specifically, researchers use *nondirectional hypotheses* when they believe that the groups will differ, but they do not have a belief regarding how the groups will differ (i.e., in which direction they will differ). By contrast, researchers use *directional hypotheses* when they believe that the groups being studied will differ, *and* they have a belief regarding how the groups will differ (i.e., in a particular direction).

A simple example should help clarify the important distinction between directional and nondirectional hypotheses. Let's say that a researcher is using a standard two-group design (i.e., one experimental group and one control group) to investigate the effects of a memory enhancement class on college students' memories. At the beginning of the study, all of the study participants are randomly assigned to one of the two groups. (We will talk about the important concept of random assignment later in this chapter and in Chapter 3, and about the concept of informed consent— which we mention briefly in Rapid Reference 2.4—in Chapter 8.) Subsequently, one group (i.e., the experimental group) will be exposed to the memory enhancement class and the other group (i.e., the control group) will not be exposed to the memory enhancement class. Afterward, all of the participants in both groups will be administered a memory test. Based on this research design, any observed differences between the two groups on the memory test can reasonably be attributed to the effects of the memory enhancement class.

≡ *Rapid Reference 2.4*

....

Informed Consent

Prior to your collecting any data from study participants, the participants must voluntarily agree to participate in the study. Through a process called *informed consent*, all potential study participants are informed about the procedures that will be used in the study, the risks and benefits of participating in the study, and their rights as study participants. There are, however, a few limited instances in which researchers are not required to obtain informed consent from the study participants, and it is therefore important that researchers become knowledgeable about when informed consent is required. The topic of informed consent will be discussed in detail in Chapter 8.

≡Rapid Reference 2.5

Nondirectional Hypotheses vs. Directional Hypotheses

A reliable way to tell the difference between directional and nondirectional hypotheses is to look at the wording of the hypotheses. If the hypothesis simply predicts that there will be a difference between the two groups, then it is a nondirectional hypothesis. It is nondirectional because it predicts that there will be a difference but does not specify how the groups will differ. If, however, the hypothesis uses so-called comparison terms, such as "greater," "less," "better," or "worse," then it is a directional hypothesis. It is directional because it predicts that there will be a difference between the two groups *and* it specifies how the two groups will differ.

In this example, the researcher has several options in terms of hypotheses. On the one hand, the researcher may simply hypothesize that there will be a difference between the two groups on the memory test. This would be an example of a nondirectional hypothesis, because the researcher is hypothesizing that the two groups will differ, but the researcher is not specifying how the two groups will differ. Alternatively, the researcher could hypothesize that the participants who are exposed to the memory enhancement class will perform better on the memory test than the participants who are not exposed to the memory enhancement class. This would be an example of a directional hypothesis, because the researcher is hypothesizing that the two groups will differ *and* specifying *how* the two groups will differ (i.e., one group will perform better than the other group on the memory test). See Rapid Reference 2.5 for a tip on how to distinguish between directional and nondirectional hypotheses.

CHOOSING VARIABLES TO STUDY

We are now very close to beginning the actual study, but there are still a few things remaining to do before we begin collecting data. Before proceeding any further, it would probably be helpful for us to take a moment and see

Rapid Reference 2.6

Variables

A *variable* is anything that can take on different values. For example, height, weight, age, race, attitude, and IQ are variables because there are different heights, weights, ages, races, attitudes, and IQs. By contrast, if something cannot vary, or take on different values, then it is referred to as a *constant*.

where we are in this process of planning a research study. So far, we have discussed how researchers (1) come up with researchable ideas; (2) conduct thorough literature reviews to see what has been done in their topic areas (and, if necessary, to refine the focus of their studies based on the results of the prior research); (3) formulate concise research problems with clearly defined concepts and terms (using operational definitions); and (4) articulate falsifiable hypotheses. We have certainly accomplished quite a bit, but there is still a little more to do before beginning the study itself.

The next step in planning a research study is identifying what variables (see Rapid Reference 2.6) will be the focus of the study. There are many categories of variables that can appear in research studies. However, rather than discussing every conceivable one, we will focus our attention on the most commonly used categories. Although not every research study will include all of these variables, it is important that you are aware of the differences among the categories and when each type of variable may be used.

Independent Variables vs. Dependent Variables

When discussing variables, perhaps the most important distinction is between independent and dependent variables. The *independent variable* is the factor that is manipulated or controlled by the researcher. In most studies, researchers are interested in examining the effects of the independent variable. In its simplest form, the independent variable has two levels: present or absent. For example, in a research study investigating the effects of a new type of psychotherapy on symptoms of anxiety, one group will be exposed to the psychotherapy and one group will not be exposed to the psychotherapy. In this example, the independent variable is the psychotherapy, because the researcher can control whether the study participants are exposed to it and the researcher is interested in examining the effects of the psychotherapy on symptoms of anxiety. As you may already know, the group in which the independent variable is present (i.e., that is exposed to the psychotherapy) is referred to as the *experimental group,* whereas the group in which the independent variable is not present (i.e., that is not exposed to the psychotherapy) is referred to as the *control group.*

Although, in its simplest form, an independent variable has only two levels (i.e., present or absent), it is certainly not uncommon for an independent variable to have more than two levels. For example, in a research study examining the effects of a new medication on symptoms of depression, the researcher may include three groups in the study—one control group and two experimental groups. As usual, the control group would not get the medication (or would get a placebo), while one experimental group may get a lower dose of the medication and the other experimental group may get a higher dose of the medication. In this example, the independent variable (i.e., medication) consists of three levels: absent, low, and high. Other levels of independent variables are, of course, also possible, such as low, medium, and high; or absent, low, medium, and high. Researchers make decisions regarding the number of levels of an independent variable based on a careful consideration of several factors, including the number of available study participants, the degree of specificity of results they desire to achieve with the study, and the associated financial costs.

It is also common for a research study to include multiple independent variables, perhaps with each of the independent variables consisting of multiple levels. For example, a researcher may attempt to investigate the effects of both medication and psychotherapy on symptoms of depression. In this example, there are two independent variables (i.e., medication and psychotherapy), and each independent variable could potentially consist of multiple levels (e.g., low, medium, and high doses of medication; cognitive behavioral therapy, psychodynamic therapy, and rational emotive therapy). As you can see, things have a tendency to get complicated fairly quickly when researchers use multiple independent variables with multiple levels.

At this point in the discussion, you should be actively resisting the urge to be intimidated by the material presented so far in this chapter. We have covered quite a bit of information, and it is getting more complicated as we go. Keeping track of the different categories and types of variables can certainly be difficult, even for those of us with considerable research experience. If you are getting confused, it may be helpful to reduce things to their simplest terms. In the case of independent variables, the important point to keep in mind is that researchers are interested in examining the effects of an independent variable on something, and that something is the dependent variable (Isaac & Michael, 1997). Let's now turn our attention to dependent variables.

The *dependent variable* is a measure of the effect (if any) of the independent variable. For example, a researcher may be interested in examining the effects of a new medication on symptoms of depression among college students. In this example, prior to administering any medication, the researcher would most likely administer a valid and reliable measure of depression—such as the Beck Depression Inventory (Beck, Ward, Mendelson, Mock, & Erbaugh, 1961)—to a group of study participants. The Beck Depression Inventory is a well-accepted self-report inventory of symptoms of depression. Administering a measure of depression to the study participants prior to administering any medication allows the researcher to obtain what is called a *baseline measure* of depression, which simply means a measurement of the levels of depression that are present prior to the administration of any intervention (e.g., psychotherapy, medication). The researcher then randomly assigns the study participants to two groups, an experimental group that receives the new medication and a control group that does not receive the new medication (perhaps its members are administered a placebo).

After administering the medication (or not administering the medication, for the control group), the researcher would then readminister the Beck Depression Inventory to all of the participants in both groups. The researcher now has two Beck Depression Inventory scores for each of the participants in both groups—one score from before the medication was administered and one score from after the medication was administered. (By the way, this type of research design is referred to as a *pre/post design,* because the dependent variable is measured both before and after the intervention is administered. We will talk about this type of research design in Chapter 5.) These two depression scores can then be compared to determine whether the medication had any effect on the levels of depression. Specifically, if the scores on the Beck Depression Inventory decrease (which indicates lower levels of depression) for the participants in the experimental group, but not for the participants in the control group, then the researcher can reasonably conclude that the medication was effective in reducing symptoms of depression. To be more precise, for the researcher to conclude that the medication was effective in reducing symptoms of depression, there would need to be a *statistically significant difference* in Beck Depression Inventory scores between the experimental group and the control group, but we will put that point aside for the moment.

Before proceeding any further, take a moment and see whether you can identify the independent and dependent variables in our example. Have you figured it out? In this example, the new medication is the independent variable because it is under the researcher's control and the researcher is interested in measuring its effect. The Beck Depression Inventory score is the dependent variable because it is a measure of the effect of the independent variable.

When students are exposed to research terminology for the first time, it is not uncommon for them to confuse the independent and dependent variables. Fortunately, there is an easy way to remember the difference between the two. If you get confused, think of the independent variable as the "cause" and the dependent variable as the "effect." To assist you in this process, it may be helpful if you practice stating your research question in the following manner: "What are the effects of _____ on _____?" The first blank is the independent variable and the second blank is the dependent variable. For example, we may ask the following research question: "What are the effects of <u>exercise</u> on <u>levels of body fat</u>?"

≡Rapid Reference 2.7

Independent Variables and Dependent Variables

The independent variable is called "independent" because it is independent of the outcome being measured. More specifically, the independent variable is what causes or influences the outcome. The dependent variable is called "dependent" because it is influenced by the independent variable. For example, in our hypothetical study examining the effects of medication on symptoms of depression, the measure of depression is the dependent variable because it is influenced by (i.e., is dependent on) the independent variable (i.e., the medication).

In this example, "exercise" is the independent variable and "levels of body fat" is the dependent variable. Rapid Reference 2.7 summarizes the distinction between the two; and Rapid Reference 2.8 uses this distinction to further our understanding of the term "research."

≡Rapid Reference 2.8

Definition of "Research"

In Chapter 1, we briefly defined research as an examination of the relationship between two or more variables. We can now be a little more specific in our definition of "research." *Research* is an examination of the relationship between one or more independent variables and one or more dependent variables. In even more precise terms, we can define research as an examination of the effects of one or more independent variables on one or more dependent variables.

Now that we know the difference between independent and dependent variables, we should focus our attention on how researchers choose these variables for inclusion in their research studies. An important point to keep in mind is that the researcher selects the independent and dependent variables based on the research problem and the hypotheses. In many ways, this simplifies the process of selecting variables by requiring the selection of independent and dependent variables to flow logically from the statement of the research problem and the hypotheses. Once the research problem and the hypotheses are articulated, it should not take too much effort to identify the independent and dependent variables.

Perhaps another example will clarify this important point. Suppose that a researcher is interested in examining the relationship between intake of dietary fiber and the incidence of colon cancer among elderly males. The research problem may be stated in the following manner: "Does increased consumption of dietary fiber result in a decreased incidence of colon cancer among elderly males?" Using our suggested phrasing from the previous paragraph, we could also ask the following question: "What are the effects of dietary fiber consumption on the incidence of colon cancer among elderly males?" Following logically from this research problem, the researcher may hypothesize the following: "High levels of dietary fiber consumption will decrease the incidence of colon cancer among elderly males." Obviously, several terms in this hypothesis need to be operationally defined, but we can skip that step for the purposes of the current example. It takes only a cursory examination of the research problem and related hypothesis to determine the independent variable and dependent variable for this study. Have you figured it out yet? Because the researcher is interested in examining the effects of consuming dietary fiber on the incidence of colon cancer, "dietary fiber consumption" is the independent variable and a measure of the "incidence of colon cancer" is the dependent variable.

Categorical Variables vs. Continuous Variables

Now that you are familiar with the difference between independent and dependent variables, we will turn our attention to another category of variables with which you should be familiar. The distinction between categorical variables and continuous variables frequently arises in the context of many research studies. *Categorical variables* are variables that can take on specific values only within a defined range of values. For example, "gender" is a categorical variable because you can either be male or female. There is no middle ground when it comes to gender; you can either be male or female; you must be one, and you cannot be both. "Race," "mari-

Putting It Into Practice

Varying Independent Variables and Measuring Dependent Variables

Assuming that a researcher has a well-articulated and specific hypothesis, it is a fairly straightforward task to identify the independent and dependent variables. Often, the difficult part is determining how to *vary* the independent variable and *measure* the dependent variable. For example, let's say that a researcher is interested in examining the effects of viewing television violence on levels of prosocial behavior. In this example, we can easily identify the independent variable as viewing television violence and the dependent variable as prosocial behavior. The difficult part is finding ways to vary the independent variable (how can the researcher vary the viewing of television violence?) and measure the dependent variable (how can the researcher measure prosocial behavior?). Finding ways to vary the independent variable and measure the dependent variable often requires as much creativity as scientific know-how.

tal status," and "hair color" are other common examples of categorical variables. Although this may sound obvious, it is often helpful to think of categorical variables as consisting of discrete, mutually exclusive categories, such as "male/female," "White/Black," "single/married/divorced," and "blonde/brunette/redhead." In contrast with categorical variables, *continuous variables* are variables that can theoretically take on any value along a continuum. For example, "age" is a continuous variable because, theoretically at least, someone can be any age. "Income," "weight," and "height" are other examples of continuous variables. As we will see, the type of data produced from using categorical variables differs from the type of data produced from using continuous variables.

In some circumstances, researchers may decide to convert some continuous variables into categorical variables. For example, rather than using "age" as a continuous variable, a researcher may decide to make it a categorical variable by creating discrete categories of age, such as "under age 40" or "age 40 or older." "Income," which is often treated as a continuous variable, may instead be treated as a categorical variable by creating dis-

≡ Rapid Reference 2.9

Categorical Variables vs. Continuous Variables

The decision of whether to use categorical or continuous variables will have an effect on the precision of the data that are obtained. When compared with categorical variables, continuous variables can be measured with a greater degree of precision. In addition, the choice of which statistical tests will be used to analyze the data is partially dependent on whether the researcher uses categorical or continuous variables. Certain statistical tests are appropriate for categorical variables, while other statistical tests are appropriate for continuous variables. As with many decisions in the research-planning process, the choice of which type of variable to use is partially dependent on the question that the researcher is attempting to answer.

crete categories of income, such as "under $25,000 per year," "$25,000–$50,000 per year," and "over $50,000 per year." The benefit of using continuous variables is that they can be measured with a higher degree of precision. For example, it is more informative to record someone's age as "47 years old" (continuous) as opposed to "age 40 or older" (categorical). The use of continuous variables gives the researcher access to more specific data. See Rapid Reference 2.9.

Quantitative Variables vs. Qualitative Variables

Finally, before moving on to a different topic, it would behoove us to briefly discuss the distinction between qualitative variables and quantitative variables. *Qualitative variables* are variables that vary in kind, while *quantitative variables* are those that vary in amount (see Christensen, 2001). This is an important yet subtle distinction that frequently arises in research studies, so let's take a look at a few examples.

Rating something as "attractive" or "not attractive," "helpful" or "not helpful," or "consistent" or "not consistent" are examples of qualitative variables. In these examples, the variables are considered qualitative because they vary in kind (and not amount). For example, the thing being rated is either "attractive" or "not attractive," but there is no indication of the level (or amount) of attractiveness. By contrast, reporting the number of times that something happened or the number of times that someone engaged in a particular behavior are examples of quantitative variables. These variables are considered quantitative because they provide information regarding the amount of something.

As stated at the beginning of this section, there are several other categories of variables that we will not be discussing in this text. What we have covered in this section are the major categories that most commonly appear in research studies. One final comment is necessary. It is important to keep in mind that a single variable may fit into several of the categories that we have discussed. For example, the variable "height" is both continuous (if measured along a continuum) and quantitative (because we are getting information regarding the amount of height). Along similar lines, the variable "eye color" is both categorical (because there is a limited number of discrete categories of eye color) and qualitative (because eye color varies in kind, not amount).

If this discussion of variables still seems confusing to you, take comfort in the fact that even seasoned researchers can still get turned around on these issues. As with most aspects of research, repeated exposure to (and experience with) these concepts tends to breed a comfortable level of familiarity. So, the next time you come across a research study, practice identifying the different types of variables that we have discussed in this section.

RESEARCH PARTICIPANTS

Selecting participants is one of the most important aspects of planning and designing a research study. For reasons that should become clear as you read this section, selecting research participants is often more difficult and more complicated than it may initially appear. In addition to needing the appropriate *number* of participants (which may be rather difficult in large-scale studies that require many participants), researchers need to have the appropriate *kinds* of participants (which may be difficult when resources are limited or the pool of potential participants is small). Moreover, the manner in which individuals are selected to participate, and the way those participants are subsequently assigned to groups within the study, has a dramatic effect on the types of conclusions that can be drawn from the research study.

At the outset, it is important to note that not all types of research studies involve human participants. For example, the research studies carried out in many fields of science, such as physics, biology, chemistry, and botany, generally do not involve human participants. For the research scientists in these fields, the unit of study may be an atom, a cell, a molecule, or a flower, but not a human participant. However, for those researchers who are involved in other types of research, such as social science research, the majority of their studies will involve human participants in some capacity. Therefore, it is important that you become familiar with the procedures that are commonly employed by researchers to select an appropriate group of study participants and assign those participants to groups within the study. This section will address these two important tasks.

Before proceeding any further, it is worth noting that when a researcher is planning a study, he or she must choose an appropriate research design *prior* to selecting study participants and assigning them to groups. In fact, the specific research design used in a study often determines how the participants will be selected for inclusion in the study and how they will be assigned to groups within it. However, because the topic of choosing an appropriate research design requires an extensive and detailed discussion, we have set aside an entire chapter to cover that topic (see Chapter 5). Therefore, when reading this section, it is important to keep in mind that the tasks of selecting participants and assigning those participants to groups typically take place *after* you have chosen an appropriate research design. Accordingly, you may want to reread this section after you have read the chapter on research designs (Chapter 5).

Selecting Study Participants

For those research studies that involve human participants, the selection of the study participants is of the utmost importance. There are several ways in which potential participants can be selected for inclusion in a research study, and the manner in which participants are selected is determined by several factors, including the research question being investigated, the research design being used, and the availability of appropriate numbers and types of study participants. In this section, we will discuss the most common methods used by researchers for selecting study participants.

For some types of research studies, specific research participants (or groups of research participants) may be sought out. For example, in a qualitative study investigating the combat experiences of World War II veterans, the researcher may simply approach identified World War II veterans and ask them to participate in the study. Another example would be an investigation of the effects of a Head Start program among preschool students. In this situation, the researcher may decide to study an already existing preschool class. The researcher could randomly select preschool students to participate in the study, but would probably save both time and money by using a preexisting group of students.

As you can probably imagine, there are some difficulties that arise when researchers use preexisting groups or target specific people for inclusion in a research study. The primary difficulty is that the study results may not be generalizable to other groups or other individuals (i.e., groups or individuals not in the study). For example, if a researcher is interested in drawing broad conclusions about the effects of a Head Start program on preschool students in general, the researcher would not want to limit participation in the study to one specific group of preschool students from one specific preschool. For the results of the study to generalize beyond the sample used in the study, the sample of preschool students in the study would have to be representative of the entire population of preschool students.

We have introduced quite a few new terms and concepts in this discussion, so we need to make sure that we are all on the same page before we proceed any further. Let's start with *generalizability*. The concept of generalizability will be covered in detail in future chapters, so we will not spend too much time on it here. But we do need to take a moment and briefly discuss what we mean when we say that the results of a study are (or are not) generalizable. To make this discussion more digestible, let's look at a brief example.

Suppose that a researcher is interested in examining the employment rate among recent college graduates. To examine this issue, the researcher collects employment data on 1000 recent graduates from ABC University. After looking at the data and conducting some simple calculations, the researcher determines that 97.5% of the recent ABC graduates obtained full-time employment within 6 months of graduation. Based on the results of this study, can the researcher reasonably conclude that the employment rate for *all* recent college graduates across the United States is 97.5%? Obviously not. But why? The most obvious reason is that the recent graduates from ABC University may not be *representative* of recent graduates from other colleges. Perhaps recent ABC graduates have more success in obtaining employment than recent graduates from smaller, lesser-known colleges. As a result, there is likely a great degree of variability in the employment rates of recent college graduates across the United States. Therefore, it would be misleading and inaccurate to reach a broad conclusion about the employability of all recent college graduates based exclusively on the employment experiences of recent ABC graduates.

In the previous example, the only reasonable conclusion that the researcher can reach is that 97.5% of the recent ABC graduates *in that particular study* obtained full-time employment within 6 months of graduation. This limited conclusion would likely be of little interest to students outside ABC University because the results of the study have no implications for those other students. For the results of this study to be generalizable (i.e., applicable to recent graduates from all colleges, not just ABC) the researcher would need to examine the employment rates for recent graduates from many different colleges. This would have the effect of ensuring that the sample of participants is representative of all recent college graduates. Obviously, it would be most informative and accurate if the researcher were able to examine the employment rates for all recent graduates from all colleges. Then, rather than having to make an inference about the employment rate in the population based on the results of the study, the researcher would have an exact employment rate.

For obvious reasons, however, it is typically not practical to include every member of the population of interest (e.g., all recent college graduates) in a research study. Time, money, and resources are three limiting factors that make this unlikely. Therefore, most researchers are forced to study a representative subset—a *sample*—of the population of interest. Accordingly, in our example, the researcher would be forced to study a sample of recent college graduates from the population of all recent college graduates. (If you need a brief refresher on the distinction between a sample and a population, see Chapter 1.) If the sample used in the study is representative of the population from which it was drawn, the researcher can draw conclusions about the population based on the results obtained with the sample. In other words, using a representative sample is what allows researchers to reach broad conclusions applicable to the entire population of interest based on the results obtained in their specific studies. For those of you who are still confused about the concept of generalizability, do not fret, because we revisit this issue in later chapters.

The discussion up to this point should lead you to an obvious question. Specifically, if choosing a representative sample is so important for the purposes of generalizing the results of a study, how do researchers go about selecting a representative sample from the population of interest? The primary procedure used by researchers to choose a representative sample is called "random selection." *Random selection* is a procedure through which a sample of participants is chosen from the population of interest in such a way that each member of the population has an equal probability of being selected to participate in the study (Kazdin, 1992). Researchers using the random selection procedure first define the population of interest and then randomly select the required number of participants from the population.

There are two important points to keep in mind regarding random selection. The first point is that random selection is often difficult to accomplish unless the population is very narrowly defined (Kazdin, 1992). For example, random selection would not be possible for a population defined as "all economics students." How could we possibly define "all economics students"? Would this population include all economics students in a particular state, or in the United States, or in the world? Would it include both current and former economics students? Would it include both undergraduate and graduate economics students? Obviously, the population of "all economics students" is too broad, and it would therefore be impossible to select a random sample from that population. By contrast, random selection could easily be accomplished with a population defined as "all students currently taking introductory economics classes at a particular university." This population is sufficiently narrowly defined, which would permit a researcher to use random selection to obtain a representative sample.

As you may have noticed, narrowly defining the population of interest, which we have stated is a requirement for random selection, has the negative effect of limiting the representativeness of the resulting sample. This certainly presents a catch-22—we need to narrowly define the population to be able to select a representative sample, but by narrowing the population, we are limiting the representativeness of the sample we choose.

This brings us to the second point that you should keep in mind regarding random selection, namely, that the results of a study cannot be generalized based solely on the random selection of participants from the population of interest. Rather, evidence for the generalizability of a study's findings typically comes from replication studies. In other words, the most effective way to demonstrate the generalizability of a study's findings is to conduct the same study with other samples to see if the same results are obtained. Obtaining the same results with other samples is the best evidence of generalizability.

Despite the limitations that are associated with random selection, it is a popular procedure among researchers who are attempting to ensure that the sample of participants in a particular study is similar to the population from which the sample was drawn.

Assigning Study Participants to Groups

Once a population has been appropriately defined and a representative sample of participants has been randomly selected from that population, the next step involves assigning those participants to groups within the research study—one of the most important aspects of conducting research. In fact, Kazdin (1992) regards the assignment of participants to groups within a research study as "the central issue in group research" (p. 85). Therefore, it is important that you understand how the assignment of participants is most effectively accomplished and how it affects the types of conclusions that can be drawn from the results of a research study.

There is almost universal agreement among researchers that the most effective method of assigning participants to groups within a research study is through a procedure called "random assignment." The philosophy underlying random *assignment* is similar to the philosophy underlying random *selection* (see Rapid Reference 2.10). *Random assignment* involves assigning participants to groups within a research study in such a way that each participant has an equal probability of being assigned to any of the groups within the study (Kazdin, 1992). Although there are several accepted methods that can be used to effectively implement random assignment, it is typically accomplished by using a table of random numbers that determines the group assignment for each of the participants. (See Chapter 5 for a discussion and example of random-numbers tables.) By using a table of random numbers, participants are assigned to groups within the study according to a predetermined schedule. In fact, group assignment is determined for each participant prior to his or her entrance into the study (Kazdin, 1992).

Now that you know how participants are most effectively assigned to groups within a study (i.e., via random assignment), we

Rapid Reference 2.10

Random Selection vs. Random Assignment

Random selection: Choosing study participants from the population of interest in such a way that each member of the population has an equal probability of being selected to participate in the study.

Random assignment: Assigning study participants to groups within the study in such a way that each participant has an equal probability of being assigned to any of the groups within the study.

should spend some time discussing why random assignment
is so important in the context of
research. In short, random assignment is an effective way of ensuring that the groups within a research study are *equivalent* (see
Rapid Reference 2.11). More
specifically, random assignment is
a dependable procedure for producing equivalent groups because
it evenly distributes characteristics
of the sample among all of the
groups within the study (see Kazdin, 1992). For example, rather
than placing all of the participants
over age 40 into one group, random assignment would, theoretically at least, evenly distribute all
of the participants over age 40 among all of the groups within the research
study. This would produce equivalent groups within the study, at least with
respect to age.

At this point, you may be wondering why it is so important for a research study to consist of equivalent groups. The primary importance of
having equivalent groups within a research study is to ensure that *nuisance
variables* (i.e., variables that are not under the researcher's control) do not
interfere with the interpretation of the study's results (Kazdin, 1992). In
other words, if you find a difference between the groups on a particular dependent variable, you want to attribute that difference to the independent
variable rather than to a baseline difference between the groups. Let's take
a moment and explore what this means. In most studies, variables such as
age, gender, and race are not the primary variables of interest. However, if
these characteristics are not evenly distributed among all of the groups
within the study, they could obscure the interpretation of the primary vari-

≡*Rapid Reference 2.11*

Group Equivalence

One of the most important aspects of group research is isolating
the effects of the independent
variable. To accomplish this, the
experimental group and control
group should be identical, except
for the independent variable. The
independent variable would be
present in the experimental group,
but not in the control group. Assuming this is the only difference
between the two groups, any observed differences on the dependent variable can reasonably be attributed to the effects of the
independent variable.

ables of interest in the study. Let's take a look at a short example that should help to clarify these concepts.

A researcher interested in measuring the effects of a new memory enhancement strategy conducts a study in which one group (i.e., the experimental group) is taught the memory enhancement strategy and the other group (i.e., the control group) is not taught the memory enhancement strategy. Then, all of the participants in both groups are administered a test of memory functioning. At the conclusion of the study, the researcher finds that the participants who were taught the new strategy performed better on the memory test than the participants who were not taught the new strategy. Based on these results, the researcher concludes that the memory enhancement strategy is effective. However, before submitting these impressive results for publication in a professional journal, the researcher realizes that there is a slight quirk in the composition of the two groups in the study. Specifically, the researcher discovers that the experimental group is composed entirely of women under the age of 30, while the control group is composed entirely of men over the age of 60.

The unfortunate group composition in the previous example is quite problematic for the researcher, who is understandably disappointed in this turn of events. Without getting too complicated, here is the problem in a nutshell: Because the two study groups differ in several ways—exposure to the memory enhancement strategy, age, and gender—the researcher cannot be sure exactly what is responsible for the improved memory performance of the participants in the experimental group. It is possible, for example, that the improved memory performance of the experimental group is not due to the new memory enhancement strategy, but rather to the fact that the participants in that group are all under age 30 and, therefore, are likely to have better memories than the participants who are over age 60. Alternatively, it is possible that the improved memory performance of the experimental group is somehow related to the fact that all of the participants in that group are women. In summary, because the memory enhancement strategy was not experimentally isolated and controlled (i.e., it was not the only difference between the experimental and control groups), the researcher cannot be sure whether it was responsible for the observed differences between the groups on the memory test.

As stated earlier in this section, the purpose of random assignment is to distribute the characteristics of the sample participants evenly among all of the groups within the study. By using random assignment, the researcher distributes nuisance variables unsystematically across all of the groups (see Kazdin, 1992). Had the researcher in our example used random assignment, the male participants over age 60 and the female participants under age 30 would have been evenly distributed between the experimental group and the control group. (See Rapid Reference 2.12 for a discussion of testing for group equivalence.)

If the sample size is large enough, the researcher can assume that the nuisance variables are evenly distributed among the groups, which increases the researcher's confidence in the equivalence of the groups (Kazdin, 1992). This last point should not be overlooked. Random assignment is most effective with a large sample size (e.g., more than 40 participants per group). In other words, the likelihood of obtaining equivalent groups increases as the sample size increases. Once participants have been

≡ Rapid Reference 2.12

Equivalence Testing

Although using random assignment with large samples can be assumed to produce equivalent groups, it is wise to statistically examine whether the two groups are indeed equivalent. This is accomplished by comparing the two groups on nuisance variables to see whether the two groups differ significantly. If there are no statistically significant differences between the two groups on any of the nuisance variables, the researcher can be confident that the two groups are equivalent. In this situation, any observed effects on the dependent variables can reasonably be attributed to the independent variable (and not to any of the nuisance variables). By contrast, if the two groups are not equivalent on one or more of the nuisance variables, there are statistical steps that a researcher can take to ensure that the differences do not affect the interpretation of the study's results.

randomly assigned to groups within the study, the researcher is then ready to begin collecting data. (Both random selection and random assignment will be discussed in more detail in Chapter 3 as strategies for controlling artifact and bias.)

MULTICULTURAL CONSIDERATIONS

One final and important topic in this chapter is the relationship between multicultural issues and research studies. In research, as in most other areas of life at the beginning of the 21st century, considerations surrounding multiculturalism (see Rapid Reference 2.13) have taken on increased visibility and importance. As a result, there is a growing need for researchers at all levels and in all settings to become familiar with the role of multiculturalism in all aspects of research studies.

Multicultural considerations are important in two distinct ways when it comes to conducting research studies. First, multicultural considerations often have a considerable effect on a researcher's choice of research question and research design (even if the researcher is unaware of the role played by multicultural considerations in those decisions). Second, multicultural considerations are important in the selection and composition of the sample of participants used in particular research studies. In other words, multicultural considerations are important with respect to both the researcher and the study sample. This section will address both of these important considerations.

 *Rapid Reference 2.13*

Multiculturalism

When considered in its broadest sense, a researcher who has achieved *multicultural competence* is cognizant of differences among study participants related to race, ethnicity, language, sexual orientation, gender, age, disability, class status, education, and religious or spiritual orientation (American Psychological Association, 2003).

Multiculturalism and Researchers

As the population of the United States becomes increasingly diverse, there is a growing need for researchers to become more aware of the impact of multicultural issues on the planning and designing of research studies (Reid, 2002). Using the current lingo, it can be stated that there is a need for researchers to achieve "multicultural competence." For researchers, the first step in achieving multicultural competence is becoming aware of how their own worldviews affect their choice of research questions (American Psychological Association [APA], 2003). These worldviews necessarily include researchers' views of their own cultures as well as their views of other cultures. Researchers must acknowledge that their worldviews likely play an integral role in shaping their views of human behavior. Hence, their theories of human behavior, as well as the research questions and hypotheses that stem from those theories, are based on assumptions particular to their own culture—and it is these assumptions of which researchers must be aware (see Egharevba, 2001).

To increase awareness of multicultural issues in the conceptualization of research designs, the researcher often benefits from consulting with members of diverse and traditionally underrepresented cultural groups (APA, 2003; Quintana, Troyano, & Taylor, 2001). This serves the purpose of providing perspectives and insights that may not have otherwise been considered by the researcher acting alone. Considering different viewpoints from members of diverse cultural groups facilitates the development of a culturally competent research design that has the potential to benefit people from many different cultures. Along similar lines, it is also important for researchers to recognize the limitations of their research designs in terms of applicability to diverse cultural groups.

Researchers also need to be aware of multicultural considerations when deciding on assessment techniques and instruments for their studies. For example, when working with a culturally diverse sample, it is important that researchers use instruments and assessment techniques that have been validated with culturally diverse groups (see Council of National Psychological Associations for the Advancement of Ethnic Minority Interests, 2000). According to the APA's *Guidelines on Multicultural Education, Training, Research, Practice, and Organizational Change for Psychologists* (2003, p. 389), "psychological researchers are urged to consider culturally sensitive assessment techniques, data-generating procedures, and standardized instruments whose validity, reliability, and measurement equivalence have been tested across culturally diverse sample groups. . . ."

Finally, when it comes to interpreting data and drawing conclusions, researchers need to consider the role of culture and cultural hypotheses. It is conceivable, for example, that there is a culturally based explanation for the research study's findings, and it therefore may be prudent to statistically examine relevant cultural variables. Researchers also need to be cognizant of the cultural limitations and generalizability of the research study's results.

Multiculturalism and Study Participants

In the preceding section, we emphasized the importance of multicultural considerations in terms of formulating a research question, choosing an appropriate research design, selecting assessment strategies, and analyzing data and drawing conclusions. In this section, we will focus on multicultural considerations as they relate to selecting the research participants who make up the study sample. As you will see, the inclusion of people from diverse cultural backgrounds in study samples has attracted a great deal of attention in recent years.

The debate regarding the appropriate composition of study samples is no longer exclusively in the domain of researchers. The federal government has voiced an opinion on this important issue. In 1993, President Clinton signed into law the NIH Revitalization Act of 1993 (PL 103-43), which directed the National Institutes of Health (NIH) to establish guidelines for the inclusion of women and minorities in clinical research. On March 9, 1994, in response to the mandate contained in the NIH Revitalization Act, the NIH issued *NIH Guidelines on the Inclusion of Women and Minorities as Subjects in Clinical Research* (henceforth "*NIH Guidelines*").

According to the *NIH Guidelines,* because research is designed to provide scientific evidence that could lead to a change in health policy or a standard of care, it is imperative to determine whether the intervention being studied affects both genders as well as diverse racial and ethnic groups differently. Therefore, all NIH-supported biomedical and behavioral research involving human participants is required to be carried out in a manner that elicits information about individuals of both genders and from diverse racial and ethnic backgrounds. According to the Office for Protection From Research Risks, which is part of the U.S. Department of Health and Human Services, the inclusion of women and minorities in research will, among other things, help to increase the generalizability of the study's findings and ensure that women and minorities benefit from the research. Although the *NIH Guidelines* apply only to studies conducted or supported by the NIH, all other researchers and research institutions are encouraged to include women and minorities in their research studies, as well.

SUMMARY

In this chapter, we have covered the research-related issues that are most commonly encountered by researchers when they are planning and designing research studies. There are certainly other topics related to planning and designing a research study that we could have included in this discussion (e.g., choosing study instruments), but we chose to take a broad approach because of the inherent uniqueness of research studies. Rather than discussing topics that are specific to specific types of studies, we believed that it would be most beneficial to make the discussion more general by focusing on the research-related topics that are encountered by virtually all researchers when planning and designing studies.

✒ TEST YOURSELF ✒

1. Researchers become familiar with the existing literature on a particular topic by conducting a _____ _____.

2. Researchers use _____ to attempt to explain, predict, and explore the phenomenon of interest.

3. The _____ hypothesis always predicts that there will be no differences between the groups being studied.

4. The _____ _____ is a measure of the effect (if any) of the independent variable.

5. The most effective method of assigning participants to groups within a research study is through a procedure called _____ _____.

Answers: 1. literature review; 2. hypotheses; 3. null; 4. dependent variable; 5. random assignment

Three

GENERAL APPROACHES FOR CONTROLLING ARTIFACT AND BIAS

I n Chapter 6, we will discuss the four main types of experimental validity and the potential threats associated with each. These threats are also referred to as *confounds,* or sources of artifact and bias. Remember that we conduct research to systematically study specified variables of interest. Any variable that is not of interest, but that might influence the results, can be referred to as a potential confound, artifact, or source of bias. The primary purpose of research design is to eliminate these sources of bias so that more confidence can be placed in the results of the study. Identifying potential sources of artifact and bias is therefore an essential first step in ensuring the integrity of any conclusions drawn from the data obtained during a study. Once the threats are identified, appropriate steps can be taken to reduce their impact.

Unfortunately, even the most seasoned researchers cannot account for or foresee every potential source of artifact and bias that might confound the results or be present in a research design. In this chapter, we will discuss general strategies and controls that can be used to reduce the impact of artifact and bias. These strategies are very useful in that they help reduce the impact of artifact and bias even when the researcher is not aware that they exist in the study. These strategies should be considered early in the design phase of a research study. Early consideration allows the researcher to take a proactive, preventive approach to potential artifacts and biases and minimizes the need to be reactionary as problems arise later in the study. Early consideration cannot be overemphasized because the worth of the findings of any research study is directly related to the reduction or elimination of confounding sources of artifact and bias. Implementing these basic strategies also reduces threats to validity and bolsters the confidence we can place in the findings of a study.

A BRIEF INTRODUCTION TO VALIDITY

Our introduction to this chapter suggests that the purpose of research is to provide valid conclusions regarding a wide range of researchable phenomena. Although we discuss it in detail in Chapter 6, a brief discussion of the concept of validity is necessary here to frame our general discussion of the experimental control of artifact and bias. *Validity* refers to the conceptual and scientific soundness of a research study or investigation, and the primary purpose of all forms of research is to produce valid conclusions.

Researchers are usually interested in studying the relationship of specific variables at the expense of other, perhaps irrelevant, variables. To produce valid, or meaningful and accurate, conclusions researchers must strive to eliminate or minimize the effects of extraneous influences, variables, and explanations that might detract from the accuracy of a study's ultimate findings. Put simply, validity is related to research methodology because its primary purpose is to increase the accuracy and usefulness of findings by eliminating or controlling as many confounding variables as possible, which allows for greater confidence in the findings of any given study. Chapter 6 further discusses the main types of validity and the specific threats related to each, so we will not go into any more detail about the subject in this chapter. The remaining material in this chapter will discuss general design strategies that can be used to help ensure that the conclusions drawn from the results of a study are valid.

SOURCES OF ARTIFACT AND BIAS

In Chapter 6, we discuss the most common threats to validity. The material in Chapter 6 is very specific to the four main types of validity encountered in research design and methodology—internal, external, construct, and statistical conclusion validity (see Rapid Reference 3.1). By contrast,

Rapid Reference 3.1

Four Types of Validity

- **Internal validity** refers to the ability of a research design to rule out or make implausible alternative explanations of the results, or plausible rival hypotheses. (A *plausible rival hypothesis* is an alternative interpretation of the researcher's hypothesis about the interaction of the dependent and independent variables that provides a reasonable explanation of the findings other than the researcher's original hypothesis.)

- **External validity** refers to the generalizability of the results of a research study. In all forms of research design, the results and conclusions of the study are limited to the participants and conditions as defined by the contours of the research. External validity refers to the degree to which research results generalize to other conditions, participants, times, and places.

- **Construct validity** refers to the basis of the causal relationship and is concerned with the congruence between the study's results and the theoretical underpinnings guiding the research. In essence, construct validity asks the question of whether the theory supported by the findings provides the best available explanation of the results.

- **Statistical validity** refers to aspects of quantitative evaluation that affect the accuracy of the conclusions drawn from the results of a study. At its simplest level, statistical validity addresses the question of whether the statistical conclusions drawn from the results of a study are reasonable.

the aim of this chapter is more general. While Chapter 6 discusses specific artifacts, biases, and confounds as they relate to the four main types of validity, this chapter provides valuable information on general sources of artifact and bias that can exist in most forms of research design. It also provides a framework for minimizing or eliminating a wide variety of these confounds without directly addressing specific threats to validity.

Although sources of artifact and bias can be classified across a number of broad categories, these categories are far from all-inclusive or exhaustive. The reason for this is that every research study is distinct and is faced with its own unique sources of artifact and bias that may threaten the va-

≡ Rapid Reference 3.2

Methods for Controlling Sources of Artifact and Bias

- Statistical controls
- Control and comparison groups
- Random selection
- Random assignment
- Experimental design

lidity of its findings. In addition, sources of artifact and bias can occur in isolation or in combination, further compounding the potential threats to validity. Researchers must be aware of these potential threats and control for them accordingly. Failure to implement appropriate controls at the outset of a study may substantially reduce the researcher's ability to draw confident inferences of causality from the study findings. Fortunately, there are several ways that the researcher can control for the effects of artifact and bias. The most effective methods include the use of statistical controls, control and comparison groups, and randomization (a more complete list is found in Rapid Reference 3.2).

A short discussion of sources of artifact and bias is necessary before we can address methods for minimizing or eliminating their impact on the validity of study findings. As mentioned, the types of potential sources of artifact and bias are virtually endless—for example, the heterogeneity of research participants alone can contribute innumerable sources. Research participants bring a wide variety of physical, psychological, and emotional traits into the research context. These different characteristics can directly affect the results of a study. Similarly, an almost endless array of environmental factors can influence a study's results. For example, consider what your level of attention and or motivation might be like in an excessively warm classroom versus one that is comfortable and conducive to learning. As you will see in Chapter 4, measurement issues can also introduce artifact and bias into the study. The use of poorly validated or unreliable measurement strategies can contribute to misleading results (Leary, 2004; Rosenthal & Rosnow, 1969). To make matters worse, sources of artifact and bias can also combine and interact (e.g., as when one is taking a poorly validated test in an uncomfortable classroom) to further reduce the validity of study findings. Despite the potentially infinite types and combinations of artifact and bias, they can generally be seen as falling into one of several primary categories.

Experimenter Bias

Ironically, the researchers themselves are the first common source of artifact and bias (Kintz, Delprato, Mettee, Persons, & Shappe, 1965). Frequently called *experimenter bias* this source of artifact and bias refers to the potential for researchers themselves to inadvertently influence the behavior of research participants in a certain direction (Adair, 1973; Beins, 2004). In other words, a researcher who holds certain beliefs about the nature of his or her research and how the results will or should turn out may intentionally or unintentionally influence the outcome of the study in a way that favors his or her expected outcome (Barber & Silver, 1968); the Rosenthal and Pygmalion effects (see Rapid Reference 3.3) are examples.

Experimenter bias can manifest itself across a wide variety of circumstances and settings. For example, a researcher might interpret data in such a way that it supports his or her theoretical orientation or a particular theoretical paradigm. Similarly, the researcher might be tempted to change the original research hypotheses to fit the actual data

$\equiv$ *Rapid Reference 3.3*

The Rosenthal and Pygmalion Effects

The *Rosenthal* and *Pygmalion* effects are examples of experimenter bias. Both of these terms refer to the documented phenomenon that researchers' expectations (rather than the experimental manipulation) can bias the outcome of study by influencing the behavior of their participants.

DON'T FORGET

Experimenter Bias

Experimenter bias exists when researchers inadvertently influence the behavior of research participants in a way that favors the outcomes they anticipate.

when it becomes apparent that the data do not support the original hypotheses. A related bias occurs when researchers blatantly ignore findings that do not support their hypotheses. Other, more innocuous examples include subtle errors in data collection and recording and unintentional deviations from standardized procedures. These biases are particularly prevalent in studies in which a single researcher is responsible for generating the hypotheses, designing the study, and collecting and analyzing the data (Barber, 1976). Let's now consider how experimenter bias might specifically manifest itself in the context of research methodology.

Consider an example in which a researcher is studying the efficacy of different types of psychotherapy. The study is comparing three different types of therapy, and our researcher has a personal belief that one of the three is superior to the other two treatments. Our researcher is involved in conducting screening assessments of symptom levels, and based on those results, assigns participants to the different treatment conditions. The researcher's personal interest in one particular form of therapy might lead to the introduction of a potential source of artifact or bias. For example, if the researcher thinks that his or her therapeutic preference is superior, then individuals with greater symptom levels might be unconsciously (or inadvertently) assigned to that treatment group. Here, the underlying bias might be that a superior form of treatment is necessary to help the participants in question. This could work in the other direction as well, when the researcher unconsciously (or inadvertently) assigns participants with low symptom levels to the treatment of choice. Either approach can bias the results and blur the findings as they relate to the relationship between the intervention and symptom level, or independent and dependent variables.

A subtler example could simply be the fact that the researcher unconsciously treats some participants differently from others during the administration of the screening or other aspects of the treatment interventions. Perhaps the researcher is having a particularly bad or stressful day and is not as engaging or amiable as he or she might otherwise be while interacting with the participants. Participants might feel somewhat different after interacting with the researcher and this might have an impact on their self-report of symptoms or their attitudes toward engaging in the study.

Another example of experimenter bias is related to training and sophistication. Like people in general, researchers possess varying levels of knowledge and sophistication, which can have a significant impact on any study. Consider our previous therapy example. Let's assume that three different researchers are conducting the therapeutic interventions. One researcher has 20 years of experience, the other has 10, and the final one is just out of graduate school and has little practical experience. Any results that we might obtain from this study might be a reflection more of therapist experience than of the nature and effectiveness of the three different types of therapy. Although subtle, experimenter biases can have a significant impact on the validity of the research findings because they can blur the relationship between the independent and dependent variables.

Controlling Experimenter Bias

As just mentioned, experimenter bias can have substantial negative impacts on the overall validity of a study. Fortunately, there are a number of strategies (listed in Rapid Reference 3.4) that can be employed to minimize the impact of these biases.

The first strategy is to maintain careful control over the research procedures. The goal of this approach is to hold study procedures constant, in an attempt to minimize unforeseen variance in the research design. In other words, all procedures should be carefully standardized. This might include the use of manualized study procedures, standardized instruments, and uniform scripts for interacting with research participants. Some studies go so far as to try to anticipate participant questions and behaviors and script out appropriate responses for researchers to follow.

Typically, this type of control is limited to the recruitment and assessment of participants and to the giving of standardized instructions throughout the study. Inclusion criteria and standards are usually developed to ensure that only appropriate participants are included in the study. Achieving this type of control is more difficult than it might sound. Remember that research participants bring a wide range of individual differences to any research study. Despite this, there are other steps related to

≡Rapid Reference 3.4

Strategies for Minimizing Experimenter Effects

- Carefully control or standardize all experimental procedures.
- Provide training and education on the impact and control of experimenter effects to all of the researchers involved in the study.
- Minimize dual or multiple roles within the study.
- When multiple researcher roles are necessary, provide appropriate checks and balances and quality control procedures, whenever possible.
- Automate procedures, whenever possible.
- Conduct data collection audits and ensure accuracy of data entry.
- Consider using a statistical consultant to ensure impartiality of results and choice of appropriate statistical analyses.
- Limit the knowledge that the researcher or researchers have regarding the nature of the hypotheses being tested, the experimental manipulation, and which participants are either receiving or not receiving the experimental manipulation.

constancy that researchers can employ to minimize the impact of experimenter bias.

One of the more common approaches to achieving constancy is to provide training and education on the impact and control of experimenter effects to all of the researchers involved in the study. Although it has been said that ignorance is bliss, this is usually not the case in research design. Ignorance of the potential impact of researcher behavior and attitudes on the results of a study is a common source of bias that can be easily addressed through education and training. Awareness of the potential impact of behavior is usually the first step in making sure that the behavior does not go unregulated or unchecked in a research context. Training and education are essential when there are varying levels of expertise among researchers or when the researchers have enlisted the help of support staff who possess little experience in conducting research. At a minimum, training in this area should include a discussion of the most common types of experimenter effects and how they are best minimized or eliminated.

As noted previously, there are numerous types of experimenter effects that can bias the results of a study. Some can be minimized through awareness and training, and others through standardized procedures. We also mentioned that experimenter effects might be more prevalent when one individual is acting in multiple roles within the study. This is particularly true in smaller studies for which funding and resources are limited, such as graduate school dissertation research.

The problem that this might produce in light of experimenter effects is an apparent one: temptation. The solution is relatively simple—use multiple researchers and provide appropriate checks and balances and quality control procedures whenever possible. It might also be helpful to divide responsibilities in a way that minimizes possible confounds and temptations to act in a way that might be inconsistent with drawing valid conclusions from the results of the study. Let's consider some examples.

Checks and balances, or quality control procedures, are essential for eliminating potential experimenter biases. As discussed previously, standardized procedures are the first step in ensuring the strength of a research design. Participant inclusion criteria, scripts, standardized interventions, and control of the experimental environment are all examples of standardizing various aspects of a research design. There are other steps related to standardization that can be taken to further bolster validity and minimize potential experimenter effects. Unfortunately, many of these approaches are labor intensive and require multiple researchers. When the inclusion of multiple researchers is not possible, informal consultation with knowledgeable colleagues should be utilized whenever possible.

Most studies begin with developing the research question, construction of the research design, and generation of hypotheses. Having multiple researchers involved in planning a research study brings a diversity of views and opinions that should minimize the likelihood of a poorly conceptualized research design. With an effective and appropriate design in place, multiple researchers can also be used to ensure that other aspects of the study are executed in a way that helps minimize or eliminate experimenter bias. For example, multiple researchers could develop participant inclusion and exclusion criteria. Similarly, participant inclusion might be dependent on agreement by two or more researchers as to whether the participant meets the required criteria.

Multiple researchers can also act as a quality control mechanism for the actual delivery of the intervention, or independent variable. Again, more than one researcher might be involved in designing the intervention related to the independent variable, and then in confirming that the intervention was actually delivered to the participants in the required fashion.

Data collection and analysis is another area where multiple researchers can be an asset to minimizing or eliminating experimenter bias. Audits can be conducted to determine whether mistakes were made in the data collection or data entry processes. Similarly, multiple researchers can help ensure that the correct statistical analyses are conducted and that the results are reported in an accurate manner (O'Leary, Kent, & Kanowitz, 1975). A statistical expert should be consulted whenever there is uncertainty about which statistical approaches might best be used to answer the research question. Finally, this approach can be useful in the communication of the results of the study because multiple authors bring a more diverse view to the conceptualization, interpretation, and application of the findings.

There are other methodological approaches that allow us to further minimize the impact of experimenter bias. Recall from previous paragraphs that knowledge about the research hypotheses and the nature of the experimental manipulation has the potential to inappropriately influence or bias the outcome of a study. It makes intuitive sense that limiting this knowledge (if permitted by the specific research design) might have a positive impact on the validity of the conclusions drawn from the study because it might help to further minimize the potential impact of experimenter effects.

There are three main approaches or procedures for limiting the knowledge that researchers have regarding the nature of the hypotheses being tested, of the experimental manipulation, and of which participants are either receiving or not receiving the experimental manipulation (Christensen, 2004; Graziano & Raulin, 2004). Each of these procedures seeks to reduce or minimize the researcher's knowledge about the participants and about which experimental conditions they are assigned to (Graziano & Raulin).

The first approach is referred to as the *double-blind technique,* which is the most powerful method for controlling experimenter expectancy and related bias. This procedure requires that neither the participants nor the researchers know which experimental or control condition the participants are assigned to (Leary, 2004). This often requires that the study be supervised by a person who tracks assignment of participants without informing the main researchers of their status (Rosenthal, Persinger, Vikan-Kline, & Mulry, 1963). Without this knowledge, it will be very difficult for the other researchers to either intentionally or inadvertently introduce experimenter bias into the study.

For a variety of reasons, it is often not practical or appropriate to use a double-blind procedure. This leads us to a discussion of the second most effective approach for controlling experimenter bias: the *blind technique.* The blind technique requires that the researcher be kept "blind" or naïve regarding which treatment or control conditions the participants are in (Christensen, 1988). As with the double-blind technique, someone other than the researcher assigns the participants to the required control or experimental conditions without revealing the information to the researcher.

If either the double-blind or blind technique is inappropriate or impractical, the researcher can resort to a third approach to minimizing experimenter bias. The final method for accomplishing this is known as the *partial-blind technique,* which is similar to the blind technique except that the researcher is kept naïve regarding participant selection for only a portion of the study. Most commonly, the researcher is kept naïve throughout participant selection and assignment to either control or experimental conditions (Christensen, 1988).

These three approaches—double-blind, blind, and partial-blind—are summarized in Rapid Reference 3.5. We will return to the topic of experimenter bias in Chapter 5.

Rapid Reference 3.5

Approaches for Limiting Researchers' Knowledge of Participant Assignment

- **Double-blind technique:** The most powerful method for controlling researcher expectancy and related bias, this procedure requires that neither the participants nor the researchers know which experimental or control condition research participants are assigned to.
- **Blind technique:** This procedure requires that only the researcher be kept "blind" or naïve regarding which treatment or control conditions the participants are in.
- **Partial-blind technique:** This procedure is similar to the blind technique, except that the researcher is kept naïve regarding participant selection for only a portion of the study.

Participant Effects

As just discussed, experimenter effects are a potential source of bias in any research study. If the researchers can be a significant source of artifact and bias, then it makes both intuitive and practical sense that the participants involved in a research project can also be a significant source of artifact and bias. Accordingly, we will now discuss a second common form of artifact and bias that can introduce significant confounds into a research design if not properly controlled. This source of artifact and bias is most commonly referred to as "participant effects."

As the name implies, the participants involved in a research study can be a significant source of artifact and bias. Just like researchers, they bring their own unique sets of biases and perceptions into the research setting. Put simply, *partic-*

DON'T FORGET

Participant Effects

Participant effects are a source of artifact and bias stemming from a variety of factors related to the unique motives, attitudes, and behaviors that participants bring to any research study.

ipant effects refers to a variety of factors related to the unique motives, attitudes, and behaviors that participants bring to any research study (Kruglanski, 1975; Orne, 1962). For example, is the participant anxious about the process, eager to please the researcher, or motivated by the fact that he or she is being compensated for participation? Do the participants think they have figured out the purpose of the study, and are they acting accordingly? In other words, are the participants, either consciously or unconsciously, altering their behavior to the demands of the research setting? (See Rapid Reference 3.6).

Rapid Reference 3.6

Participant Effects by Any Other Name . . .

Participant effects are also referred to as "demand characteristics." *Demand characteristics* are the tendencies of research participants to act differently than they normally might simply because they are taking part in a study. At their most severe, demand characteristics are changes in behavior that are based on assumptions about the underlying purpose of the study, which can introduce a significant confound into the study's findings.

In this regard, participant effects are very similar to experimenter effects because they are simply the expression of individual differences, predispositions, and biases imposed upon the context of a research design. Often, participants are unaware of their own attitudes, predispositions, and biases in their day-to-day lives, let alone in the carefully controlled context of a research study.

The impact of participant effects has been thoroughly researched and well documented. At the broadest level of conceptualization, research suggests that the level of participant motivation and behavior changes simply as a result of the person's being involved in a research study. This phenomenon is most commonly referred to as the *Hawthorne effect*. The term "Hawthorne effect" was coined as a result of a series of studies that lent support to the proposition that participants often change their behavior merely as a response to being observed and to be helpful to the researcher. There are numerous, more specific ways that participant effects could manifest themselves in the context of a research design. Many of these manifestations are directly related to the different roles that a participant might assume within the context of the research study.

Consider for a moment that most participants in research studies are volunteers (Rosen, 1970; Rosnow, Rosenthal, McConochie, & Arms, 1969). As such, these individuals might be different from other people who decide not to participate or do not have the opportunity to participate in the study. This is further confounded by the fact that a significant amount of research is conducted on college undergraduates enrolled in introductory-level psychology courses. Often, participation in research is tied to course credit or some other form of external motivation or reward. Accordingly, volunteer participants might be different from the general population as a whole, and the conclusions drawn from the study might be limited to this specific population. Therefore, even volunteer status may result in a participant effect because volunteers are a unique subset of the population with distinct characteristics that can have a significant impact on the results of the study.

Some commentators have taken the concept of participant effects to an even more refined level by identifying the different "roles" that a participant might consciously or unconsciously adopt in the context of a research study (Rosnow, 1970; Sigall, Aronson, & Van Hoose, 1970; Spinner, Adair, & Barnes, 1977). Although there is some disagreement about the existence and exact classification of participant roles, the most commonly discussed roles include the "good," the "negativistic," the "faithful," and the "apprehensive" participant roles (Kazdin, 2003c; Weber & Cook, 1972).

The "good" participant might attempt to provide information and responses that might be helpful to the study, while the "negativistic" participant might try to provide information that might confound or undermine it. The "faithful" participant might try to act without bias, while the "apprehensive" participant might try to distort his or her responses in a way that portrays him or her in an overly positive or favorable light (Kazdin, 2003c). Regardless of the role or origin, participant effects, either alone or in combination, can have a direct impact on the attitudes of research participants, which in turn can have an impact on the overall validity of the study. Specifically, participant effects can undermine both the internal and external validity of a study. Internal and external validity are discussed in detail in Chapter 6.

Controlling Participant Effects

As with experimenter effects, researchers should consider and attempt to control for the impact of participant effects. And, as with the sources of bias, the potential impact of these effects should be considered early on during the design phase of the study. Conveniently, one of the methods for controlling participant effects is exactly the same as one for controlling experimenter effects, namely, the use of the double-blind technique. Remember that this procedure requires that neither the participants nor the researchers know which experimental or control conditions the participants are assigned to. Without this knowledge, it would be difficult for participants to alter their behavior in ways that would be related to the experimental conditions to which they were assigned. This approach, however, would still not prevent a participant from adopting one of the preconceived participant roles we discussed previously.

Deception is another relatively common method for controlling participant effects. The use of deception should not be taken lightly because there are potential ethical issues that should be considered before proceeding. At a minimum, deception cannot jeopardize the well-being of the study participants, and at the conclusion of the study, researchers are usually required to explain to the participants why deception was used. When researchers use deception, it usually takes the form of providing participants with misinformation about the true hypotheses of interest or the focus of the study (see Christensen, 2004). Without knowledge of the true hypotheses, it is much more difficult for participants to alter their behaviors in ways that either support or refute the research hypotheses.

Double-blind and deception techniques are common ways of controlling for participant effects, and these approaches operate by altering the knowledge available to the participants. One drawback to these approaches is that the researchers will never know for certain whether their attempts at

CAUTION

Use Deception Cautiously and Only Under Appropriate Circumstances!

The use of deception in research design is controversial and should not be undertaken without serious consideration of the possible implications and consequences. Certain ethical codes and federal rules and regulations are very clear that the potential gains of using deception in research must be balanced against potential negative consequences and effects on the participants. Generally, the use of deception must be justified in the context of the research study's possible scientific, educational, or applied value. In addition, the researchers must consider other approaches and demonstrate that the research question necessarily involves the use of deception. Researchers must never use deception when providing information about the possible risks and benefits of participating in the study or in obtaining the informed consent of the research participants.

control were successful or what the participants were actually thinking as they progressed through the various aspects of the research study. Fortunately, there is one more approach for controlling for participant effects that allows the researchers to gather information about participant attitudes and behavior as they progress through the research study.

This third approach is straightforward and focuses on a process of *inquiry*. The researchers can simply ask the participants about any number of issues related to participant effects and the overall purpose and hypotheses of the study. Typically, the researchers will ask questions related to the hypotheses and the natures of the roles adopted by the participants. The timing of the questioning can vary. For example, participants might be asked about specific or essential aspects of the study in a retrospective fashion, after they have completed the study. On the other hand, the researchers might decide to question participants concurrently, throughout the course of the study. The choice of approach is up to the researchers. Regardless of timing, the intent of this approach is to allow the researchers to gather information directly from the participants regarding role, motivation, and behavior (Christensen, 2004). This information can then be controlled for in the statistical analysis or used to remove a certain participant's data from the analysis.

ACHIEVING CONTROL THROUGH RANDOMIZATION: RANDOM SELECTION AND RANDOM ASSIGNMENT

Our discussion so far has focused on approaches for controlling two common sources of potential artifact and bias, namely, experimenter and participant effects. Although important, these two types of artifact and bias represent only a very limited number of potential sources of artifact and bias that should be controlled for in a research study. Other types of artifact and bias can come from a variety of sources and are unique to the research design in question. We discuss these other types of artifacts and biases in detail in Chapter 6.

Controlling and minimizing these sources of artifact and bias is directly related to the quality of any study and it bolsters the confidence we can have in the accuracy and relevance of the results. In an ideal world, researchers would be able to eliminate all extraneous influences from the contexts of their studies. That is the ultimate goal, but one that no research study will likely ever obtain. As you can imagine, eliminating all sources of artifact and bias is virtually impossible. Fortunately, there are other methods that can be used to help researchers control for the influence of extraneous variables that do not require the a priori identification and elimination of all potential sources of artifact and bias. The most powerful and effective method for minimizing the impact of extraneous variables and ensuring the internal and external validity of a research study is randomization.

Randomization is a control method that helps to ensure that extraneous sources of artifact and bias will not confound the validity of the results of the study. In other words, randomization helps ensure the internal validity of the study by helping to eliminate alternative rival hypotheses that might explain the results of the study. (We will discuss internal validity in detail in Chapter 6.) Unlike other forms of experimental control, randomization does not attempt to eliminate sources of artifact and bias from the study.

DON'T FORGET

Randomization

Randomization is a control method that helps to eliminate alternative rival hypotheses that might otherwise explain the results of the study. Randomization does not attempt to eliminate sources of artifact and bias from the study. Instead, it attempts to control for the effects of extraneous variables by ensuring that they are equivalent across all of the experimental and control groups in the study.

Instead, randomization attempts to control for the effects of extraneous variables by ensuring that they are equivalent across all of the experimental and control groups in the study. Randomization can be used when selecting the participants for the study and for assigning those participants to various conditions within the study. These two approaches are referred to as "random selection" and "random assignment," respectively. As you may recall, the topic of randomization was briefly discussed in Chapter 2 in the context of choosing study participants and assigning those participants to groups within the study. In this section, we will discuss randomization as a strategy for controlling artifact and bias.

We will now discuss how participant selection and assignment constitute the most effective way of controlling for and minimizing the impact of sources of artifact and bias. As mentioned previously, it is impossible to identify, let alone eliminate, all of the potential confounds that can be at work within a research study. Despite this, researchers can still attempt to minimize the effects of these confounds by using random selection and random assignment in participant selection and assignment procedures.

Random selection is a control technique that increases external validity, and it refers to the process of selecting participants at random from a defined population of interest (Christensen, 2004; Cochran, 1977). We will discuss external validity in detail in Chapter 6. The *population of interest* is usually defined by the purpose of the research and the research question itself. For example, if the purpose of a research project is to study depression in the elderly, then the population of interest will most likely be elderly people with depression.

The research question might further define the population of interest; in this example, the research question might be the following: Does a new therapy technique alleviate symptoms of depression in people over the age of 65? In the broadest sense, the population of interest is therefore people with depression who are at least 65 years old. Ideally, we would be able to draw our sample of participants from the entire population of elderly individuals suffering from depression, and each of these individuals would have an equal chance of being selected to participate in the study. The fact that each participant has an equal chance of being selected to participate is the hallmark of random selection.

Random selection helps control for extraneous influences because it minimizes the impact of selection biases and increases the external validity of the study. In other words, using random selection would help ensure that the sample was representative of the population as a whole. In this case, a sample composed of randomly selected elderly individuals with depression should be representative of the population of all elderly individuals with depression. Theoretically, the results we obtain from a randomly selected sample should be generalizable to all elderly individuals with depression. Figure 3.1 provides a graphic representation of this example.

As you might suspect, random selection in its most general form is almost impossible to accomplish. Consider the resources and logistical network that would be necessary to randomly select from an entire population of interest. Would you want the task of randomly selecting and recruiting elderly, depressed individuals from across the world? From the United States? From the state or city in which you live? Although possible, random selection is a daunting prospect even when we narrow the population of interest.

For this reason, researchers tend to randomly select from samples of convenience. A *sample of convenience* is simply a potential source of participants that is easily accessible to the researcher. A common example of a sample of convenience is undergraduate psychology majors, who are usually subtly or not so subtly coerced to participate in a wide variety of re-

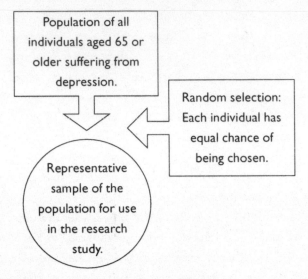

Figure 3.1   A graphic example of random selection.
In any research study, the population of interest is usually defined by the purpose of the research and the research question itself. In our current example, the purpose of the research study is to examine depression in the elderly, and the research question is whether a new therapy technique alleviates symptoms of depression in people over the age of 65.

search activities. We could conduct our study of depression and the elderly using a readily accessible sample of convenience, rather than attempting to sample the entire population of depressed elderly individuals.

For example, we might approach two or three local geriatric facilities and try to randomly select participants from each. In many instances, the study might simply focus on randomly selecting participants from one facility. The advantage of this approach is that we might actually be able to conduct the research and gain valuable, albeit limited, information on treating depression in the elderly. The primary disadvantage is that this approach has a negative impact on external validity. The sample will be smaller and

DON'T FORGET

Sample of Convenience

A *sample of convenience* is simply a potential source of research participants that is easily accessible to the researcher.

likely less representative of the population of depressed, elderly individuals, which can have a negative impact on statistical conclusion validity.

As will be discussed in Chapter 6, the aspect of quantitative evaluation that affects the accuracy of the conclusions drawn from the results of a study is called *statistical conclusion validity*. At its simplest level, statistical conclusion validity addresses the question of whether the statistical conclusions drawn from the results of a study are reasonable. Although an exhaustive discussion is inappropriate at this point, the results of certain statistical analyses can be influenced by sample size. Accordingly, the use of an exceptionally small, or large, sample can produce misleading results that do not necessarily accurately represent the actual relationship between the independent and dependent variables.

The second type of randomization control technique is *random assignment*, which is concerned with how participants are assigned to experimental and control conditions within the research study. The basic tenet of random assignment is that all participants have an equal likelihood of being assigned to any of the experimental or control groups (Sudman, 1976). The basic purpose of random assignment is to obtain equivalence among groups across all potential confounding variables that might impact the study. Remember that we can never eliminate all forms of artifact and bias, and random assignment does not attempt to do this. Instead, it seeks to distribute or equalize these potential confounds across experi-

DON'T FORGET

Random Assignment

Random assignment is a control technique in which all participants have an equal likelihood of being assigned to any of the experimental or control groups. Random assignment increases internal validity because it distributes or equalizes potential confounds across experimental and control groups. Studies that use random assignment are referred to as *true experiments*, while studies that do not use random assignment are referred to as *quasi experiments*. See Chapter 5 for a more detailed discussion of true experimental and quasi-experimental research designs.

mental and control groups. Let's consider our study of depression and the elderly to illustrate the concept of random assignment.

We manage to randomly select 30 participants from local geriatric facilities. Remember that we are interested in the effects of our new therapy on depression. Accordingly, we form two groups: The first group receives the treatment, while the other receives a psychologically inert form of intervention that does not involve therapy. We have 30 participants who must now be randomly assigned to the two conditions. According to the tenets of random assignment, we must ensure each participant has an equal probability of winding up in either of the two groups. This is usually accomplished by using a computer-generated random selection process or by simply referring to a table of random numbers. (Contrast this with a nonrandom approach to assignment.)

For example, taking the first 15 participants and assigning them to the treatment condition and the last 15 to the control condition would not be random assignment because the participants did not have an equal opportunity to be placed in either of the two groups. If we proceeded this way, then we could be introducing a selection bias into the study. The first 15 participants might be significantly different on a variety of factors than the second 15. Are the first 15 more motivated to participate because they are actively seeking symptom reduction? Motivation level itself might be a confounding variable. The second group of 15 might not be as motivated to participate for a variety of reasons.

Therefore, the results we obtained might be affected by these differences and not be a reflection of our intervention (the independent variable), even if we found a positive effect. If we randomly assigned the participants to each of the two groups, we would expect that the two groups should be equivalent in terms of participant characteristics and any other confounding variables, such as motivation. This equivalence is a researcher's best defense against the impact of extraneous influences on the validity of a study. Accordingly, random assignment should be utilized whenever possible in the context of research design and methodology. Figure 3.2 gives a graphic representation of random assignment in our example.

Obviously, random selection and random assignment—collectively re-

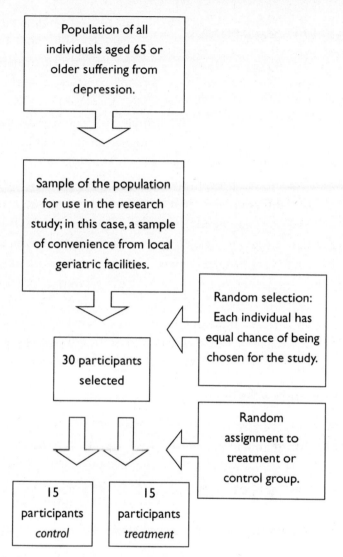

Figure 3.2 A graphic example of random assignment.

Using our new sample of convenience, we can build on the example provided in Figure 3.1 to illustrate the process of random assignment. We manage to randomly select 30 participants from local geriatric facilities. We must now randomly assign them to either the therapy group or the control group.

ferred to as "randomization"—are essential techniques for minimizing the impact of extraneous variables and ensuring the validity of the conclusions drawn from the results of a research study. Although optimal, randomization is not the only approach for minimizing, or controlling for, the impact of extraneous variables. In our previous discussion, we highlighted the theoretical and logistical difficulties inherent in trying to achieve true random selection and random assignment. These realities often make it difficult, if not impossible, to achieve true randomization. In some circumstances, randomization might not be the best approach to use because the researchers might be more interested in or concerned with the impact of specific extraneous variables and confounds. When this is the situation, some measure of experimental control can be achieved by holding the influence of the variable or variables in question constant in the research design.

Holding Variables Constant

The primary and most common method for holding the influence of a specific variable or variables constant in a study is referred to as *matching*.

This assignment procedure involves matching research participants on variables that may be related to the dependent variable and then randomly assigning each member of the matched pair to either the experimental condition or control condition (Beins, 2004; Graziano & Raulin, 2004). The application of matching is best illustrated through example. Let's revisit the example we considered earlier regarding a new treatment for depression in an elderly population.

In our previous discussion, we randomly assigned participants to either an experimental or a control condition. We will use the same basic premise in this example, in which we are still interested in knowing whether our treatment will produce greater reduction of symptoms of depression than will receiving an inert intervention that does not involve therapy. As we previously discussed, we sampled from the population in the same way, and still ended up using a sample of convenience; we then randomly assigned the participants to the experimental or control group.

Now let's add another layer of complexity to the scenario. We still want to know whether our new treatment is effective, but we might also be interested in the potential impact of other specific, potentially confounding variables. Consider, for example, that therapeutic outcome can sometimes be influenced by intelligence. Difficulties with memory and other modes of cognitive functioning might also significantly impact the outcome of therapy when working with elderly clients.

Given this, the researchers decide to control for the effects of memory in the study. Accordingly, the methodology is altered to include a general measure of memory functioning that demonstrates adequate reliability and validity. In practice, this assessment would have to be given before matching or assignment could occur.

The first step in the matching procedure would be to create matched pairs of participants based on their memory screening score. In this case, we have a two-group design—therapy versus an inert treatment (control group). The researchers would take the two highest scores on the memory test and those participants would constitute a matched pair. Next, this matched pair would be split and each participant randomly assigned such that one member ends up in the experimental group and one member ends up in the control group. In other words, each participant in this first matched pair still has an equal likelihood of being assigned to either the treatment or the control condition. The process is repeated, so the next two highest scores on the memory screen would be matched and then randomly assigned to the two conditions. The process would continue until each of the participants was assigned to either one of the two conditions.

Note that matching can be used with more than two groups. With three groups, the three highest scores would be randomly assigned, with four groups the four highest scores, and so on. Similarly, participants can be matched on more than one variable. In this case, for example, we might also be interested in gender as a potentially confounding variable. The researchers could take the two highest male memory scores and randomly assign each participant such that one is in the experimental and the other in the control group, and then repeat the procedure for females based on memory score. Ultimately, the goal is the same: to make the experimental and control conditions equivalent on the variables of interest. In our example, the researchers could safely assume that the two groups had equivalent representation in terms of gender and memory functioning.

Although matching is one of the more common approaches for holding the influence of extraneous variables constant, there are other approaches that can be used. The first of these approaches is referred to as "blocking." Unlike matching, which is concerned with holding extraneous variables constant, *blocking* is an approach that allows the researchers to determine what specific impact the variable in question is having on the dependent variable (Christensen, 1988). In essence, blocking takes a potentially confounding variable and examines it as another independent variable.

An example should help clarify how blocking is actually implemented in the context of a research study. Let's return once again to our treatment effective-

DON'T FORGET

Blocking

This assignment technique allows the researchers to determine what specific impact the variable in question is having on the dependent variable by taking a potentially confounding variable and examining it as another independent variable.

ness study for depression in the elderly. In the original design, we were interested in whether the new treatment was effective for reducing symptoms of depression in the elderly. There were two groups—one group received the new treatment and the other group received an inert or control intervention.

In this example, the independent variable is the new treatment and the dependent variable is the symptom level of depression. Blocking allows for a potentially confounding variable to become an independent variable. We will use memory as our potentially confounding or blocking variable. In other words, we not only want to know whether the treatment is effective, we also want to know whether memory functioning has an impact on therapeutic effectiveness. Therefore, the researchers might first divide the participants into two categories based on memory score. For instance, scores below a certain cutoff number would constitute the "impaired memory" group and scores above the cutoff number would constitute the "adequate memory" group. The participants would then be randomly assigned to either the experimental group or the control group. Note that now there are two independent variables, therapy and memory, and four groups instead of two groups in our study. In the original design, there were only two groups, experimental and control. Now the researchers have four groups: therapy/impaired memory, therapy/adequate memory, no therapy/impaired memory, and no therapy/adequate memory. As you can see, the researchers can now compare the performance of these groups to determine whether memory had an effect on therapeutic effectiveness. Without the use of blocking, these additional comparisons would not have been possible.

Another selection approach for controlling extraneous variables requires the researchers to hold the extraneous variable in question constant by selecting a sample that is very uniform or homogeneous on the variable of interest. For example, the researchers might first select only those elderly individuals with intact memory functioning for the therapy study, most likely based on a pretest cutoff score. All participants who did not meet the cutoff score would be excluded from the study. The participants would then be randomly assigned to the different experimental conditions. The rationale behind this approach is relatively straightforward. Specifically, if all of the participants are roughly equivalent on the variable under consideration (e.g., memory), then the potential impact of the variable is consistent across all of the groups and cannot operate as a confound. Although this is an effective way of eliminating potential confounds, it has a negative effect on the generalizability of the results of a study. In this example, any results would pertain only to elderly individuals with adequate memory functioning and not to a broader representation of elderly people suffering from depression.

Statistical Approaches

The final method for attaining control of extraneous variables that we will discuss involves statistical analyses rather than the selection and assignment of participants. Rapid Reference 3.7 lists the methods we'll describe in some detail here.

One statistical approach for determining equivalence between groups is to use simple analyses of means and standard deviations for the variables of interest for each group in the study. A *mean* is simply an average score, and a *standard deviation* is a measure of variability indicating the average amount that scores vary from the mean. (These concepts will be discussed in more detail in Chapter 7.) We could use means and standard deviations to obtain a snapshot of group scores on a variable of interest, such as memory.

Let's assume we randomly assign our elderly participants to our two original groups and that we are still interested in memory functioning as a potential confounding variable. Theoretically,

Rapid Reference 3.7

Statistical Approaches for Holding Extraneous Variables Constant

- Descriptive statistics
- T-test
- ANOVA
- ANCOVA
- Partial correlation

random assignment should make the two groups equivalent in terms of memory functioning. If we were cynical (or perhaps obsessive-compulsive), we could check the means and standard deviations for memory scores for both groups to see if they were consistent. For some researchers, eyeballing the results would be sufficient—in other words, if the means and standard deviations were close for both groups, we would assume that there was no confound. For others, a statistical test (*t*-test for two groups, or analysis of variance [ANOVA] for three or more groups) to compare the means would be run to determine whether there was a statistically significant difference between the groups on the variable of interest (Howell, 1992). If significant differences were found, then the groups would not be equivalent on the variable of interest, suggesting a possible confound. This approach can be particularly useful when random assignment is not possible or practical.

There are two other statistical approaches that can be used to minimize the impact of or to control for the influence of extraneous variables. The first is referred to as "analysis of covariance," or ANCOVA, and it is used during the data analysis phase (Huitema, 1980). This statistical technique adjusts scores so that participant scores are equalized on the measured variable of interest. In other words, this statistical technique controls for individual differences and adjusts for those differences among nonequivalent groups (see Pedhazur & Schmelkin, 1991; Winer, 1971).

A partial correlation is another statistical technique that can be used to control for extraneous variables. In essence, a *partial correlation* is a correlation between two variables after one or more variables have been mathematically controlled for and partialed out (Pedhazur & Schmelkin, 1991). For example, a partial correlation would allow us to look at the relationship between memory and symptom level while mathematically eliminating the impact of another possibly confounding variable such as intelligence or level of motivation. This assumes, of course, that appropriate data on each variable have been collected and can be included in the analyses. These statistical approaches can be used regardless of whether random selection and assignment were employed in the study.

SUMMARY

This chapter discussed general strategies and controls that can be used to reduce the impact of artifact and bias in any given research design. These basic strategies are particularly useful because they help reduce the impact of unwanted bias even when the researcher is not aware that bias is present. The implementation of these basic strategies ultimately reduces threats to validity and bolsters the confidence that we can place in a study's findings.

🐊 TEST YOURSELF 🐊

1. Theoretically, a sample is most representative of the total population when random _____ is used.
2. Deception can be used in any aspect of the study as long as the benefits of the study outweigh the potential risks. True or False?
3. The most effective way to equalize the impact of potentially confounding variables and ensure the internal validity of the study is through _____ _____.
4. Research participants can assume various roles that can influence the results of a study. True or False?
5. Research studies that are quasi-experimental are preferred over true experiments because they utilize random assignment. True or False?

Answers: 1. selection; 2. False (There are ethical prohibitions against using deception under certain circumstances.); 3. random assignment; 4. True; 5. False (True experiments utilize random assignment.)

Four

DATA COLLECTION, ASSESSMENT METHODS, AND MEASUREMENT STRATEGIES

The importance of measurement in research design cannot be overstated. Even the most well-designed studies will prove useless if inappropriate measurement strategies are used in the data collection stages. This chapter will discuss issues related to data collection and measurement strategies in research design. To be clear, this chapter is not meant to be an exhaustive treatment of the topic. Indeed, this area of research design could be, and has been, the topic of a number of in-depth texts devoted solely to the subject. Rather, this chapter is meant to highlight important concepts related to measurement and data collection. We start with general issues related to the importance of measurement in research design. Next, we consider specific scales of measurement and how they are related to various statistical approaches and techniques. Finally, we turn to psychometric considerations and specific measurement strategies for collecting data.

MEASUREMENT

Measurement is often viewed as being the basis of all scientific inquiry, and measurement techniques and strategies are therefore an essential component of research methodology. A critical juncture between scientific theory and application, *measurement* can be defined as a process through which researchers describe, explain, and predict the phenomena and constructs of our daily existence (Kaplan, 1964; Pedhazur & Schmelkin, 1991). For example, we measure how long we have lived in years, our financial success in dollars, and the distance between two points in miles. Important life decisions are based on performance on standardized tests that measure intelligence, aptitude, achievement, or individual adjustment. We predict that certain things will happen as we age, become more educated, or make other significant lifestyle changes. In short, measurement is as important in our daily existence as it is in the context of research design.

The concept of measurement is important in research studies in two key areas. First, measurement enables researchers to quantify abstract constructs and variables. As you may recall from Chapter 2, research is usually conducted to explore the relationship between independent and dependent variables. Variables in a research study typically must be operationalized and quantified before they can be properly studied (Kerlinger, 1992). As was discussed in Chapter 2, an *operational definition* takes a variable from the theoretical or abstract to the concrete by defining the variable in the specific terms of the actual procedures used by the researcher to measure or manipulate the variable. For example, in a study of weight loss, a researcher might operationalize the variable "weight loss" as a decrease in weight below the individual's starting weight on a particular date.

The process of quantifying the variable would be relatively simple in this situation—for example, the amount of weight lost in pounds and ounces during the course of the research study. Without measurement, researchers would be able to do little else but make unsystematic observations of the world around us.

Second, the level of statistical sophistication used to analyze data derived from a study is directly dependent on the scale of measurement used to quantify the variables of interest (Anderson,

DON'T FORGET
....

Importance of Measurement in Research Design

Measurement is important in research design in two critical areas. First, measurement allows researchers to quantify abstract constructs and variables. Second, the level of statistical sophistication used to analyze data derived from a study is directly dependent on the scale of measurement used to quantify the variables of interest.

1961). There are two basic categories of data: nonmetric and
metric. *Nonmetric data* (also referred to as *qualitative data*) are typically attributes, characteristics, or
categories that describe an individual and cannot be quantified.
Metric data (also referred to as
quantitative data) exist in differing
amounts or degrees, and they re-
flect relative quantity or distance. Metric data allow researchers to examine amounts and magnitudes, while nonmetric data are used predominantly as a method of describing and categorizing (Hair, Anderson,
Tatham, & Black, 1995).

DON'T FORGET

Nonmetric Data vs. Metric Data

Nonmetric data (which cannot be quantified) are predominantly used to describe and categorize. Metric data are used to examine amounts and magnitudes.

Scales of Measurement

There are four main scales of measurement subsumed under the broader
categories of nonmetric and metric measurement: nominal scales, ordinal
scales, interval scales, and ratio scales. Nominal and ordinal scales are nonmetric measurement scales. *Nominal scales* (see Rapid Reference 4.1) are the

≡ Rapid Reference 4.1

Distinguishing Characteristics of Nominal Measurement Scales and Data

- Used only to qualitatively classify or categorize not to quantify.
- No absolute zero point.
- Cannot be ordered in a quantitative sequence.
- Impossible to use to conduct standard mathematical operations.
- Examples include gender, religious and political affiliation, and marital status.
- Purely descriptive and cannot be manipulated mathematically.

least sophisticated type of measurement and are used only to qualitatively classify or categorize. They have no absolute zero point and cannot be ordered in a quantitative sequence, and there is no equal unit of measurement between categories. In other words, the numbers assigned to the variables have no mathematical meaning beyond describing the characteristic or attribute under consideration—they do not imply amounts of an attribute or characteristic. This makes it impossible to conduct standard mathematical operations such as addition, subtraction, division, and multiplication. Common examples of nominal scale data include gender, religious and political affiliation, place of birth, city of residence, ethnicity, marital status, eye and hair color, and employment status. Notice that each of these variables is purely descriptive and cannot be manipulated mathematically.

The second type of nonmetric measurement scale is known as the ordinal scale. Unlike the nominal scale, *ordinal scale* measurement (see Rapid Reference 4.2) is characterized by the ability to measure a variable in terms of both *identity* and *magnitude*. This makes it a higher level of measurement

≡Rapid Reference 4.2

Distinguishing Characteristics of Ordinal Measurement Scales and Data

- Build on nominal measurement.
- Categorize a variable and its relative magnitude in relation to other variables.
- Represent an ordering of variables with some number representing more than another.
- Information about relative position but not the interval between the ranks or categories.
- Qualitative in nature.
- Example would be finishing position of runners in a race.
- Lack the mathematical properties necessary for sophisticated statistical analyses.

than the nominal scale because the ordinal scale allows for the categorization of a variable and its relative magnitude in relation to other variables. Variables can be ranked in relation to the amount of the attribute possessed. In simpler terms, ordinal scales represent an ordering of variables, with some number representing more than another.

One way to think about ordinal data is by using the concept of greater than or less than, which incidentally also highlights the main weakness of ordinal data. Notice that knowing whether something has more or less of an attribute does not quantify *how much* more or less of the attribute or characteristic there is. We therefore know nothing about the differences between categories or ranks; instead, we have information about relative position, but not the interval between the ranks or categories. Like nominal data, ordinal data are qualitative in nature and do not possess the mathematical properties necessary for sophisticated statistical analyses. A common example of an ordinal scale is the finishing positions of runners in a race. We know that the first runner to cross the line did better than the fourth, but we do not know how much better. We would know how much better only if we knew the time it took each runner to complete the race. This requires a different level or scale of measurement, which leads us to a discussion of the two metric scales of measurement.

Interval and ratio scales are the two types of metric measurement scales, and are quantitative in nature. Collectively, they represent the most sophisticated level of measurement and lend themselves well to sophisticated and powerful statistical techniques. The *interval scale* (see Rapid Reference 4.3) of measurement builds on ordinal measurement by providing information about both order and distance between values of variables. The numbers on an interval scale are scaled at equal distances, but there is no absolute zero point. Instead, the zero point is arbitrary. Because of this, addition and subtraction are possible with this level of measurement, but the lack of an absolute zero point makes division and multiplication impossible. It is perhaps best to think of the interval scale as related to our traditional number system, but without a zero. On either the Fahrenheit or Celsius scale, zero does not represent a complete absence of temperature, yet the quantitative or measurement difference between 10 and 20 degrees

≡ Rapid Reference 4.3

Distinguishing Characteristics of Interval Measurement Scales and Data

- Quantitative in nature.
- Build on ordinal measurement.
- Provide information about both order and distance between values of variables.
- Numbers scaled at equal distances.
- No absolute zero point; zero point is arbitrary.
- Addition and subtraction are possible.
- Examples include temperature measured in Fahrenheit and Celsius.
- Lack of an absolute zero point makes division and multiplication impossible.

≡ Rapid Reference 4.4

Distinguishing Characteristics of Ratio Measurement Scales and Data

- Identical to the interval scale, except that they have an absolute zero point.
- Unlike with interval scale data, all mathematical operations are possible.
- Examples include height, weight, and time.
- Highest level of measurement.
- Allow for the use of sophisticated statistical techniques.

is the same as the difference between 40 and 50 degrees. There might be a qualitative difference between the two temperature ranges, but the quantitative difference is identical—10 units or degrees.

The second type of metric measurement scale is the *ratio scale* of measurement (see Rapid Reference 4.4). The properties of the ratio scale are identical to those of the interval scale, except that the ratio scale has an absolute zero point, which means that all mathematical operations are possible. Numerous examples of ratio scale data exist in our daily lives. Money is a pertinent example. It is possible to have no (or zero) money—a zero balance in a checking account, for example. This is an example of an absolute zero point. Unlike with interval scale data, multiplication and division are now possible. Ten dollars is 10 times more than 1 dollar, and 20 dollars is twice as much as 10 dollars. If we have 100 dollars and give away half, we are left with 50 dollars, which is 50 times more than 1 dollar. Other examples include height, weight, and time. Ratio data is the highest level of measurement and allows for the use of sophisticated statistical techniques.

PSYCHOMETRIC CONSIDERATIONS

A Note on Measurement and Operational Definitions

The assessment instruments and methods used in all forms of research should meet certain minimum psychometric requirements. As we will discuss later in this chapter, there is a wide variety of measurement strategies and techniques that are common in research design. As with considerations in research design, the research question and the constructs under study usually drive the choice of measurement technique or strategy. More specifically, the researcher is usually concerned with operationalizing and quantifying the independent and dependent variables through some type of measurement strategy. For example, depression can be operationalized through measurement by using the score from a standardized instrument. Similarly, a score on a personality trait measure might be used to operationalize a particular personality trait. Recall from Chapter 2 that an operational definition is simply the definition of a variable in terms of the actual procedures used to measure or manipulate it (Graziano & Raulin, 2004). Given this definition, it is easy to see that operational definitions are essential in research because they help to quantify abstract concepts. Operationalization can be easily accomplished through measurement.

For example, a researcher studying a new treatment for depression would be interested in operationalizing what depression is and how it is measured, or quantified. Although this might seem self-evident at first, consider all of the potential ways that depression could be operationalized and measured. Is it a score on an instrument designed to measure depression? Is it the presence or absence of certain symptoms as determined through a structured clinical interview? Could it be based on behavioral observations of activity level? This merely scratches the surface of the possible operational definitions of a single variable. Let's stay with the same example and consider how we would measure improvement in level of depression. After all, if we are interested in a new treatment for depression, we will have to see whether our participants improve, remain the same, or deteriorate after receiving the intervention. So, how should we quantify improvement? Depending on the operational definition, improvement could be determined by observing reduced scores on a depression assessment, reduced symptoms on a diagnostic interview, observations of increased activity level, or perhaps observations of two or all of these indices.

Ultimately, the choice lies with the researcher, the nature of the research question to be answered, the availability of resources, and the availability of measurement techniques and strategies for the construct of interest. In any event, the accuracy and quality of the data collected from the study are directly dependent on the measurement procedures and related operational definitions used to define and measure the constructs of interest. Regardless of the approach used, measurement approaches and instruments should meet certain minimum psychometric requirements that help ensure the accuracy and relevance of the measurement strategies used in a study. Reliability and validity are the most common and important psychometric concepts related to assessment-instrument selection and other measurement strategies.

Reliability and Validity and Their Relationship to Measurement

At its most general level, *reliability* (see Rapid Reference 4.5) refers to the consistency or dependability of a measurement technique (Andrich, 1981; Leary, 2004). More specifically, reliability is concerned with the consistency or stability of the score obtained from a measure or assessment tech-

≡ Rapid Reference 4.5

....

Measurement of Reliability

Reliability refers to the consistency or dependability of a measurement technique, and it is concerned with the consistency or stability of the score obtained from a measure or assessment over time and across settings or conditions. If the measurement is reliable, then there is less chance that the obtained score is due to random factors and measurement error.

So, how do we know if a measurement method or instrument is reliable? In its simplest form, reliability is concerned with the relationship between independently derived sets of scores, such as the scores on an assessment instrument on two separate occasions. Accordingly, reliability is usually expressed as a correlation coefficient, which is a statistical analysis that tells us something about the relationship between two sets of scores or variables. Adequate reliability exists when the correlation coefficient is .80 or higher.

nique over time and across settings or conditions (Anastasi & Urbina, 1997; White & Saltz, 1957). If the measurement is reliable, then there is less chance that the obtained score is due to random factors and measurement error. Measurement error is uncontrolled for variance that distorts scores and observations so that they no longer accurately represent the construct in question. Scores obtained from most forms of data collection are subject to measurement error. Essentially, this means that any score obtained consists of two components. The first component is the *true score,* which is the score that would have been obtained if the measurement strategy were perfect and error free. The second component is *measurement error,* which is the portion of the score that is due to distortion and imprecision from a wide variety of potential factors, such as a poorly designed test, situational factors, and mistakes in the recording of data (Leary, 2004).

Although all measures contain error, the more reliable the method or instrument, the less likely it is that these influences will affect the accuracy of the measurement (see Rapid Reference 4.6). Let's consider an example. In psychology, personality is a construct that is thought to be relatively

Rapid Reference 4.6

Strategies for Increasing Reliability and Minimizing Measurement Error

There are numerous practical approaches that can be used alone or in combination to minimize the impact of measurement error. These suggestions should be considered during the design phase of the study and should focus on data collection and measurement strategies used to measure the independent and dependent variables. First, the administration of the instrument or measurement strategy should be standardized—all measurement should occur in the most consistent manner possible. In other words, the administration of measurement strategies should be consistent across all of the participants taking part in the study. Second, the researchers should make certain that the participants understand the instructions and content of the instrument or measurement strategy. If participants have difficulty understanding the purpose or directions of the measure, they might not answer in an accurate fashion, which has the potential to bias the data. Third, every researcher involved in data collection should be thoroughly trained in the use of the measurement strategy. There should also be ample opportunity for practice before the study begins and repeated training over the course of the study to maintain consistency. Finally, every effort should be made to ensure that data are recorded, compiled, and analyzed accurately. Data entry should be closely monitored and audits should be conducted on a regular basis (Leary, 2004).

stable. If we were to assess a person's personality traits using an objective, standardized instrument, we would not expect the results to change significantly if we administered the same instrument a week later. If the results did vary considerably, we might wonder whether the instrument that we used was reliable (see Rapid Reference 4.7). Notice that we chose this example because personality is a relatively stable construct that we would not expect to change drastically over time. Keep in mind that some constructs and phenomena, such as emotional states, can vary considerably with time. We would expect reliability to be high when measuring a stable construct, but not when measuring a transient one.

≡Rapid Reference 4.7

Assessing Reliability

Reliability can be determined through a variety of methods:

- **Test-retest reliability** refers to the stability of test scores over time and involves repeating the same test on at least one other occasion. For example, administering the same measure of academic achievement on two separate occasions 6 months apart is an example of this type of reliability. The interval of time between administrations should be considered with this form of reliability because test-retest correlations tend to decrease as the time interval increases.

- **Split-half reliability** refers to the administration of a single test that is divided into two equal halves. For example, a 60-question aptitude test that purports to measure one aspect of academic achievement could be broken down into two separate but equal tests of 30 items each. Theoretically, the items on both forms measure the same construct. This approach is much less susceptible to time-interval effects because all of the items are administered at the same time and then split into separate item pools afterward.

- **Alternate-form reliability** is expressed as the correlation between different forms of the same measure where the items on each measure represent the same item content and construct. This approach requires two different forms of the same instrument, which are then administered at different times. The two forms must cover identical content and have a similar difficulty level. The two test scores are then correlated.

- **Interrater reliability** is used to determine the agreement between different judges or raters when they are observing or evaluating the performance of others. For example, assume you have two evaluators assessing the acting-out behavior of a child. You operationalize "acting-out behavior" as the number of times that the child refuses to do his or her schoolwork in class. The extent to which the evaluators agree on whether or when the behavior occurs reflects this type of reliability.

DON'T FORGET

....

Validity

The concept of *validity* refers to *what* the test or measurement strategy measures and *how well* it does so. Conceptually, validity seeks to answer the following question: "Does the instrument or measurement approach measure what it is supposed to measure?"

Although reliability is a necessary and essential consideration when selecting an instrument or measurement approach, it is not sufficient in and of itself. Validity is another critical aspect of measurement that must be considered as part of an overall measurement strategy. Whereas *reliability* refers to the consistency of the measure, *validity* focuses on what the test or measurement strategy measures and how well it does so (Anastasi & Urbina, 1997). Therefore, the conceptual question that validity seeks to answer is the following: "Does the instrument or measurement approach measure what it is supposed to measure?" If so, then the instrument or measurement approach is said to be valid because it accurately assesses and represents the construct of interest.

Validity and reliability are interconnected concepts (Sullivan & Feldman, 1979). This can be demonstrated by the fact that a measurement cannot be valid unless it is reliable. Remember that validity is concerned not only with what is being measured, but also how well it is being measured. Think of it this way: If you have a test that is not reliable, how can it accurately measure the construct of interest? Reliability, or consistency, is therefore a hallmark of validity. Note, however, that a measurement strategy can be reliable without being valid. The measurement strategy might provide consistent scores over time, but that does not necessarily mean it is accurately measuring the construct of interest.

Consider an example in which you choose to use in your study an instrument that purports to measure depression. It produces reliable scores as evidenced by a high test-retest reliability coefficient. In other words, there is a high positive correlation between the pretest and posttest scores on the same measure. On further inspection, however, you notice that the content of the instrument is more closely related to anxiety. You are measuring something reliably, but at this point it might not be depression. In other words, the instrument, though reliable, might not be a valid measure of depression; instead, it might be a valid measure of anxiety.

As we discussed earlier in this chapter, the accurate measurement of the constructs and variables in a study is a critical component of research. The most well-designed study is meaningless and a waste of time and resources if the independent and dependent variables cannot be identified, conceptualized, operationalized, and quantified. The validity of measurement approaches is therefore a critical aspect of the overall design process. How, then, is the validity of a measurement strategy established? Like reliability, validity is determined by considering the relationship, either quantitatively or qualitatively, between the test or measurement strategy and some external, independent event (Groth-Marnat, 2003). The most common methods for demonstrating validity are referred to as content-related, criterion-related, and construct-related validity (Campbell, 1960).

Content-related validity refers to the relevance of the instrument or measurement strategy to the construct being measured (Fitzpatrick, 1983). Put simply, the measurement approach must be related to the construct being measured. Although this concept is usually applied to the development and critique of psychological and other forms of tests, it is also applicable to most forms of measurement strategies used in research.

The approach for determining content validity starts with the operationalization of the construct of interest. The test developer defines the construct and then attempts to develop item content that will accurately capture it. For example, an instrument designed to measure anxiety should contain item content that reflects the construct of anxiety. If the content does not accurately reflect the construct, then chances are that there is little or no content validity.

Content validity can also be related to other types of measurement strategies used in research

DON'T FORGET
....

Content Validity

Content-related validity refers to the relevance of the instrument or measurement strategy to the construct being measured.

design and methodology. A significant amount of research, especially in psychology, is conducted using preexisting, commercially available instruments (see Rapid Reference 4.8). However, a researcher might be interested in studying a variable that cannot be measured with an existing instrument or test—or perhaps the use of commercially available instruments might be cost prohibitive. This is a relatively common situation that should not bring the study to a grinding halt. Most forms of research do not require the use of preexisting or expensive measurement strategies. It is not un-

≡ Rapid Reference 4.8

Commercially Available Instruments and Measurement Strategies

A huge number of measurement instruments are commercially available to researchers. They are particularly abundant in the areas of psychological and educational research. Researchers must be careful to consider a number of factors when deciding on whether an existing test is appropriate for data collection in a research study. A consideration of the psychometric properties (validity and reliability) is always an essential first step. Interested readers are referred to the latest editions of the *Mental Measurements Yearbook* and *Tests in Print,* which provide psychometric data and reviews for a wide variety of measurement materials (Impara & Plake, 1998; Murphy, Impara, & Plake, 1999). What follows is a nonexhaustive list of other factors that should be considered when evaluating a test:

• Reliability

• Validity

• Cost

• Time needed to administer

• Reading level

• Test length

• Theoretical soundness

• Norms

• Standardized administration procedure

• Well-documented manual

usual for researchers to develop their own measures or measurement strategies. This is a legitimate approach to data collection as long as the measure or strategy accurately captures the construct of interest.

Consider the following example. A researcher is interested in studying aggression in young children. The researcher consults the literature only to find that there is no preexisting measure for quantifying aggression for the age group under consideration. Rather than abandoning the project, the researcher decides to create a measure to capture the behavior of interest. First, "aggression" must be operationalized. In this case, our researcher is interested in studying physical aggression, so the researcher decides to operationalize aggression as the number of times a child strikes another child during a certain period of time. A checklist of items related to this type of aggression is then developed. The researcher observes children in a variety of settings and records the frequency of aggressive behavior and the circumstances surrounding each event. Although there are no psychometric data available for this approach, it is apparent that the measurement strategy has content validity. The items and the approach clearly measure the construct of aggression in young children as operationalized by the researcher.

Another effective approach to determining the validity of an instrument or measurement strategy is examining the criterion validity of the instrument or measurement strategy. *Criterion validity* is determined by the relationship between the measure and performance on an outside criterion or measure. The outside criterion or measure should be related to the construct of interest, and it can be measured at the same time the measure is given or some-

DON'T FORGET

Criterion Validity

Criterion validity is is determined by the relationship between a measure and performance on an outside criterion or measure. *Concurrent* criterion validity refers to the relationship between measures taken at the same time. *Predictive* criterion validity refers to the relationship between measures that are taken at different times.

time in the future. If the measure is compared to an outside criterion that is measured at the same time, it is then referred to as *concurrent validity*. If the measure is compared to an outside criterion that will be measured in the future, it is then referred to as *predictive validity*.

Again, an example may help clarify this concept. Let's assume that a researcher is using an instrument or has developed another measurement strategy to capture the construct of depression. There are a number of ways that criterion validity could be determined in this case. The measure would have concurrent criterion validity if the measure indicated depression and the participant met diagnostic criteria for depression at the same time. When both suggest the presence of depression, then we have the beginnings of criterion validity. The measure would have predictive criterion validity if the measure indicated depression and the participant met diagnostic criteria for depression at some point in time in the future.

The final concept that we will discuss with respect to demonstrating the validity of an instrument or measurement strategy is construct validity. *Construct validity* assesses the extent to which the test or measurement strategy measures a theoretical construct or trait (Groth-Marnat, 2003). Although there are numerous approaches for determining construct validity, we will focus on the two most common methods: convergent and divergent validity (Bechtold, 1959; Campbell & Fiske, 1959). Again, these concepts are best illustrated through an example. The first approach is to explore the relationship between the measure of interest and another measure that purportedly captures the same construct (i.e., *convergent validity*). Consider our depression example. If the instrument or strategy we were using in our depression study were accurately capturing the construct of depression, we would expect that there would be a strong relationship between the measurement in question and other measures of depression. This relationship would be expressed as the correlation between the two approaches, or a *correlation coefficient*. A strong positive correlation between the two measures would suggest construct validity. Construct validity can also be demonstrated by showing that two constructs are unrelated (i.e., *divergent validity*). For example, we would not expect our measure of depression to have a strong positive correlation with a measure of happiness. In this case, construct validity would be expressed as a strong negative correlation because we would expect the two constructs of happiness and depression to be inversely related—the happier you are, the less likely it is that you are suffering from depression.

MEASUREMENT STRATEGIES FOR DATA COLLECTION

> **DON'T FORGET**
>
> ### Construct Validity
>
> *Construct validity* assesses the extent to which the test or measurement strategy measures a theoretical construct or trait. There is a variety of approaches for determining construct validity. These approaches focus on the extent to which the measurement of a certain construct converges or diverges with the measurement of similar or different constructs.

So far, we have considered various basic issues related to measurement. We have highlighted the importance of scales of measurement and how they can guide data collection. Our discussion of psychometrics pointed out the importance of considering reliability and validity when choosing a measurement instrument or approach to quantify the independent and dependent variables under consideration. These are important considerations, but this chapter would not be complete without a discussion of some of the different methods and approaches used for collecting the data for the constructs of interest. Remember that the constructs of interest in any research study tend to be defined in terms of independent and dependent variables.

So, how do we measure our independent and dependent variables? They are, after all, the focus of any study. The number of available measurement strategies is staggering, and is sometimes limited only by the researcher's imagination and choice of research question. The choice of strategy also tends to vary by research question and research design, which is why it is difficult to account for every type of measurement approach. Despite this, the choice of measurement strategy is usually driven by a variety of factors that progress from general to specific.

The broadest consideration is always the nature of the research question and the independent and dependent variables. In other words, the researcher decides how best to measure the independent and dependent variables with the ultimate goal being to answer the research question. Addressing this broad and all-important choice requires the consideration of more specific factors.

For example, our earlier discussion highlighted the importance of scales of measurement. At what level should we try to measure our variables, knowing that this decision can affect our ability to employ certain statistical techniques during the data analysis stage? At this point, the thought might come to mind that all the researcher has to do is find a way to measure the variables of interest at the interval or ratio level of measurement. Although this might allow for the use of preferred statistical techniques, it is not always possible or even desirable to measure variables at the interval and ratio levels because not all variables lend themselves to these levels of measurement. Take a moment to think about all of the interesting and critically important variables that are measured by the nominal or ordinal scales of measurement. Gender, race, ethnicity, religious affiliation, employment status, and political party affiliation are all examples of nominal or ordinal data that are common in many forms of social science research.

Another factor might be related to the psychometric properties of the measurement strategy. Although reliability and validity are usually considered primarily in the context of psychological tests and other instruments, the concepts are important to consider in all types of measurement. The fact that you are not using a psychological test or other psychometrically validated instrument does not mean that reliability and validity are no longer important considerations. Regardless of what you are measuring and how you do so, that measurement approach should measure what it purports to measure and do so in a consistent fashion.

For psychological and other tests, a related issue is whether the instrument is appropriate for the population the researcher is studying. For example, consider a case in which a researcher wants to use an established, commercially available instrument to assess levels of depression in the elderly. The researcher would have to make certain that the test developers considered and captured this population when developing the instrument.

If they did not, then it would be inappropriate to use the instrument to study depression in this population.

Availability is another important consideration when selecting a measurement strategy. What approaches, if any, already exist for measuring the construct of interest? One might want to consider established forms of measurement, such as psychometrically based tests. Instruments of this type can be researched by consulting the most recent version of the *Mental Measurements Yearbook*. For example, there is a wide variety of psychometrically sound instruments available for the measurement of depression and personality. Another approach might be to review related research to see how others have measured the construct or similar constructs. The literature might suggest what instrument has been used most often to measure the construct of interest with the same population that you are interested in. Or, if there is no instrument available, it might suggest an appropriate strategy for capturing the construct. For example, previously conducted research might provide a framework for designing a unique assessment strategy for quantifying specific behavioral problems with young children. Note that original research questions might require the development of unique and specialized assessment instruments and strategies.

Cost is another consideration. Funding tends to vary from study to study. Some studies are well funded, while others are conducted with little or no funding. Those of you who conducted dissertation research with actual participants probably have some experience with the little-or-no-funding category. One of the primary drawbacks of using commercially available instruments is that they can be costly, hence the expression "commercially" available. There is considerable variation in the cost associated with various instruments. Some are very reasonable and others are cost prohibitive. The cost consideration is partially dependent on how many participants are in the study. The more participants to be measured on some construct, the higher the cost. In studies for which money is a serious consideration, the use of some commercially available instruments might be prohibitive. This might require the researcher to develop or create a measure or assessment strategy to capture the constructs of interest.

Although this is relatively common, there are some potential problems that arise from creating a new measure or measurement strategy. The first concern is that new instruments and strategies might have questionable reliability and validity. It cannot be assumed that the instrument or strategy is reliable or valid. At a minimum, the researcher will have to take steps to demonstrate the reliability and validity of the measurement approach. After all, you have to measure variables in a reliable and valid fashion before you can make any statements about the relationship between them, regardless of what statistical analysis might suggest.

Another issue regarding unique measurement approaches and instruments relates to the existing body of scientific literature in a given topic area. There are certain instruments and approaches that tend to appear in the scientific literature for the study of given topics. For example, there are a number of common measures of personality and depression that appear consistently in the research literature. Studies using these instruments can add to an existing body of literature. Conversely, studies using obscure or unique instruments and approaches, although valuable in and of themselves, might not be as relevant to that body of literature because the measurement strategies are not consistent and therefore not directly comparable.

Training is another factor to consider when selecting a measurement instrument or strategy. Training is important for two reasons: The first relates to the training of the researcher and is usually related primarily to the use of commercially available psychological and related tests. Many test providers have minimum user requirements. In our case, that would mean that the researcher must meet certain educational and/or training requirements before the company will permit the use of the instrument in the study. Although the requirements vary by test, the typical user must have an advanced degree in the social sciences or education, and/or have specific training in psychometrics. In some instances, test developers will allow the use of these instruments by less-qualified individuals if they attend a training seminar that provides a certification in the proper use of the instrument.

The second reason relates to training in a broad sense. The use of measurement instruments and strategies, whether commercially available or not, requires a theoretical foundation related to the construct of interest. For example, a researcher measuring some aspect of personality should be familiar with personality theory and the theoretical approach adopted by the instrument or strategy in question. Similarly, a researcher interested in evaluating the effectiveness of a behavioral modification system for children should be familiar with the theoretical underpinnings and practical application of concepts related to behavior modification before designing the measurement strategy. Remember that all validation begins after a concept has been given an accurate operational definition that reflects the construct of interest. Appropriate training assists in this process and is the first step in addressing the validity of the measurement strategy or instrument.

The time needed to conduct the measurement and the ease of its use are the last two factors that we will consider. Researchers should let the concept of parsimony guide them here. Generally, *parsimony* refers to selecting the simplest explanation for a phenomenon when there are competing explanations available (Kazdin, 2003c). The key concept here is simplicity. Researchers should attempt to measure the variables of interest as efficiently and accurately as possible. Remember the importance of reliability and validity. Depending on the construct, a longer and more complicated assessment will not necessarily provide a more accurate measurement than a strategy that is less complicated and takes half the time. In addition, the likelihood of mistakes, fatigue, or inattention among both researchers and participants might become more prevalent as the measurement strategy becomes more time intensive and complicated. This, in turn, could affect the accuracy of the data. In short, avoid unnecessarily long and complicated assessment procedures whenever possible.

METHODS OF DATA COLLECTION

With these factors in mind, we will now discuss some of the more common approaches to data collection and measurement in research. Again, there are many different approaches to data collection, and this discussion is not intended to be exhaustive of the subject matter. Despite this, there are certain broad categories that encompass the more common types of data collection techniques. Generally, and not surprisingly, the research question and the nature of the variables under investigation usually drive the choice of measurement strategy for data collection.

We have mentioned the use of psychological testing and other similar commercially available instruments throughout this chapter. The use of this type of testing in research is very common, especially in psychology, education, and other social sciences. A brief survey of available instruments suggests that we can capture a wide variety of factors related to the human experience. For example, instruments exist that allow researchers to measure personality, temperament, adjustment, symptom level, behavior, career interest, memory, academic achievement and aptitude, emotional competence, and intelligence. These instruments are attractive to researchers because they tend to have established reliability and validity, and they eliminate the need to develop and validate an instrument from scratch. Many of these instruments also produce data at the interval and ratio levels, which is a prerequisite feature for certain types of statistical analyses. The development of new instruments is best left to specialists with extensive training in psychological testing, psychometrics, and test development. In other words, always consider existing instruments as data collection methods before developing one of your own. A poorly designed measurement strategy can confound the results of even the best research design. Again, let reliability and validity be your guides.

Although testing is common, it is not the only method for data collection available to researchers. There are often times when it is necessary to adopt another approach to data collection. As we discussed earlier, there are many reasons that this might be the case. For example, not all variables of interest have been operationalized in the form of standardized tests, or some research questions might require unique or different approaches. Cost and time constraints might also be important considerations. In cases like these, the researcher might have to consider and adopt other data collection strategies. In many cases, these strategies are just as valid as, and are even preferable to, the use of formal testing.

Some of these alternative approaches, as summarized in Rapid Reference 4.9, include interviewing, global ratings, observation, and biological measures. As we will see, sometimes the most efficient data collection techniques are also the simplest.

A thorough *interview* is a form of self-report that is a relatively simple approach to data collection. Although simple, it can produce a wealth of information. An interview can cover any number of content areas and is a relatively

≡ *Rapid Reference 4.9*

Main Approaches to Measurement and Data Collection in Research Methods

- Formal testing (psychological, educational, academic, intelligence)
- Interviewing
- Global ratings
- Observation
- Biological measures

inexpensive and efficient way to collect a wide variety of data that does not require formal testing. One of the most common uses of the interview is to collect life-history and biographical data about the research participants (Anastasi & Urbina, 1997; Stokes, Mumford, & Owens, 1994). The effectiveness of an interview depends on how it is structured. In other words, the interview should be thought out beforehand and standardized so that all participants are asked the same questions in the same order. Similarly, the researchers conducting the interview should be trained in its proper administration to avoid variation in the collection of data. Interviews are a relatively common way of collecting data in research and the data they collect and the forms they take are limited only by the requirements of the research question and the related research design. One drawback of using an interview procedure is that the data obtained may not be appropriate for extensive statistical analysis because they simply describe a construct rather than quantifying it.

Examples of interviews are not difficult to identify. Employment interviews are a classic example. Although they are not typically used in research studies, their main goal is to gather data that will allow a company to answer the research question (so to speak) of whether someone would make a good employee. Interviews are also an essential component of most types of qualitative research, which is briefly discussed in Chapter 5. For example, if we were interested in the impact of childhood trauma on a participant's current functioning, we might construct an interview to capture his or her experiences from childhood through adulthood.

Like interviews, *global ratings* are another form of self-report that is commonly used as a data collection technique in research. Unlike an interview, this approach to measurement attempts to quantify a construct or variable of interest by asking the participant to rate his or her response to a summary statement on a numerical continuum. This is less complex than it sounds, and everyone has been exposed to this data collection approach at one point in time or another. If a researcher were interested in measuring attitudes toward a class in research methods, he or she could develop a set of summary statements and then ask the participants to rate their attitudes along a bipolar continuum. One statement might look like this:

On a scale of 1 to 5, please rate the extent to which you enjoy the research-methods class.

1	2	3	4	5
Hate it		Neutral		Love it

In this example, the participant would simply circle the appropriate number that best reflects his or her attitude toward the research-methods class. The use of global ratings is also common when asking participants to rate emotional states, symptoms, and levels of distress.

The strength of global ratings is that they can be adapted for a wide variety of topics and questions. They also yield interval or ratio data. Despite this, researchers should be aware that such a rating is only a global measure of a construct and might not capture its complexity or more subtle nuances. For example, the previous example may tell us how much someone enjoys a certain research-method class, but it will not tell us why the person either loves it or hates it.

Observation is another versatile approach to data collection. This approach relies on the direct observation of the construct of interest, which is often some type of behavior. In essence, if you can observe it, you can find some way of measuring it. The use of this approach is widespread in a variety of research, educational, and treatment settings.

Let's consider the use of observation in a research setting. This approach is an efficient way to collect data when the researcher is interested in studying and quantifying some type of behavior. For example, a researcher might be interested in studying cooperative behavior of young children in a classroom setting. After operationalizing "cooperative behavior" as sharing toys, the researcher develops a system for quantifying the behavior. In this case, it might be as simple as sitting unobtrusively in a corner of the classroom, observing the behavior of the children, and counting the number of times that they engage in cooperative behavior. Alternatively, if we were interested in studying levels of boredom in a research-methods class, we could simply count the number of yawns or number of times that someone nods off.

As with other forms of data collection, the process of quantifying observations should be standardized. The behavior in question must be accurately operationalized and everyone involved in the data collection should be trained to ensure accuracy of observation. Proper operationalization of the variable and adequate training should help ensure adequate validity and interrater reliability. Videotaping and multiple raters are frequently used to confirm the accuracy of the observations. The use of observational methods usually produces frequency counts of a particular behavior or behaviors. These data are frequently at the interval and ratio level.

Obtaining *biological measures* is another strategy for collecting research data. This approach is common in medical and psychobiological research. It often involves measuring the physiological responses of participants to any number of potential stimuli. The most common examples of responses include heart rate, respiration, blood pressure, and galvanic skin response. As with all of the forms of measurement that we have discussed,

DON'T FORGET

Multiple Measurement Strategies

Multiple measurement strategies can be used in a research study, even if they are all used to measure the same construct or variable. For example, a psychological test, an interview, and a global rating could all be used to measure the construct of depression. This may be considered an optimal approach, as convergence on multiple measures would increase overall confidence in a study's findings.

operationalization and standardization are essential. Consider a study investigating levels of anxiety in response to a certain aversive stimulus. We could use any of the other measurement approaches to gather the data we need regarding anxiety, but we chose instead to collect biological data because it is very difficult for people to regulate or fake their responses. We operationalize anxiety as scores on certain physiological responses, such as heart rate and respiration. Each participant is exposed to the stimulus in the exact same fashion and then is measured across the biological indicators we chose to operationalize anxiety. The data obtained from biological measures are frequently at the interval or ratio level.

SUMMARY

This chapter focused on important issues and considerations related to various aspects of data collection and measurement. Measurement strategies are an integral aspect of research design and methodology that should be considered at the earliest stages of design conceptualization. Special consideration should be given to scales of measurement, psychometric properties, and specific measurement strategies for collecting data. Ultimately, measurement is critical in research because it allows researchers to quantify abstract constructs and variables. This is an essential step in exploring the relationship between various independent and dependent variables.

Putting It Into Practice

An Example

Suppose a researcher is asked to design a study to examine student attitudes toward two different research-methods classes taught by two different instructors. The researcher is told that the purpose of the study is to determine whether there are significant differences in satisfaction between the two classes. The referral source cannot provide a significant level of funding. The researcher starts by clarifying the research question and the variables to be quantified and studied. The referral source wants to quantify whether there are significant differences between the two classes' satisfaction levels with regard to a variety of class components, such as class size, quality of the instructor, usefulness of the textbook, pace of the class, and so on. These components are the variables of interest. The referral source wants to compare the two classes, which suggests that certain parametric statistical tests (e.g., a *t*-test) will be used to determine whether there are differences between the two classes on the variables of interest. Accordingly, the researcher decides that the variables of interest should be measured at the interval or ratio level.

The key question is what measurement strategy to use. The researcher needs a measurement strategy that allows for measurement at the interval or ratio level. Not surprisingly, a review of the *Mental Measurements Yearbook* and the literature reveals that there are no existing measures of student satisfaction toward certain components of a research-methods class. Furthermore, an interview will not provide interval or ratio data, and it might be inappropriate to take biological measurements in this setting because it would certainly be cost prohibitive and would disrupt the flow of the classes. Behavioral observation might allow us to infer satisfaction, but it is not a direct measure of the variables we have been asked to assess. Remember that what is being measured is satisfaction with a number of different course components, and not just general satisfaction with the class.

The researcher decides to use global ratings. Questions are designed to capture the variables of interest and the students will be asked to respond on a scale from 1 to 5, with 5 suggesting *extreme satisfaction* and 1 suggesting *extreme dissatisfaction*. This approach is cost effective and will provide data at the interval level (because there is no absolute zero on the scale), which will allow for the use of the preferred parametric statistical technique. Wanting to be thorough, the researcher includes an open-

(continued)

ended question (an interview question) with each global rating so that the students can elaborate on their numerical rating with narrative material. Although this type of information does not lend itself to statistical analysis, it should provide more specifics as to why the students are satisfied or dissatisfied with various class components. The data are collected and analyzed, and the results, perhaps not surprisingly, suggest that everyone is dissatisfied with everything about research methods!

🐟 TEST YOURSELF 🐟

1. _____ is often defined as a process through which researchers describe, explain, and predict the phenomena and constructs of our daily existence.

2. _____ data constitute the highest level of measurement and allow for the use of sophisticated statistical techniques.

3. _____, or qualitative, data are the attributes, characteristics, or categories that describe an individual and are used predominantly as a method of describing and categorizing. _____, or quantitative, data refer to differing amounts or degrees of an attribute, and these data reflect relative quantity or distance.

4. A measurement can be valid, but not reliable. True or False?

5. _____ and _____ are two important psychometric considerations when selecting psychological and other tests.

Answers: 1. Measurement; 2. Ratio; 3. Nonmetric, Metric; 4. False (A measure must be reliable to be valid.); 5. Reliability, validity

Five

GENERAL TYPES OF RESEARCH DESIGNS AND APPROACHES

Once the researcher has determined the specific question to be answered and has operationalized the variables and research question into a clear, measurable hypothesis, it is time to consider a suitable research design. Although there are endless ways of classifying research designs, they usually fall into one of three general categories: experimental, quasi-experimental, and nonexperimental. This classification system is based primarily on the strength of the design's experimental control. To determine the classification of a particular research design, it is helpful to ask several key questions. First, does the design involve random assignment to different conditions? If random assignment is used, it is considered to be a randomized, or true, experimental design. If random assignment is not used, then a second question must be asked: Does the design use either multiple groups or multiple waves of measurement? If the answer is yes, the design is considered quasi-experimental. If the answer is no, the design would be considered nonexperimental (see Trochim, 2001).

Although each of the three types of research designs can provide useful information, they differ greatly in the degree to which they enable researchers to draw confident causal inferences from a study's findings (as discussed in Chapter 1). In this chapter, we will review each of the three classes of research design, the ways that each type of research design are applied, and the overall strengths and weaknesses of each type of research design.

EXPERIMENTAL DESIGNS

A true experimental design is one in which study participants are randomly assigned to experimental and control groups. We have discussed randomization in previous chapters, so this chapter will simply highlight the importance of randomization in terms of the strength of a research design. Although randomization is typically described using examples such as rolling dice, flipping a coin, or picking a number out of a hat, most studies now rely on the use of random numbers tables to help them assign their research participants (as discussed in Chapters 2 and 3).

A *random numbers table* is nothing more than a random list of numbers displayed or printed in a series of columns and rows. Typically, computer programs that generate such lists allow you to request a specific quantity and range of numbers to be generated. To use a random numbers table to assign study participants to groups, you must first determine the exact numbers that you will use to determine the assignments. For example, if you have three groups or conditions, you may use the numbers 1, 2, and 3. Alternatively, if you were assigning participants to two groups, you could use the numbers 1 and 2, or simply odd or even numbers, to determine the group assignments. The important point is that you define the assignment criteria ahead of time, so that your selections are not biased and remain purely random.

DON'T FORGET

....

Random Numbers Table

A *random numbers table* is nothing more than a random list of numbers displayed or printed in a series of columns and rows. Using a random numbers table is one effective way to randomly assign participants to groups within a research study.

After selecting your assignment criteria, you must randomly identify a starting place in the random numbers table. This is usually done by either selecting a starting place on the table before beginning (e.g., top right of third column) or simply closing your eyes and randomly pointing to a location on the table, which will serve as the starting point. Once you have selected a starting point, you will simply move through the list (either down the columns or across the rows) and identify each instance that numbers in your selected range appear until you have group assignments for your entire sample of participants.

To illustrate, assume that you are planning to assign 100 participants to one of four different groups. You begin by defining the numbers 1, 2, 3, and 4 as the criteria for your group assignments. You then randomly point to a spot on the table from which to begin, and go down the columns of numbers one by one listing each appearance of 1, 2, 3, or 4, while skipping all other numbers. Once you have listed 100 numbers, you will be done. The first number that you listed will determine the first participant's assignment, the second number will determine the second participant's assignment, and so forth. For example, using the table below, assume that we begin with number 0480 in the top row, left-most column of the table. If we worked our way down the columns, from left to right, listing appearances of 1, 2, 3, or 4 (in bold type) in the *last digit* of each number, we would wind up with the following series of assignments: 2, 4, 1, 1, 3, 3, 2, 3, 1, 3, 4, 1, 3, 1, 4, 2.

0480	5011	1536	2011	1647	9174
2362	6573	5595	5393	0995	9198
4134	8360	2527	7265	6393	4809
2167	3093	6243	1684	7856	6376
7570	9975	1837	6656	6121	1782
7921	6902	1008	2751	7756	3498

Although the standard randomization procedure will ensure randomized groups, it will not necessarily result in groups of equal size. To obtain randomized groups of equal sizes, you could use a *block randomization* procedure. This procedure is carried out in the same manner as discussed, except that participants are grouped into blocks. Each block will consist of one assignment to each of the study groups. Therefore, the number of participants per block is the same as the number of groups in the study. Using the prior example, you would proceed down the columns listing each appearance of 1, 2, 3, or 4 only once until the first block is full, before moving to the second block of four assignments, and so forth, until you have assigned 100 participants into a total of 25 blocks of four. Regardless of the technique used to randomly assign participants to groups within a study, random assignment increases the likelihood that changes in the dependent variable are attributable to the independent variables rather than to extraneous factors or nuisance variables.

For example, a researcher examining the effectiveness of a certain treatment will want to be confident that the experimental group (the group receiving the new treatment) does not differ from the control group (the group receiving an alternative or placebo intervention) at the start of the study. Otherwise, the researcher will be unable to confidently attribute any between-group differences that appear at the end of the study to the treatment rather than to some preexisting differences. Although the researcher could attempt to make the groups more comparable by matching the two groups on any number of variables, it would ultimately be impossible to make the groups identical. There are simply too many (perhaps an infinite number of) other individual differences that remain uncontrolled for and that may influence the study's outcome.

For example, the researcher may carefully match the two groups on characteristics such as age, gender, race, and socioeconomic status with the belief that these variables may have an impact on treatment outcomes. Although this procedure may make the groups more similar, the groups may still differ on other potentially important yet unmeasured variables, such as level of intelligence, degree of motivation, or prior treatment experiences. The fact that the groups may differ on some unknown and unmeasured variable substantially reduces the researcher's ability to attribute changes in the dependent variable to the independent variable and to draw valid causal conclusions from the data. Randomization, however, tends to distribute individual differences equally across groups so that the groups differ systematically in only one way: the intervention being examined in the study.

It is primarily for this reason that in most instances, when feasible, the randomized experimental design is the preferred method of research. Put simply, it provides the highest degree of control over a research study, and it allows the researcher to draw causal inferences with the highest degree of confidence. In general, randomized or true experiments can be conducted using one of three main designs: (1) a randomized two-group posttest only or pretest-posttest design, (2) a Solomon four-group design, or (3) a factorial design. The following notation will be used to describe the different designs:

X = experimental manipulation (independent variable); subscripts identify different levels or groups of the independent variable (e.g., X_1, X_2, X_3 is used to denote either a no-intervention or alternative-intervention control group)

Y = experimental manipulation (independent variable) other than X

O = observation

R = indication that participants have been randomly assigned

NR = indication that participants have not been randomly assigned

Randomized Two-Group Design

In their simplest form, true experiments are composed of two groups or two levels of an independent variable. Of course, as discussed in Chapter 2, these designs could incorporate any number of levels of an independent variable and could thus consist of three, four, or any other number of groups. The primary purpose of this design is to demonstrate causality—that is, to determine whether a specific intervention (the independent variable) causes an effect (as opposed to being merely correlated with an effect).

For example, a researcher studying smoking cessation may randomly assign identified cigarette smokers either to a novel medication (experimental) group or to a comparison (control) group. There are several different types of control or comparison groups that can be used in this type of design. The type of comparison group that is used largely depends on the specifics of the research hypothesis and the factors that the researcher wishes to control. For example, if the researcher wishes to examine whether the intervention is more effective than no treatment at all, the researcher may choose to use some form of placebo control group. The placebo control condition may involve a seemingly useful intervention, but one that has no demonstrable effects (e.g., a sugar pill). This would control for effects that may occur in the experimental groups as a result of experimenter attention or other forms of bias. Alternatively, if the researcher wants to know whether the intervention is superior to a standard treatment, the researcher would choose the standard intervention as the comparison group. There are two basic types of randomized two-group designs: the posttest only and the pretest-posttest design.

Randomized Two-Group Posttest Only Design

In its most basic form, the two-group experimental design may involve little more than random assignment and a posttest, as depicted here:

$$R—X_1—O$$

$$R—X_2—O$$

Because individual characteristics are assumed to be equally distributed through randomization, there is theoretically no real need for a pretest to assess the comparability of the groups prior to the intervention. In this design, random assignment ensures, to some degree, that the two groups are equivalent before treatment so that any posttreatment differences can be attributed to the treatment. This simple design encompasses all the necessary elements of a true randomized experiment: (1) random assignment, to distribute extraneous differences across groups; (2) intervention and control groups, to determine whether the treatment had an effect; and (3) observations following the treatment.

Randomized Two-Group Pretest-Posttest Design

Despite the relative simplicity of the posttest only approach, most randomized experiments typically utilize the pretest-posttest design, which is depicted here:

$$R-O-X_1-O$$

$$R-O-X_2-O$$

The addition of a pretest has several important benefits. First, it allows the researcher to compare the groups on several measures following randomization to determine whether the groups are truly equivalent. Although it is likely that randomization distributed most differences equally across the groups, it is possible that some differences still exist. This process of measuring the integrity of random assignment is typically referred to as a *randomization check* (see Rapid Reference 5.1). Researchers can often statistically control for such preintervention differences if they are found.

The second major benefit of a pretest is that it provides baseline information that allows researchers to compare the participants who completed the posttest to those who did not. Accordingly, researchers can determine whether any between-group differences found at the end of the study are due to the intervention or merely to differential attrition of

≡ *Rapid Reference 5.1*

Randomization Checks

The *randomization check*, as its name suggests, is the process of examining the overall effectiveness of random assignment. The goal of this process is to determine whether random assignment resulted in nonequivalent groups. In performing randomization checks, researchers compare study groups or conditions on a number of pretest variables. These typically include demographic variables such as age, gender, level of education, and any other variables that are measured or available prior to the intervention. Importantly, randomization checks should look for between-group differences on the baseline measures of the dependent variables because they are likely to have the most impact on outcomes. Generally, randomization checks involve the use of statistical analyses that can examine differences between groups (as will be discussed in Chapter 7). If differences are found on certain variables, the researcher should determine whether they are correlated with the outcomes. Any such variables that are correlated with outcomes should be controlled for in the final analyses.

participants across groups. *Attrition* is the loss of participants during the course of the study. This process is typically referred to as an *attrition analysis* (see Rapid Reference 5.2).

For example, consider a study in which we compare outpatient treatment to inpatient treatment for depression. After examining the posttest data, we conclude that outpatient treatment produced greater reductions in depression than the inpatient treatment. Although random assignment may have ensured that all participant differences were distributed equally at baseline, it did not ensure that all groups would be the same at follow-up. Therefore, it is possible that certain participants were more likely to drop out of one group than the other, resulting in differential attrition. In this example, clients with higher levels of depression may have been more likely to drop out of the outpatient treatment, which would explain the relative success of outpatient over inpatient treatment.

Inevitably, a certain proportion of study participants will not make it to follow-up. Often referred to as *mortality*, attrition can have many negative effects on the validity of a research study. First, it may substantially diminish the size of an experimental sample, which could reduce the study's statistical power and its ability to identify group differences if they exist. Second, because participants who drop out are likely to be different from those who complete, attrition may substantially limit the overall generaliz-

≡ *Rapid Reference 5.2*

....

Attrition and Attrition Analysis

Attrition analysis is a method of examining the overall impact of research attrition on the makeup of a study sample and the validity of a study's findings. The goal of this procedure is to identify any differences between those participants who complete the study and those who do not complete the study. To conduct this type of analysis, researchers compare completers versus noncompleters on a number of pretest variables. These may include demographic and any other variables that are measured or available on participants prior to the intervention. Generally, this process involves the use of several statistical analyses.

ability of a study's findings. Third, and perhaps most important, attrition from research is generally *not* randomly distributed (Cook & Campbell, 1979) and appears to be systematically influenced by the participant characteristics, the nature of research interventions, the type of follow-up methods employed, and many other variables. This can contribute to highly systematic differences in attrition rates between research conditions. Unfortunately, such differential attrition cannot be confidently controlled for by random selection, random assignment, or any other experimental research method (Cook & Campbell, 1963). As a practical matter, when attrition occurs, it can *never* be definitively established whether between-group differences in a particular study were caused by the experimental intervention(s) or by differential attrition across conditions (Campbell & Stanley, 1963; Cook & Campbell, 1963).

One obvious disadvantage of the pretest-posttest design is that the use of a pretest may ultimately make participants aware of the purpose of the study and influence their posttest results. If the pretest influences the posttests of both the experimental and control groups, it becomes a threat to the external validity or generalizability of a study's findings. This is because the posttest will no longer reflect how participants would respond if they had not received a pretest. Alternatively, if the pretest influences the posttests of only one of the groups, it poses a threat to the internal validity of a study. We discuss internal validity in detail in Chapter 6.

Despite this drawback, the two-group experimental design may be seen as the gold standard in determining whether a new procedure (or independent variable) causes an effect. Researchers often employ this design in the early stages of an intervention's empirical validation. At these initial stages, the researcher's primary aim may simply be to examine the effectiveness of the intervention. This can be done easily and relatively inexpensively by comparing the treatment to just one other group (typically a standard intervention or a placebo control). If the study's findings suggest that the treatment is effective, the researcher may want to test more-specific hypotheses regarding the treatment, such as isolating its effective components by dismantling the intervention (see Rapid Reference 5.3), examining its effectiveness with other populations, comparing it with

≡ *Rapid Reference 5.3*

Dismantling Studies

The term *dismantling,* as used in the research context, refers to studies aimed at isolating the effective components of an intervention. In studying specific interventions, researchers often begin by examining the effectiveness of the overall model. However, once the model is found to be effective, the research community will often want to know why it is effective. To answer this question, researchers may begin dismantling the intervention. Dismantling can be done in a variety of ways, but typically involves a series of studies that compare an intervention with and without certain components.

other types of treatment, or examining it in combination with other interventions. Testing these hypotheses may require the use of other, perhaps more sophisticated experimental designs.

Solomon Four-Group Design

It is perhaps easiest to understand the Solomon four-group design if we think of it as a combination of the randomized posttest only and pretest-posttest two-group designs, as depicted below.

$$R—O—X_1—O$$

$$R—O—X_2—O$$

$$R\text{———}X_1—O$$

$$R\text{———}X_2—O$$

The principal advantage of this design is that it controls for the potential effects of the pretest on posttest outcomes. This design allows the researcher to determine whether posttest differences resulted from the intervention, the pretest, or a combination of the treatment and the pretest. This last possibility is an example of an interaction, which will be discussed shortly. Importantly, this design offers the best features of both of the two-group designs, in that it allows the researcher to examine between-group differences at baseline, without the results' being influenced or confounded by the pretest administration. For this reason, the Solomon four-group design can also be viewed as a very basic example of a factorial design (discussed in the next section), as it examines the separate and combined effects of more than one independent variable (i.e., the pretest and the intervention).

Factorial Design

Most outcomes in research are likely to have several causes that interact with each other in a variety of ways that cannot be identified through the use of two-group experimental designs. For example, as discussed, the two-group pretest-posttest design might result in an undetectable interaction effect (see Rapid Reference 5.4 and Figure 5.1) between the pretest

≡ Rapid Reference 5.4

Interaction Effects

An *interaction effect* is the result of two or more independent variables combining to produce a result different from those produced by either independent variable alone. An interaction effect occurs when one independent variable differs across the levels of at least one other independent variable. Interactions can be found only in those factorial designs that include two or more independent variables. When reviewing the results of a factorial study, we begin by determining whether there are any significant interactions. If significant interactions are found, we can no longer interpret the simple effects (i.e., between-group differences for either independent variable alone), because they (as a result of the interaction) are determined to vary across levels of the other independent variable(s). This is illustrated in Figure 5.1, where the dose of a specific intervention is found to interact with client gender on the client success rate.

In this example, we cannot interpret the simple effects of gender or dose (on client success rate) because they vary as a function of each other. We can interpret only the interaction, which appears to indicate that males are more successful with lower doses, while females are more successful with higher doses.

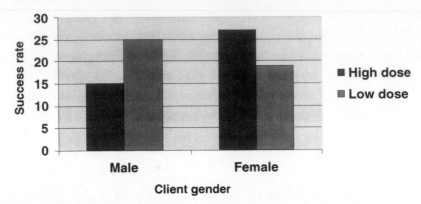

Figure 5.1   An example of an interaction effect.

and the independent variable, such that posttest differences, if found, could not be confidently attributed to the independent variable. The Solomon four-group design, which may also be viewed as a factorial design, was able to control for this potential interaction. The primary advantage of factorial designs is that they enable us to empirically examine the effects of more than one independent variable, both individually and in combination, on the dependent variable, as depicted in the following illustration. The design, as its name implies, allows us to examine all possible combinations of factors in the study:

$$R—X_1—Y_1—O$$

$$R—X_1—Y_2—O$$

$$R—X_2—Y_1—O$$

$$R—X_2—Y_2—O$$

To further illustrate the utility of this design, let us consider a situation in which a researcher is interested in examining how both treatment dose (4 vs. 8 sessions) and treatment setting (client's home vs. clinical setting) influence the effectiveness of a particular intervention. Although the researcher could conduct separate two-group randomized studies, this would not provide information on the potential interaction of different doses of treatment with different treatment settings. The researcher might, for example, want to test the hypothesis that higher doses of treatment provided in a clinical setting will result in the best treatment outcomes. To best examine this hypothesis, the researcher could make use of a factorial design. This specific example would be considered a two-by-two (2×2) factorial design, because each of the two independent variables has two levels, as illustrated here:

		Dose	
		Low (4 weeks)	High (8 weeks)
Setting	Home		
Setting	Clinical		

Following this same notation, a study with two independent variables in which one independent variable had three levels and the other had two levels would be considered a two-by-three (2×3) factorial design. Similarly, a study with three two-level independent variables would be considered a two-by-two-by-two ($2 \times 2 \times 2$) factorial design. Although a study could have any number of independent variables with any number of levels, it is important to note that each additional independent variable that is added to the factorial design increases the number of groups exponentially. Where a 2×2 design has four groups, a $2 \times 2 \times 3$ design will have 12 groups.

The factorial design has several important strengths. First, it permits the simultaneous examination of more than one independent variable. This can be critical because most, if not all, human behavior is determined by more than one variable. A second and related strength is the efficiency of the factorial design. Because it allows us to test several hypotheses in a single research study, it can be more economical to use a factorial design than to conduct several individual studies, in terms of both number of participants and researcher effort. Last, and perhaps most important, the factorial design allows us to look for interactions between independent variables. Just as most human behavior is influenced by more than one variable, it is equally probable that no combination of variables influences all persons in the same manner or influences human behavior the same way in all possible conditions. In other words, there are no universal truths. It is therefore critical to examine between-variable interactions to more accurately describe causal relationships (Fisher, 1953; Ray & Ravizza, 1988).

Are Experimental Designs Perfect?

Despite their seemingly ideal nature, even studies that employ experimental designs may face threats to validity in certain situations (Cook & Campbell, 1979). Threats to validity will be discussed in detail in Chapter 6, so we will not spend too much time discussing them in this chapter. We will, however, introduce you to some of the more common threats to validity. The first such threat occurs when a study's control group is inadvertently exposed to the intervention or when key aspects of the intervention also exist in the control group. This can substantially diminish the unique aspects of an experimental intervention and reduce any potential between-group differences.

Another situation that may threaten a study's validity (even with randomized experimental designs) occurs when one of the groups is perceived by participants as better or more desirable than the other. If participants in one condition feel that those in the other condition are somehow receiving superior treatment, they may experience feelings of resentment toward the researcher, may feel demoralized, or may even try harder or change their behavior to compensate. When condition assignment affects participant behavior in this manner, a *contrast effect* has occurred. Contrast effects can have a substantial impact on a study's findings.

Still another potential threat to the validity of an experimental design occurs when there are substantial differences in the implementation of the experimental and control conditions. For example, this may occur if the clinician delivering the experimental treatment were far more experienced or educated than the one delivering the control treatment. This could obviously confound the study's findings by diminishing the researcher's ability to attribute any measured change to the experimental intervention.

Finally, and very importantly, experimental designs are also not immune to the effects of differential participant mortality (or dropout). This is particularly likely when one of the conditions is noxious or onerous. Regardless of randomization, participant dropout can substantially reduce a study's internal validity by systematically creating two or more very different groups and ultimately undoing what randomization initially achieved.

Another important point about randomized experimental designs is that randomization, while far superior to other methods in ensuring that extraneous variables are distributed equally across groups, does not always work. This is of particular concern when sample sizes are small (i.e., fewer than 40 participants per group). Although researchers may attempt to examine the integrity of randomization by comparing the study groups on a number of pretest measures, they can never be certain that differences do not exist. Ironically, because they lack sufficient *statistical power* (i.e., the ability to detect between-group differences if differences actually exist), studies with small sample sizes are less likely to find between-group differences on such measures (Kazdin, 2003c).

The most obvious limitation of studies that employ a randomized experimental design is their logistical difficulty. Randomly assigning participants in certain settings (e.g., criminal justice, education) may often be unrealistic, either for logistical reasons or simply because it may be considered inappropriate in a particular setting. Although efforts have been made to extend randomized designs to more real-world settings, it is often not feasible. In such cases, the researcher often turns to quasi-experimental designs.

QUASI-EXPERIMENTAL DESIGNS

As just noted, although random assignment is the best way to ensure the internal validity of a research study, it is often not feasible in real-world environments. Therefore, when randomized designs are not feasible, researchers must often make use of quasi-experimental designs. A good rule of thumb is that researchers should attempt to use the most rigorous research design possible, striving to use a randomized experimental design whenever possible (Campbell, 1969).

Cook and Campbell (1979) present a variety of quasi-experimental designs, which can be divided into two main categories: nonequivalent comparison-group designs and interrupted time-series designs. In this section, we will discuss these two major groups of quasi-experimental designs, followed by a brief overview of single-subjects designs.

Nonequivalent Comparison-Group Designs

Nonequivalent comparison-group designs are among the most commonly used quasi-experimental designs. Structurally, these designs are quite similar to the experimental designs, but an important distinction is that they do not employ random assignment. In using these designs, the researcher attempts to select groups that are as similar as possible. Unfortunately, as indicated by the design's name, it is likely that the resulting groups will be nonequivalent. With careful analysis and cautious interpretation, however, nonequivalent comparison-group designs may still lead to some valid conclusions (Graziano & Raulin, 2004).

Nonequivalent Groups Posttest-Only (Two or More Groups)

In the nonequivalent groups posttest-only design, one group (the experimental group) receives the intervention while the other group (the control group) does not, as depicted here (NR = not randomized):

$$NR—X_1—O$$

$$NR—X_2—O$$

Unfortunately, there is a low probability that any resulting between-group differences on the dependent variable could be attributed to the intervention, so the results of a study using this design may be considered largely uninterpretable.

One potential application of this design (Cook & Campbell, 1979; McGuigan, 1983) is a case in which each of the groups might represent a different type of teaching method. If differences are found in the resulting test scores of students, it may suggest that the specific teaching method caused the differences. However, it is equally possible that students who were likely to achieve higher grades were selected for a specific teaching method. Ultimately, even this variation cannot rule out the serious threats to internal validity that plague this design.

Nonequivalent Groups Pretest-Posttest (Two or More Groups)

In the nonequivalent groups pretest-posttest design, the dependent variable is measured both before and after the treatment or intervention, as depicted here:

$$NR—O—X_1—O$$

$$NR—O—X_2—O$$

This gives it two advantages over its posttest only counterpart. First, with the use of both a pretest and a posttest, the temporal precedence of the independent variable to the dependent variable can be established. This may give the researcher more confidence when inferring that the independent variable was responsible for changes in the dependent variable. Second, the use of a pretest allows the researcher to measure between-group differences before exposure to the intervention. This could substantially reduce the threat of selection bias by revealing whether the groups differed on the dependent variable prior to the intervention.

Interrupted Time-Series Designs

The *time-series design* is perhaps best described as an extension of a one-group pretest-posttest design—the design is extended by the use of numerous pretests and posttests. In this type of quasi-experimental design, periodic measurements are made on a group prior to the presentation (interruption) of the intervention to establish a stable baseline. Observing and establishing the normal fluctuation of the dependent variable over time allows the researcher to more accurately interpret the impact of the independent variable. Following the intervention, several more periodic measurements are made. There are four basic variations of this design: the simple interrupted time-series design, the reversal time-series design, the multiple time-series design, and the longitudinal design.

Simple Interrupted Time-Series Design

The *simple interrupted time-series design* is a within-subjects design in which periodic measurements are made on a single group in an effort to establish a baseline, as depicted here:

$$O—O—O—O—X—O—O—O—O$$

At some point in time, the independent variable is introduced, and it is followed by additional periodic measurements to determine whether a change in the dependent variable occurs.

According to Cook and Campbell (1979), there are two principal ways in which the independent variable can influence the series of observations after it has been introduced: (1) a change in the level and (2) a change in the slope. A sharp discontinuity in the values of the dependent variable at the point of interruption (introduction of the independent variable) would indicate a change in level.

To better understand this, consider a study in which an employer was using a particular rating system to evaluate the employees' monthly productivity, before and after offering them stock options. One potential outcome might be a dramatic change in employee productivity. As depicted in Figure 5.2, employee productivity ratings that hovered between 2 and 3

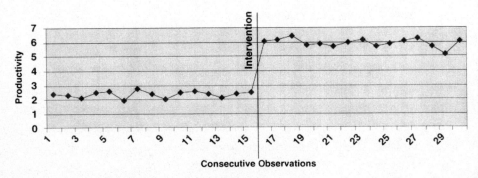

Figure 5.2 An example of a change in level.

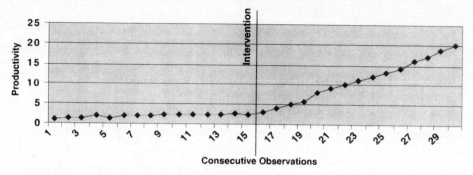

Figure 5.3 An example of a change in slope.

prior to the availability of stock options might abruptly rise to the 5–6 range following the company offer. Alternatively, as depicted in Figure 5.3, the employer might find a steady increase in productivity following the company bonus.

In addition to the level and slope, the researcher can examine the duration of effects and whether they ultimately persist or decay over time. Finally, the researcher can examine the ultimate latency of effects and whether the effect was immediate or delayed. The more immediate the change in the dependent variable, the more likely that the change is due to the influence of the independent variable. The ability to examine changes and trends across a series of observations made before and after the intervention permits the researcher to more closely identify the possibility of maturation, testing, and history as alternative explanations. (Maturation, testing, and history are discussed further in Chapter 6.)

Although changes in either level or slope are often used as the basis for inferring a causal relationship between the independent and dependent variables, such inferences must be made with extreme caution because this design does little to control for alternative explanations for measured change. For instance, in the prior example, it may have been the employer's attention rather than the bonus that led to increased employee productivity. Consequently, this design does not permit a researcher to draw causal inferences with any substantial degree of certainty.

Reversal Time-Series Design

Also known as an *ABA design* (detailed on page 145), the *reversal time-series design* is basically a multi-subject variation of the single-subject reversal design, which will be discussed later in this chapter. The basic goal of this design is to establish causality by presenting and withdrawing an intervention, or independent variable, one to several times while concurrently measuring change in the dependent variable (as depicted in the following). As in the simple time-series design, this design begins with a series of pretests to observe normal fluctuations in baseline. The name "reversal" refers to the idea that causality can be inferred if changes that occur following the presentation of an intervention diminish or "reverse" when the independent variable is withdrawn.

O—O—O—X—O—O—O—REV—O—O—O—X—O—O—O

      (A)   (B)   (A)

To fully appreciate the elegance of this design, consider the prior example in which an employer offers a company bonus. Imagine if, rather than offering a one-time bonus, the employer offered a monthly bonus to employees for 2 months, removed it for 2 months, and then again offered it for 2 months. If increases in productivity were found following each bonus, and decreases in productivity were found each time the bonus was removed, one could be fairly confident that company bonuses influenced employee productivity.

Despite the elegance of the reversal design, it is similar to its single-subject counterpart (to be discussed) in that it is not appropriate for the study of all independent or dependent variables. The fact is that the effects of some interventions simply cannot be reversed, as with learning to read or learning to ride a bike. You can offer and remove instruction on these skills as often as you like and you are still likely to observe a learning curve, with little reversal. It is therefore necessary for the researcher to carefully consider the characteristics of the independent variable to be studied when considering the use of this design.

Multiple Time-Series Design

This design is essentially the same as the nonequivalent pretest-posttest design, with the exception that the dependent variable is measured at multiple time points both before and after presentation of the independent variable, or *longitudinally* (see Rapid Reference 5.5), as depicted here:

$$O—O—O—O—X_1—O—O—O—O$$

$$O—O—O—O—X_2—O—O—O—O$$

Although this design is not randomized, it can be quite strong in terms of its ability to rule out other explanations for the observed effect. This design enables us to examine trends in the data, at multiple time points, before, during, and after an intervention (allowing us to evaluate the plausibility of certain threats to internal validity). Over and above the single-group time-series design, however, this design allows us to make both within-group *and* between-group comparisons, which may further reduce concerns of alternative explanations associated with history. Therefore, the major strength of this design is that it permits both within- and between-group comparisons. Regrettably, this design does not involve random assignment and thus is unable to eliminate all threats to internal validity.

Rapid Reference 5.5

Longitudinal Designs

Longitudinal designs involve taking multiple measurements of each study participant over time. Generally, the purpose of longitudinal studies is to follow a case or group of cases over a period of time to gather normative data on growth, to plot trends, or to observe the effects of special factors. For example, a researcher may want to study the development of more than one birth cohort (i.e., a group of individuals born in the same calendar year or group of years) to determine whether personality features are stable over time.

Single-Subject Experimental Designs

Not to be confused with nonexperimental single-subject case studies, which are covered later in this chapter, the single-subject experimental design has a long and respected tradition in empirical research. According to Kazdin (2003c), single-subject experiments might be seen as true experiments because they "can demonstrate causal relationships and can rule out or make implausible threats to validity with the same elegance of group research" (p. 273). Similar to other experimental designs, the single-subject design seeks to (1) establish that changes in the dependent variable occur following introduction of the independent variable (*temporal precedence*) and (2) identify differences between study conditions.

The one way that single-subject designs differ from other experimental designs is in how they establish control, and thereby demonstrate that changes in a dependent variable are not due to extraneous variables. For example, experimental designs rely on randomization to equally distribute extraneous variables and on statistical techniques to control for such factors if they are found. Alternatively, single-subject designs eliminate between-subject variables by using only one participant, and they control for relevant environmental factors by establishing a stable baseline of the dependent variable. If change occurs following the introduction of the intervention, or independent variable, the researcher can reasonably assume that the change was due to the intervention and not to extraneous factors.

As with time-series designs, single-subject designs typically begin by establishing a stable baseline. *Establishing a stable baseline* involves taking repeated measures of a participant's behavior (dependent variable) prior to the administration of any intervention to make certain that the participant's behavior is occurring at a consistent rate. To obtain a stable baseline, the researcher must make special efforts to control all relevant environmental variables that otherwise might affect the participant's responses. If the researcher does not know, or is uncertain, about which variables are relevant, the researcher must attempt to keep the participant's environment as constant as possible by maintaining highly controlled conditions.

Single-Subject Reversal Design

The reversal design (also known, like the reversal time-series design, as the ABA) is one of the most widely used single-subject designs. As in the reversal time-series design, the *single-subject reversal design* measures behavior during three phases: before the intervention is introduced (A), after introducing the intervention (B), and again after withdrawing the intervention (A). The primary goal of this design is, first, to determine whether there is a change in the dependent variable following the introduction of the independent variable; and second, to determine whether the dependent variable reverses or returns to baseline once the independent variable is withdrawn. To rule out the possibility that apparent effects might be due to a certain cyclical pattern involving either maturation or practice (to be discussed in Chapter 6), the ABA design may be extended to an ABAB design. To rule out even more complicated maturation or practice effects, the researcher could extend the design even further to an ABABA. Obviously, the more measurements that are made, the less likely it is that measured change is due to anything other than the intervention, or independent variable.

The single-subject reversal design has the same limitations as its time-series counterpart. First, and most obviously, not all behaviors are reversible. Certain behaviors, such as reading, riding a bike, or learning a language, are somewhat permanent. Second, withdrawal of certain useful interventions or curative treatments may be unethical. To address this issue, many studies opt for the ABAB variant, in which the intervention is repeated and is designated as the final condition.

Single-Subject Multiple-Baseline Design

A second, very common single-subject approach is the *multiple-baseline design*. This design demonstrates the effectiveness of a treatment by showing that behaviors across more than one baseline change as a consequence of the introduction of a treatment. In this design, several behaviors of a single subject are monitored simultaneously. Once stable baselines are established for all of the behaviors, one of the behaviors is exposed to the intervention. The primary goal of this design is to determine whether the behavior that is exposed to the intervention changes while the other behaviors remain constant. Once the first behavioral shift is identified, the intervention is applied to the next behavior, and so on. The logic behind this design is that it would be highly unlikely for baseline behaviors to successively shift by chance.

For example, suppose a tutor wants to test whether providing small prizes or rewards can change two distinct behaviors that one of her students is displaying (i.e., asking questions, and attending tutoring sessions on time). The tutor, after establishing a stable baseline for both behaviors, observes that the student asks an average of 3 questions per week, and attends tutoring sessions on time an average of 2 times per week. The tutor might begin by giving the student prizes for asking questions regardless of her tardiness for the first two weeks. At this point, the tutor may find that the student begins to ask an average of 5 questions per week, while her tardiness remains the same. After two weeks, the tutor might also begin giving the student prizes for attending her tutoring sessions on time. In other words, the tutor might begin rewarding both behaviors. After another two weeks, the tutor might observe that the student's average rate of question-asking remains at 5 times per week, but that her average on-time attendance increases to 4 times per week.

The primary limitation of the multiple-baseline design is that it requires the use of relatively independent behaviors. The behaviors that are being monitored must not be so interrelated that a change in one behavior results in similar changes in others even though the other behaviors were not exposed to the intervention. For example, Kazdin (1973) points out that the design would not be useful for the study of children's classroom behaviors because many of the classroom behaviors are interrelated.

Overall, single-subject designs may be an important and logical alternative to randomized experimental designs. Importantly, because of their focus on single-subject behavior, these designs may be particularly suited for clinicians who want to determine whether certain treatments are working for specific clients or patients.

In this section, we have provided a brief overview of several of the most widely used quasi-experimental designs. However, many other quasi-experimental designs are available. In fact, there appears to be a nearly endless number of ways to arrange the independent and dependent variables in an attempt to answer experimental questions with some degree of confidence. Unfortunately, despite their often elegant structure, quasi-experimental designs cannot automatically rule out threats to internal validity with the same degree of certainty that true experimental designs can. At this point, however, the overall utility of quasi-experimental designs should be evident. Although they do not enable us to draw causal inferences with the same degree of confidence as do randomized designs, they do allow us to begin to examine real-world phenomena and begin to establish causal inferences when true experimental designs are simply not feasible.

NONEXPERIMENTAL OR QUALITATIVE DESIGNS

In the past two sections, we discussed experimental and quasi-experimental designs. Each of these design classes can provide information from which to draw causal inferences, although to very different degrees of certainty. This is not the case for nonexperimental designs (i.e., descriptive and correlational designs). No matter how convincing the data from descriptive and correlational studies may appear, these nonexperimental designs cannot rule out extraneous variables as the cause of what is being observed because they do not have control over the variables and the environments that they study. Although there are many types of nonexperimental methods, an extensive review of these techniques and designs is beyond the scope of this chapter. Therefore, we will provide a brief overview of four of the most widely used approaches: case studies, naturalistic observation, surveys, and focus groups.

Case Studies

Case studies involve an in-depth examination of a single person or a few people. The goal of the case study is to provide an accurate and complete description of the case. The principal benefit of case studies is that they can expand our knowledge about the variations in human behavior. Although experimental researchers are typically interested in overall trends in behavior, drawing sample-to-population inferences, and generalizing to other samples, the focus of the case-study approach is on individuality and describing the individual as comprehensively as possible. The case study requires a considerable amount of information, and therefore conclusions are based on a much more detailed and comprehensive set of information than is typically collected by experimental and quasi-experimental studies.

Case studies of individual participants often include in-depth interviews with participants and collaterals (e.g., friends, family members, colleagues), review of medical records, observation, and excerpts from participants' personal writings and diaries. Case studies have a practical function in that they can be immediately applicable to the participant's diagnosis or treatment.

According to Yin (1994), the case-study design must have the following five components: its research question(s), its propositions, its unit(s) of analysis, a determination of how the data are linked to the propositions, and criteria to interpret the findings. According to Kazdin (1982), the major characteristics of case studies are the following:

- They involve the intensive study of an individual, family, group, institution, or other level that can be conceived of as a single unit.
- The information is highly detailed, comprehensive, and typically reported in narrative form as opposed to the quantified scores on a dependent measure.
- They attempt to convey the nuances of the case, including specific contexts, extraneous influences, and special idiosyncratic details.
- The information they examine may be retrospective or archival.

Although case studies lack experimental control, their naturalistic and uncontrolled methods have set them aside as a unique and valuable source of information that complements and informs theory, research, and practice (Kazdin, 2003c). According to Kazdin, case studies may be seen as having made at least four substantial contributions to science: They have served as a source of research ideas and hypotheses; they have helped to develop therapeutic techniques; they have enabled scientists to study extremely rare and low-base-rate phenomena, including rare disorders and one-time events; and they can describe and detail instances that contradict universally accepted beliefs and assumptions, thereby serving to plant seeds of doubt and spur new experimental research to validate or invalidate the accepted beliefs.

Case studies also have some substantial drawbacks. First, like all nonexperimental approaches, they merely describe what occurred, but they cannot tell us why it occurred. Second, they are likely to involve a great deal of experimenter bias (refer back to Chapter 3). Although no research design, including the randomized experimental designs, is immune to experimenter bias, some, such as the case study, are at greater risk than others.

The reason the case study is more at risk with respect to experimenter bias is that it involves considerably more interaction between the researcher and the participant than most other research methods. In addition, the data in a case study come from the researcher's observations of the participant. Although this might also be supplemented by test scores and more objective measures, it is the researcher who brings all this together in the form of a descriptive case study of the individual(s) in question.

Finally, the small number of individuals examined in these studies makes it unlikely that the findings will generalize to other people with similar issues or problems. A case study of a single person diagnosed with a certain disorder is unlikely to be representative of all individuals with that disorder. Still, the overall contributions of the case study cannot be ignored. Regardless of its nonexperimental approach—in fact, *because* of its nonexperimental approach—it has substantially informed theory, research, and practice, serving to fulfill the first goal of science, which is to identify issues and causes that can then be experimentally assessed.

Naturalistic Observation

Naturalistic observation studies, as their name implies, involve observing organisms in their natural settings. For example, a researcher who wants to

Putting It Into Practice

A Refresher on Eliminating Experimenter Bias

As discussed in Chapter 3, there are several effective strategies for reducing or eliminating the effects of experimenter bias. The first strategy is to develop and employ highly specific study procedures. Using clearly operationalized and standardized procedures can reduce the opportunity for bias to influence the way that study participants are treated and the way that data are considered or analyzed. A second strategy is to reduce or eliminate experimenter-participant interactions. For example, studies could be conducted via the Internet, or participants could receive study instructions and assessments via computer (Kazdin, 2003c). A third strategy is to keep the researcher unaware of participants' specific group assignments, typically referred to as making the researcher blind or naïve. Although this may be easiest in medication studies in which participants receive either a placebo or a real medication, it can (with a bit more effort) be employed in other studies. For example, a study could use multiple researchers within sessions, so that those who deliver the interventions are aware of the group assignments and those who administer the dependent measure are not.

examine the socialization skills of children may observe them while they are at a school playground, and then record all instances of effective or ineffective social behavior. The primary advantage of the naturalistic observation approach is that it takes place in a natural setting, where the participants do not realize that they are being observed. Consequently, the behaviors that it measures and describes are likely to reflect the participants' true behaviors.

In general, naturalistic observation has four defining principals (Ray & Ravizza, 1988). The first and most fundamental principle is that of *noninterference*. Researchers who engage in naturalistic observation must not disrupt the natural course of events that they are observing. By adhering to this principle, researchers can observe events the way they truly happen. Second, naturalistic observation involves the observation and detection of *invariants,* or behavior patterns or other phenomena that exist in the real world. For example, individuals may be found to engage in similar ways, on certain times or days, in certain contexts, or when in the company of certain people or groups. Third, the naturalistic observation approach is particularly useful for exploratory purposes, when we know little or nothing about a certain subject. In this vein, naturalistic observation can provide a useful but global description of the participant and a series of events as opposed to isolated ones. Finally, the naturalistic observation method is basically descriptive. Although it can provide a somewhat detailed description of a phenomenon, it cannot tell us why the phenomenon occurred. Determining causation is left to experimental designs, which were discussed in detail earlier in this chapter.

The main limitation of the naturalistic approach is that the researcher has no real control over the setting. In the hypothetical study of children's socialization skills, factors other than a child's gender may be affecting the child's social behavior, but the researcher may not be aware of those other factors. In addition, participants may not have an opportunity to display the behaviors or phenomena the researcher is trying to observe because of factors that are beyond the researcher's control. For example, some of the children who are usually the most aggressive may not be at school that day or may instead be in detention because of previous misconduct, and thus they are not in the sample of children on the playground. A final limitation is that the topics of study are limited to overt behavior. A researcher cannot study unobservable processes like attitudes or thoughts using a naturalistic observation study.

Survey Studies

Survey studies ask large numbers of people questions about their behaviors, attitudes, and opinions. Some surveys merely describe what people say they think and do. Other survey studies attempt to find relationships between the characteristics of the respondents and their reported behaviors and opinions. For example, a survey could examine whether there is a relationship between gender and people's attitudes about some social issue. When surveys are conducted to determine relationships, as for this second purpose, they are referred to as *correlational studies*.

Campbell and Katona (1953) delineated nine general steps for conducting a survey. Although this list is more than 50 years old, it is as useful now as it was then in providing a clear overview of survey procedures. The nine steps are as follows:

1. *General objectives:* This step involves defining the general purpose and goal of the survey.
2. *Specific objectives:* This step involves developing more specificity regarding the types of data that will be collected, and specifying the hypothesis to be tested.
3. *Sample:* The major foci of this step are to determine the specific population that will be surveyed, to decide on an appropriate sample, and to determine the criteria that will be used to select the sample.
4. *Questionnaire:* The focus of this step is deciding how the sample is to be surveyed (e.g., by mail, by phone, in person) and developing the specific questions that will be used. This is a particularly important step that involves determining the content and structure (e.g., open-ended, closed-ended, Likert scales; see Rapid Reference 5.6) of the questions, as well as the general format of the survey instrument (e.g., scripted introduction, order of the questions). Importantly, the final survey should be subjected to a protocol analysis in which it is administered to numerous individuals to determine whether (a) it is clear and understandable and (b) the questions get at the type of information that they were designed to collect. For certain scales, such as Likert scales, you may also want to look for certain response patterns to see whether there is a problematic response set that emerges, as indicated by restricted variability in responses (e.g., all items rated high, all items rated low, or all items falling in between).
5. *Fieldwork:* This step involves making decisions about the individuals who will actually administer the surveys, and about their qualifications, hiring, and training.

≡ Rapid Reference 5.6

....

Measurement Modalities

Three of the most common measurement modalities include open-ended questions, closed-ended questions, and Likert scales. An open-ended question does not provide the participant with a choice of answers. Instead, participants are free to answer the question in any manner they choose. An example of an open-ended question is the following: "How would you describe your childhood?" By contrast, a closed-ended question provides the participant with several answers from which to choose. A common example of a closed-ended question is a multiple-choice question, such as the following: "How would you describe your childhood? (a) happy; (b) sad; (c) boring." Finally, a Likert scale asks participants to provide a response along a continuum of possible responses. Here's an example of a Likert scale: "My childhood was happy. (1) strongly agree; (2) agree; (3) neutral; (4) disagree; (5) strongly disagree."

6. *Content analysis:* This involves transforming the often qualitative, open-ended survey responses into quantitative data. This may involve developing coding procedures, establishing the reliability of the coding procedures, and developing careful data screening and cleaning procedures.

7. *Analysis plan:* In general, these procedures are fairly straightforward because the analysis of survey data is typically confined to descriptive and correlational statistics. Still, even survey studies should have clear statistical analysis plans.

8. *Tabulation:* This step involves decisions about data entry.

9. *Analysis and reporting:* As with all studies, the final steps are to conduct the data analyses, prepare a final report or manuscript, and disseminate the study's findings.

Although a variety of methods for administering surveys are available, the most popular are face-to-face, telephone, and mail. In general, each of these methods has its own advantages and disadvantages. The major consideration for the researcher in deciding on the form of survey administration is response rate versus cost. As a rule of thumb (Ray & Ravizza, 1988), if high rate of return is the main goal, then face-to-face or telephone surveys are the optimal choices, while mail surveys are the obvious choice when cost is an issue.

The principal advantage of survey studies is that they provide information on large groups of people, with very little effort, and in a cost-effective manner. Surveys allow researchers to assess a wider variety of behaviors and other phenomena than can be studied in a typical naturalistic observation study.

Focus Groups

Focus groups are formally organized, structured groups of individuals brought together to discuss a topic or series of topics during a specific period of time. Like surveys, focus groups can be an extremely useful technique for obtaining individuals' impressions and concerns about certain issues, services, or products.

Originally developed for use in marketing research, focus groups have served as a principal method of qualitative research among social scientists for many decades. In contrast to other, unilateral methods of obtaining qualitative data (e.g., observation, surveys), focus groups allow for interactions between the researcher and the participants and among the participants themselves.

Like most other qualitative research methods, there is no one definitive way to design or conduct a focus group. However, they are typically composed of several participants (usually 6 to 10 individuals) and a trained moderator. Fewer than 6 participants may restrict the diversity of the opinions to be offered, and more than 10 may make it difficult for everyone to express their opinions comprehensively (Hoyle, Harris, & Judd, 2002). Focus groups are also typically made up of individuals who share a particular characteristic, demographic, or interest that is relevant to the topic being studied. For example, a marketing researcher may want to conduct a focus group with parents of young children to determine the desirability of a new educational product. Similarly, a criminal justice researcher interested in developing methods of reducing criminal recidivism may choose to conduct focus groups with recent parolees to discuss problems that they encountered after being released from prison.

The presence of a trained moderator is critical to the focus-group process (Hoyle et al., 2002). The moderator is directly responsible for setting the ground rules, raising the discussion topics, and maintaining the focus of the group discussions. When setting the ground rules, the moderator must, above all, discuss issues of confidentiality, including the confidentiality of all information shared with and recorded by the researchers (also covered when obtaining informed consent). In addition, the moderator will often request that all participants respect each other's privacy by keeping what they hear in the focus groups confidential. Other ground rules may involve speaking one at a time and avoiding criticizing the expressed viewpoints of the other participants.

Considerable preparation is necessary to make a focus group successful. The researcher must carefully consider the make-up of the group (often a nonrepresentative sample of convenience), prepare a list of objectives and topics to be covered, and determine clear ground rules to be communicated to the group participants. When considering the questions and topics to be covered, the researcher should again take into account the make-up of the group (e.g., intelligence level, level of impairment) as well as the design of the questions. For example, when possible, moderators should avoid using closed-ended questions, which may not generate a great deal of useful dialogue. Similarly, moderators should avoid using "why" questions. Questions that begin with "why" may elicit socially appropriate rationalizations, best guesses, or other attributions about an individual's behavior when the person is unsure or unaware of the true reasons or underlying motivations for his or her behavior (Nisbett & Wilson, 1977). Instead, it may be more fruitful to ask participants about what they do and the detailed events surrounding their behaviors. This may ultimately shed more light on the actual precipitants of participants' behaviors. Overall, focus groups should attempt to cover no more than two to three major topics and should last no more than 1 1/2 to 2 hours.

The obvious advantage of a focus group is that it provides an open, fairly unrestricted forum for individuals to discuss ideas and to clarify each others' impressions and opinions. The group format can also serve to crystallize the participants' opinions. However, focus groups also have several disadvantages. First, because of their relatively small sample sizes and the fact that they are typically not randomly selected, the information gleaned from focus groups may not be representative of the population in general. Second, although the group format may have some benefits in terms of helping to flesh out and distill perceptions and concerns, it is also very likely that an individual's opinions can be altered through group influence. Finally, it is difficult to quantify the open-ended responses resulting from focus group interactions.

The information obtained from focus groups can provide useful insight into how various procedures, systems, or products are viewed, as well as the desires and concerns of a given population. For these reasons, focus groups, similar to other qualitative research methods, often form the starting point in generating hypotheses, developing questionnaires and surveys, and identifying the relevant issues that may be examined using more quantifiable research methodologies.

SUMMARY

In this chapter, we have provided a brief introduction to the three main classes of research design: experimental, quasi-experimental, and nonexperimental/qualitative. In addition to providing a general overview of these design types, we hope that we have given the reader a stronger appreciation for the subtleties of experimental design, and the ways that small variations can affect the researcher's ability to rule out alternative explanations and infer causation. We also hope to have conveyed an appropriate respect for quasi- and nonexperimental designs. Although these designs do not provide researchers with the same amount of confidence in their conclusions, they are often necessary given the specific parameters of the topic under investigation or the inability to study a specific phenomenon in a true experimental fashion. Perhaps most important, these quasi-

and nonexperimental designs often provide the foundation, preliminary data, and conceptual framework from which scientifically testable hypotheses are built.

🐟 TEST YOURSELF 🐟

1. The most important element of a true experimental design is _____ assignment.

2. If groups are perfectly matched on all known factors, the researcher can be certain that any group differences on outcomes are due to the independent variable. True or False?

3. In randomized two-group designs, participants are typically assigned by random selection to either an experimental or a _____ group.

4. Reversal or ABA designs cannot be used in all instances because some phenomena and behaviors are simply not reversible. True or False?

5. A guided discussion to explore a group's opinions and impressions on a specific topic area is known as a _____ _____.

Answers: 1. random; 2. False (It is still possible that any number of *unknown* variables may be responsible for the group differences.); 3. control; 4. True; 5. focus group

Six

VALIDITY

alidity is an important term in research that refers to the conceptual and scientific soundness of a research study (Graziano & Raulin, 2004). As previously discussed, the primary purpose of all forms of research is to produce valid conclusions. Furthermore, researchers are interested in explanations for the effects and interactions of variables as they occur across a wide variety of different settings. To truly understand these interactions requires special attention to the concept of validity, which highlights the need to eliminate or minimize the effects of extraneous influences, variables, and explanations that might detract from a study's ultimate findings.

Validity is, therefore, a very important and useful concept in all forms of research methodology. Its primary purpose is to increase the accuracy and usefulness of findings by eliminating or controlling as many confounding variables as possible, which allows for greater confidence in the findings of a given study. There are four distinct types of validity (internal validity, external validity, construct validity, and statistical conclusion validity) that interact to control for and minimize the impact of a wide variety of extraneous factors that can confound a study and reduce the accuracy of its conclusions. This chapter will discuss each type of validity, its associated threats, and its implications for research design and methodology.

INTERNAL VALIDITY

Internal validity refers to the ability of a research design to rule out or make implausible alternative explanations of the results, or plausible rival hy-

DON'T FORGET

....

Internal Validity and Plausible Rival Hypotheses

Internal validity: The ability of a research design to rule out or make implausible alternative explanations of the results, thus demonstrating that the independent variable was directly responsible for the effect on the dependent variable and, ultimately, for the results found in the study.

Plausible rival hypotheses: An alternative interpretation of the researcher's hypothesis about the interaction of the independent and dependent variables that provides a reasonable explanation of the findings other than the researcher's original hypothesis.

potheses (Campbell, 1957; Kazdin, 2003c). A *plausible rival hypothesis* is an alternative interpretation of the researcher's hypothesis about the interaction of the independent and dependent variables that provides a reasonable explanation of the findings other than the researcher's original hypothesis (Rosnow & Rosenthal, 2002).

Although evidence of absolute causation is rarely achieved, the goal of most experimental designs is to demonstrate that the independent variable was directly responsible for the effect on the dependent variable and, ultimately, the results found in the study. In other words, the researcher ultimately wants to know whether the observed effect or phenomenon is due to the manipulated independent variable or variables or to some uncontrolled or unknown extraneous variable or variables (Pedhazur & Schmelkin, 1991). Ideally, at the conclusion of the study, the researcher would like to make a statement reflecting some level of causation between the independent and dependent variables. By designing strong experimental controls into a study, internal validity is increased and rival hypotheses and extraneous influences are minimized. This allows the researcher to attribute the results of the study more confidently to the independent variable or variables (Kazdin 2003c; Rosnow & Rosenthal, 2002). Uncontrolled extraneous influences other than the independent variable that could explain the results of a study are referred to as *threats to internal validity*.

Putting It Into Practice

An Example of Internal Validity and Plausible Rival Hypotheses

A researcher is interested in the effectiveness of two different parental skills training and education programs on improving symptoms of depression in adolescents. The researcher recruits 100 families that meet specified inclusion criteria in the study. The primary inclusion criterion is that the family must have an adolescent who currently meets criteria for depression. After recruitment, the researcher then randomly assigns the families into one of the two skills training programs. The parents receive the interventions over a 10-week period and are then sent home to apply the skills they have learned. The researcher reevaluates the adolescents 6 months later to see whether there has been improvement in the adolescents' symptoms of depression. The results suggest that both groups improved. The researcher concludes that both parental skills training interventions were effective for treating depression in adolescents. Given the limited information here, is this an appropriate conclusion?

The answer, of course, is no. This study has poor internal validity because it is impossible to say with any certainty that the independent variable (the two skills training classes) had an effect on the dependent variable (depression). There are a number of alternative rival hypotheses that have not been controlled for and could just as easily explain the results of the study. Many things could have transpired over the course of the 6 months. For example, were certain adolescents placed on medication? Would they have improved without the intervention? Did their life circumstances change for the better? We will never know because the study has poor internal validity and does not control for even the simplest and most obvious alternative explanations.

Threats to Internal Validity

Although the terminology may vary, the most commonly encountered threats to internal validity are history, maturation, instrumentation, testing, statistical regression, selection biases, attrition, diffusion or imitation of treatment, and special treatment or reactions of controls (Christensen, 1988; Cook & Campbell, 1979; Kazdin, 2003c; Pedhazur & Schmelkin, 1991). Researchers must be aware that every methodological design is sub-

DON'T FORGET
....

Threats to Internal Validity

As discussed in Chapters 3 and 5, most threats to internal validity are controlled through statistical analyses, control and comparison groups, and randomization. The underlying assumption of randomization as it applies to internal validity is that extraneous factors are evenly distributed across all groups within the study. Control groups allow for direct comparison between experimental groups and the evaluation of suspected extraneous influences. Statistical controls are typically used when participants cannot be randomly assigned to experimental conditions, and involve statistically controlling for variables that the researcher has identified as differing between groups.

ject to at least some of these potential threats and control for them accordingly. Failure to implement appropriate controls affects the researcher's ability to infer causality.

History

Generally, history as a threat to internal validity refers to *events or incidents* that take place during the course of the study that might have an unintended and uncontrolled-for impact on the study's final outcome (or the dependent variable; Kazdin, 2003c). These events tend to be global enough that they affect all or most of the participants in a study. They can occur inside or outside the study and typically occur between the pre- and postmeasurement phases of the dependent variable. The impact of history as a threat to internal validity is usually seen during the postmeasurement phase of the study and is particularly prevalent if the study is longitudinal and therefore takes place over a long period of time. Accordingly, the longer the period of time between the pre- and postmeasure, the greater the possibility that a history effect could have confounded the results of the study (Christensen, 1988).

For example, an anxiety-provoking catastrophic national event could have an impact on many if not all participants in a study for the treatment of anxiety. The event could produce an escalation in symptoms that might be interpreted as a failure of the intervention, when, in actuality, it is an artifact of the external event itself. Depending on the timing, this external event could have a significant impact on the measurement of the dependent variable.

Another example can be found in our previous discussion of the effectiveness of parent skills training on adolescent symptoms of depression (see Putting It Into Practice on page 160). In that example, symptoms of depression were evaluated 6 months after the parental skills training intervention. It is possible that some other significant event occurred during that time period that might account for the reduced symptoms of depression. One possibility is that school ended for the year and summer vacation started, which produced a decrease in depressive symptoms among the sample of adolescents. So, the decrease in depression might be due to a historical artifact and not to the independent variable (i.e., the parent skills training intervention). Historical events can also take place within the confines of the study, although this is less common. For example, an argument between two researchers that takes place in plain view of participants and is not part of the intended intervention is an event that can produce a history effect.

Maturation

This threat to internal validity is similar to history in that it relates to changes over time. Unlike history, however, maturation refers to *intrinsic changes within the participants* that are usually related to the passage of time. The most commonly cited examples of this involve both biological and psychological changes, such as aging, learning, fatigue, and hunger (Christensen, 1988). As with history, the presence of maturational changes occurs between the pre- and postmeasurement phases of the study and interferes with interpretations of causation regarding the independent and dependent variables. Historical and maturational threats tend to be found in combination in longitudinal studies.

In our parent skills training example, might the symptoms of depression have improved because the parents had an additional 6 months to develop as parents, regardless of the skills training? Although it's unlikely, this is an alternative rival hypothesis that must be considered and controlled for, most likely through the inclusion of a control or comparison group that did not receive the parent skills training.

Another example would be a study examining the effects of visualization on strength training in male adolescents over a specified period of time. As adolescent males mature naturally, we would expect to see incremental increases in strength regardless of the visualization intervention. So, a causal statement regarding the effects of visualization on strength in adolescent males would have to be qualified in the context of the maturational threat to internal validity. Again, this threat could be minimized through the use of control or comparison groups.

Instrumentation

This threat to internal validity is unrelated to participant characteristics and refers to *changes in the assessment* of the independent variable, which are usually related to changes in the measuring instrument or measurement procedures over time (Christensen, 1988; Kazdin, 2003c). In essence, instrumentation compromises internal validity when changes in the dependent variable result from changes over time in the assessment instruments and scoring criteria used in the study. There is a wide variety of measurement and assessment techniques available to researchers, and some of these are more susceptible to instrumentation effects than others. The susceptibility of a measure to instrumentation bias is usually a function of standardization.

DON'T FORGET

Important Considerations Regarding Instrumentation

- *Standardization* refers to the guidelines established in the administration and scoring of an instrument or other assessment method.

- *Reliability* is present when an assessment method measures the characteristics of interest in a consistent fashion.

- *Validity* is present when the approach to measurement used in the study actually measures what it is supposed to measure.

Standardization refers to the guidelines established in the administration and scoring of an instrument or other assessment method, and also encompasses the psychometric concepts of reliability and validity. An approach to measurement is *reliable* if it assesses the characteristics of interest in a consistent fashion. *Validity* refers to whether the approach to measurement used in the study actually measures what it is supposed to measure. Instruments that are standardized and psychometrically sound are least susceptible to instrumentation effects, while other types of assessment methods (e.g., independent raters, clinical impressions, "homemade" instruments) dramatically increase the possibility of instrumentation effects.

For example, a researcher could use a number of measurement approaches in a treatment study of depression. The researcher could use, for example, a standardized measure to assess symptoms of depression, such as the Beck Depression Inventory (BDI), which is a self-report, paper-and-pencil test known for its reliability and validity (Beck et al., 1961). The BDI is also standardized in that respondents are all exposed to the same stimuli, which is a set of questions related to symptoms of depression. This high level of standardization in administration and scoring makes it unlikely that instrumentation effects would be present. In other words, unless the researchers altered the items of the BDI, modified the administration procedures, or switched to a different version of the instrument midway through the study, we would not expect instrumentation to be a significant threat to the internal validity of the study.

Conversely, other approaches to measurement are more susceptible to possible instrumentation effects. There are many different ways to measure the construct of depression. Let's assume that the BDI was unavailable, so the researcher had to rely on some other method for assessing the impact of treatment on symptoms of depression. A common solution to this problem might be to have independent raters assess the level of symptoms based on clinical diagnostic criteria and then assess the participants over the course of the intervention. This type of approach to measurement, if poorly implemented, dramatically increases the likelihood of instrumentation effects.

The primary concern is that the raters might have different standards for what qualifies as meeting the criteria for symptoms of depression. Let's assume that rater A requires significantly more impairment in functioning from a participant before acknowledging that depression or depressive symptoms are actually present. Furthermore, the rater standards for identifying the symptoms and making the diagnosis of depression might fluctuate significantly over time, which adds yet another layer of difficulty when the researcher attempts to interpret the impact of treatment (the independent variable) on depression (the dependent variable). Without standardization, there is a significant likelihood that any changes in the dependent variable over the course of treatment might be the result of changes in scoring criteria and not the intervention itself. These issues are usually addressed through ongoing training and frequent *interrater reliability checks* (a statistical method for determining the level of consistency and agreement between different raters).

CAUTION

Instrumentation Effects

Instrumentation effects are least prevalent when using standardized, psychometrically sound instruments to measure the variables of interest. When such measures are not available, the likelihood of instrumentation effects rises dramatically. In such cases, ongoing training of raters and interrater reliability checks are an absolute necessity.

Testing

This threat to internal validity refers to the effects that taking a test on one occasion may have on subsequent administrations of the same test (Kazdin, 2003c). In essence, when participants in a study are measured several times on the same variable (e.g., with the same instrument or test), their performance might be affected by factors such as practice, memory, sensitization, and participant and researcher expectancies (Pedhazur & Schmelkin, 1991). This threat to internal validity is most often encountered in longitudinal research where participants are repeatedly measured on the same variables over time. The ultimate concern with this threat to internal validity is that the results of the study might be related to the repeated testing or evaluation and not the independent variable itself.

For example, let's consider a hypothetical study designed to assess the impact of guided imagery techniques on the retention of a series of random symbols. First, each participant is exposed to the random symbols and then asked to reproduce as many as possible from memory after a 15-minute delay. This serves as a pretest or baseline measure of memory performance. Next, participants are exposed to the intervention, which is a series of guided imagery techniques that the researchers believe will improve retention of the symbols. The researchers believe that recall of the symbols will increase as participants learn each of six imagery techniques, with the highest level of recall coming after participants have learned all of the imagery techniques. In this case, the guided imagery technique is the intervention or independent variable, and the recall of the random symbols is the dependent variable. The participants are exposed to six learning trials. During each trial, the participant is taught a new imagery technique, exposed to the same random symbol stimuli, and then asked to reproduce as many as possible after a 15-minute delay. Ideally, the participants are using their imagery techniques to aid in retention of the symbols. Keep in mind here that the participants are being tested on the same set of symbols on six different occasions, and that the symbol set in this example is the testing instrument and outcome measure. The researchers run their trials and confirm their hypotheses. The participants perform above baseline expectations after the first trial and their performance improves consistently as they are exposed to additional imagery techniques. The best performance is seen after the final imagery technique is implemented.

Can it be said that the imagery techniques are the cause of the improved retention of the random symbols? The researchers could make that assertion, but the presence of a testing effect seriously undermines the credibility of their results. Remember that the participants are exposed to the same test or outcome—the random symbols—on at least seven different occasions. This introduces a strong plausible rival hypothesis that the improvement in retention is simply due to a *practice effect*, or the repeated exposure to the same stimuli. As the researchers did not account for this possibility with a control group or by varying the content of the symbol stimulus, this remains a legitimate explanation for the findings. In other words, the practice effect provides a plausible alternative hypothesis.

Statistical Regression

This threat to internal validity refers to a statistical phenomenon whereby extremely high or low scores on a measure tend to revert toward the arithmetic mean or average of the distribution with repeated testing (Christensen, 1988; Kazdin, 2003c; Neale & Liebert, 1973).

For example, let's assume that we obtained the following array of scores on our symbol retention measure from the preceding example: 5, 12, 18, 19, 27, 42, 55, and 62. The mean for this set of scores is 30 (240 ÷ 8 = 30). On average, the participants in the study recalled 30 random symbols when assessed for retention. Generally, statistical regression suggests that over time and repeated administration of the memory assessment, we would expect the scores in this array to revert closer to the mean score of 30. This is particularly true of extreme scores that lie far outside the normal range of a distribution. These extreme scores are also known as *outliers*. In a distribution of scores with a mean of 30, it would be reasonable to identify, at a minimum, the scores of 5 and 62 as outliers. So, on our next administration of the memory test, we would expect all of these scores to revert closer to the mean, *regardless of the effect of the intervention* (or independent variable). In addition, we would probably see the largest movement toward the mean in the more extreme scores.

This phenomenon is particularly prevalent in research in which a pre- and posttest design is used to assess the variable of interest or when participants are assigned to experimental groups based on extreme scores. Let's consider a different example to il-

DON'T FORGET

Outliers

An *outlier* is a score lying far outside the normal range of a distribution of scores.

lustrate this point. A study is designed to assess the impact of a new, 10-week treatment for anxiety. The researchers are interested in the effects of their new treatment on low, medium, and high anxiety levels as determined by a score on a standardized measure of anxiety. The researchers hope that their new treatment will reduce symptoms of anxiety across each of the three conditions. Accordingly, each participant is administered the anxiety measure as a pretest to determine his or her current anxiety level and then is assigned to one of three groups—low, medium, or high anxiety—on the basis of predetermined cutoff scores. For the sake of clarity, let's assume the mean anxiety level for the entire sample was 30, the mean for the low-anxiety group was 12, the mean for the medium-anxiety group was 29, and the mean for the high-anxiety group was 42.

Each of these groups then receives ongoing treatment and assessment over the 10-week protocol. The results of the study suggest that anxiety scores increased in the low-anxiety condition, stayed roughly the same in the medium-anxiety condition, and decreased in the high-anxiety condition. Our somewhat befuddled researchers conclude that their treatment is effective only for cases of severe anxiety, exacerbates symptoms in individuals with minimal symptoms of anxiety, and has little to no effect on moderate levels of anxiety. Although these findings might be accurate, it is also possible that they are the result of statistical regression. The scores in the high-anxiety group might have reverted to the overall group mean over the 10 weeks, giving the impression that symptom reduction resulted from the intervention. Similarly, the perceived increase in symptoms in the low-anxiety group might be the result of those low scores' moving toward the overall group mean. In other words, the mean scores for both of these groups included extreme scores, or outliers, which were then influenced by regression to the mean. It is therefore possible that we would have seen the same results even without the impact of the independent variable. Note that the medium-anxiety group did not change and that this was the group whose mean score was closest to the overall sample mean, which makes it least susceptible to the effects of statistical regression. This could account for the possibly erroneous conclusion that the treatment protocol was ineffective on moderate symptoms of anxiety.

Selection Biases

This threat to internal validity refers to systematic differences in the assignment of participants to experimental conditions. As noted in Chapter 5, selection biases are prevalent in quasi-experimental research in which participants are assigned to experimental conditions or comparison groups in a nonrandom fashion (Christensen, 1988; Kazdin, 2003c; Rosnow & Rosenthal, 2002). Remember, randomization is designed to control for systematic participant differences across experimental and control groups. In essence, randomization evenly distributes and equates groups on any potential confounding variables. Without randomization, it is more difficult to account and control for these systematic variations in participant characteristics. As with all threats to internal validity, selection bias can have a negative impact on the researcher's ability to draw causal inferences about the effects of the independent variable.

As mentioned previously, selection biases are common in quasi-experimental research in which randomization cannot be accomplished. The most common example of this is when the experimenter attempts to conduct research in a setting or under a set of circumstances where the groups are already formed and cannot be altered. In other words, for whatever reason, randomization is not feasible or possible.

For example, let's consider a design to test the effectiveness of a classroom intervention to improve mathematics skills in two classes of third graders. Because the students are already assigned to classes, randomization is not possible, and the study is therefore quasi-experimental in nature. Both classes receive a grade-appropriate pretest. Class 1 receives the mathematics intervention and Class 2 does not. In this case, Class 2 is acting as a control group because it does not receive the intervention. Both classes then receive a posttest.

CAUTION

Selection Biases

Selection biases are common in quasi-experimental designs and can interact with other threats to internal validity, such as maturation, history, or instrumentation, to produce effects that might not be attributable to the independent variable.

If Class 1 performs better, is it safe to conclude that the intervention, or independent variable, is responsible for the improvement? Although it is possible, there are a number of plausible rival hypotheses that have not been controlled for. Most of these hypotheses revolve around preexisting differences between the two groups (i.e., before the intervention was delivered). For example, it is possible that the students in Class 1 are more motivated or mature than their counterparts in Class 2. In fact, any preexisting difference between the compositions of the two groups is a threat to internal validity. Any of these differences might provide a valid explanation for the results of the math intervention.

Attrition

This threat to internal validity refers to the differential and systematic loss of participants from experimental and control groups. In essence, participants drop out of the study in a systematic and nonrandom way that can affect the original composition of groups formed for the purposes of the study (Beutler & Martin, 1999). The potential net result of attrition is that the effects of the independent variable might be due to the loss of participants and not to the manipulation of the independent variable.

Commentators have noted that this threat to internal validity is common in longitudinal research and is a direct function of time (Kazdin, 2003c; Phillips, 1985). In general, attrition rates average between 40 and 60% in longitudinal intervention research, with most participants dropping out during the earliest stages of the study (Kazdin). Attrition applies to most forms of group and single-case designs and can be a threat to internal validity even after the researcher has randomly assigned participants to experimental and control groups. This is because attrition occurs as the study progresses and *after* participants have been assigned to each of the conditions. Attrition raises the possibility that the groups differ on certain characteristics that were originally controlled for through randomization. In other words, the remaining participants no longer represent the original sample and the groups might no longer be equivalent.

Let's consider an example. A researcher decides to conduct a study of the effectiveness of a new drug on symptoms of anxiety. Randomization is used to assign participants to either a medication (i.e., experimental) group or placebo (i.e., control) group. Let's assume that over the course of the study, participants in the experimental group experience some relatively severe side effects from the medication and an increase in anxiety, causing some to drop out of the study. The placebo group does not experience the side effects, so the dropout rate is lower in that group. The average anxiety levels of the two groups are compared at the conclusion of the study, and the results suggest that the participants in the medication group are less anxious than those in the placebo group. The results seem to support the conclusion that the medication was effective for the treatment of anxiety. The problem with this conclusion is that the results are potentially confounded by attrition. If no study participants had dropped out of the medication group, it is likely that the results would have been different. In this example, notice that attrition was still a factor after randomization and that the final sample was probably very different from the original sample used to form the experimental and control groups.

Diffusion or Imitation of Treatment

This threat to internal validity is common in various forms of medical and psychotherapy treatment effectiveness research, and it manifests itself in two distinct but related sets of circumstances.

The first set of circumstances is the unintended exposure of a control group to the actual or similar intervention (independent variable) intended only for the experimental condition (Kazdin, 2003c; Pedhazur & Schmelkin, 1991). Let's consider a study examining the relative benefits of exercise and nutritional counseling on weight loss. The researchers hypothesize that exercise is more effective than nutritional counseling and assign participants to an exercise, nutritional counseling, or no-intervention control group. The experimental group receives a customized exercise regimen, the nutritional group receives general nutritional counseling, and the control group is simply monitored for weight loss or gain for the same time period.

During the course of the study, a well-intentioned, but misguided, nutritional counselor extols the benefits of exercise to the members of the nutritional counseling group. This additional counseling was not part of the original design and the researchers are unaware that it is taking place. Although the nutritional counseling group is not receiving the actual exercise intervention, the discussion of exercise with this group might have an unintended and uncontrolled-for effect. For example, this knowledge might encourage participants in the nutritional group to seek out their own exercise program or to change their day-to-day habits in such a way that increases their general activity level, such as taking the stairs instead of the elevator. If that is indeed the case, then the nutritional group has received a similar intervention as the experimental group. At a minimum, the results could be confounded because the nutritional condition is not being delivered as the researchers had originally intended, because the exercise condition has diffused into the nutritional group. The threat to internal validity in this example lies in the possibility that the exercise and nutritional groups have now received similar interventions, which might equalize performance across the groups (Kazdin, 2003c).

The second set of circumstances arises when the experimental group does not receive the intended intervention at all (Kazdin, 2003c; Pedhazur & Schmelkin, 1991). In the first case, participants in a control group either gain knowledge about or are unintentionally exposed to the experimental intervention (the independent variable). In this case, the researcher believes that the experimental group has received the intervention when, in reality, it has not. This is a common threat in many forms of psychotherapy research. Take, for example, a study comparing the effectiveness of behavioral and psychodynamic therapies for depression. Two therapists are recruited and trained to deliver the interventions. Both therapists are psychodynamic in their orientation, so one receives supplemental training in behavioral techniques. Participants receive one of the two

CAUTION
....

Diffusion or Imitation of Treatment

Diffusion or imitation of treatment is a threat to internal validity because it can equalize the performance of experimental and control groups.

treatments and the results suggest that they are both equally effective. What the researchers do not know is that the behavioral therapist has either intentionally or unintentionally strayed from the specified protocol at times and included elements of the psychodynamic treatment in the behavioral condition. In other words, the behavioral group might not have received a behavioral intervention at all. At best, they have received a hybrid of psychodynamic and behavioral treatment. As in our previous example, rather than comparing two distinct conditions, the researchers might be comparing two conditions that are more similar than intended by the original research design. Again, this might equalize the performance of the experimental and control groups, which could have the effect of distorting or clouding the results of the study.

Special Treatment or Reactions of Controls

These relatively common threats to internal validity may be caused by the special, often compensatory, treatment or attention given to the control group. Even in the absence of special attention or treatment, controls may realize that they are in a "lesser" condition and react by competing or otherwise improving their performance. Either of these situations can equalize the performance of the experimental and control conditions and thereby "washout" between-group differences on the dependent variable (Christensen, 1988; Kazdin, 2003c; Pedhazur & Schmelkin, 1991). Special treatment itself is a relatively common threat to internal validity and can be related to any number of activities conducted with the control (nonintervention) group. Remember that in this case, the intervention is also the independent variable. These factors range from simple human interaction to more concrete examples such as financial compensation or special privileges. For example, attention alone might produce an unintended change in behavior.

Let's assume that there are two groups in a study of depression. The intervention or experimental group receives therapy while the control group is simply monitored weekly for symptom severity. The monitoring consists of an hour-long structured interview with a research assistant. This weekly social attention might act as an intervention despite the fact that it was intended for monitoring purposes only. Perhaps the interview gives the control participants the opportunity to discuss their symptoms, which produces some symptom relief even without therapy per se. After all, social support has been linked to positive outcomes for depression. The same effect might be observed even in the absence of human contact. For example, just filling out a self-report measure of depressive symptoms in an empty room might have the same effect by raising the awareness of the control participants in regard to their current symptom level. Reinforcers and other incentives might have a similar effect. Giving the control participants money or special privileges might have an impact on levels of depression by raising self-esteem or reducing hopelessness. Like diffusion or imitation of treatment, this threat to internal validity might equalize the performance of the experimental and control groups, which could have the effect of distorting or clouding the results of the study.

In conclusion, threats to the internal validity of a study (summarized in Rapid Reference 6.1) are common and, at times, unavoidable. They can occur alone or in combination, and they can create unwanted plausible alternative hypotheses for the results of a study. These rival hypotheses may make it difficult to determine causation. Some of these threats can be handled effectively through design components (e.g., control groups and randomization) at the outset of the study, while others (e.g., attrition) take place during the course of the study. Accounting for these threats is a critical aspect and function of research methodology that should take place, if possible, at the design stage of the study. Refer to Chapter 3 for a general discussion of these strategies.

EXTERNAL VALIDITY

External validity is concerned with the generalizability of the results of a research study. In all forms of research design, the results and conclusions of the study are limited to the participants and conditions as defined by the contours of the study. *External validity* (compare to *ecological validity* in Rapid Reference 6.2) refers to the degree to which research results generalize to other conditions, participants, times, and places (Graziano & Raulin, 2004).

≡ Rapid Reference 6.1

....

Threats to Internal Validity

- **History:** Global internal or external events or incidents that take place during the course of the study that might have unintended and uncontrolled-for impacts on the study's final outcome (i.e., on the dependent variable).

- **Maturation:** *Intrinsic* changes within the participants that are usually related to the passage of time.

- **Instrumentation:** Changes in the assessment of the independent variable that are usually related to changes in the measuring instrument or measurement procedures over time.

- **Testing:** The effects that taking a test on one occasion may have on subsequent administrations of the test. It is most often encountered in longitudinal research, in which participants are repeatedly measured on the same variables of interest over time.

- **Statistical regression:** Statistical phenomenon, prevalent in pretest and posttest designs, in which extremely high or low scores on a measure tend to revert toward the mean of the distribution with repeated testing.

- **Selection bias:** Systematic differences in the assignment of participants to experimental conditions.

- **Attrition:** Loss of research participants that may alter the original composition of groups and compromise the validity of the study.

- **Diffusion or imitation of treatment:** Unintended exposure of a control group to an intervention intended only for the experimental group, or a failure to expose the experimental group to the intended intervention. This confound most commonly occurs in medical and psychological intervention studies.

- **Special treatment or reactions of controls:** Relatively common threats to internal validity in which either (1) special or compensatory treatment or attention is given to the control condition, or (2) participants in the control condition, as a result of their assignment, react or compensate in a manner that improves or otherwise alters their performance.

Rapid Reference 6.2

Ecological and Temporal Validity

Although the terms "ecological validity" and "external validity" are sometimes used interchangeably, a clear distinction can be drawn between the two. Of the two, *external validity* is a more general concept. It refers to the degree to which research results generalize to other conditions, participants, times, and places, and it is ultimately concerned with the conclusions that can be drawn about the strength of the inferred causal relationship between the independent and dependent variables to circumstances beyond those experimentally studied. *Ecological validity* is a more specific concept that refers to the generalization of findings obtained in a laboratory setting to the real world.

Temporal validity is another term that is related broadly to external validity. It refers to the extent to which the results of a study can be generalized across time. More specifically, this type of validity refers to the effects of seasonal, cyclical, and person-specific fluctuations that can affect the generalizability of the study's findings.

Therefore, a study has more external validity when the results generalize beyond the study sample to other populations, settings, and circumstances. External validity refers to conclusions that can be drawn about the strength of the inferred causal relationship between the independent and dependent variables to circumstances beyond those experimentally studied. In other words, would the results of our study apply to different populations, settings, or sets of circumstances? If so, then the study has strong external validity.

For example, let's consider a study designed to determine the

DON'T FORGET

External Validity

External validity is the degree to which research results generalize to other conditions, participants, times, and places. External validity is related to conclusions that can be drawn about the strength of the inferred causal relationship between the independent and dependent variables to circumstances beyond those experimentally studied.

effectiveness of a new intervention for test anxiety. Again, the intervention is the independent variable, while test anxiety is the dependent variable. The study is being conducted at a major East Coast university, and the participants are college freshmen currently taking an introductory-level psychology class. Although this might not seem realistic at first glance, many studies are conducted with college students because they are easily accessible and form samples of convenience (Kazdin, 2003c). Students are assessed to determine their levels of test anxiety and then are assigned to either a no-treatment control group or an experimental group that receives the intervention. The new therapy is remarkably effective and significantly reduces test anxiety in the experimental group. The researchers immediately market their intervention as being a generally effective treatment for test anxiety. Can the researchers support their claim based on the results of their study? Hopefully, you have already realized that this study has serious flaws related to internal validity, but let's put that aside for the purposes of this example and focus only on issues surrounding external validity.

Remember that *external validity* is the degree to which research results generalize to other conditions, participants, times, and places. A study has external validity when the results generalize to other populations, settings, and circumstances. In our example, the researchers have found that their intervention effectively reduces test anxiety, and they are assuming that it is effective across a wide variety of settings and populations. They might be correct, but the design of this study does not have strong external validity for a number of reasons, which undermines the assertion that the intervention is effective for other populations.

First, the study was conducted with a sample of college freshmen enrolled in an introductory-level psychology course. This is a very narrow sample; would the results apply to broader populations, such as elementary school children, high school students, or college seniors? Would the results apply to college freshmen who were not enrolled in an introductory-level psychology class? We do not know for certain because these individuals were not included in the sample used in the study.

Second, do the results apply to other settings, such as different universities, high schools, classes, and business environments? The effectiveness of the intervention might be limited to the setting where the study was conducted. For example, we might find that the results do not generalize to universities on the West Coast or to high schools. In other words, the effectiveness of the intervention might be specific to the population represented by the sample used in the study.

Third, is there something unique about the conditions of the study? For example, was the study conducted around midterm or final exams, when anxiety levels might be unusually high? Would the intervention have been as effective if the study had occurred at a different time during the semester? As mentioned previously, the answer is that we do not know for sure. In terms of external validity, the most accurate statement that can be made from the results of our hypothetical study is that the intervention was effective for college freshmen in introductory-level psychology classes at a major East Coast university. Any other conclusions would not necessarily be supported, and additional research across different times, places, and conditions would be necessary to support any other conclusions.

Threats to External Validity

As with internal validity, there are confounds and characteristics of a study that can limit the generalizability of the results. These characteristics and confounds are collectively referred to as *threats to external validity,* and they include sample characteristics, stimulus characteristics and settings, reactivity of experimental arrangements, multiple-treatment interference, novelty effects, reactivity of assessment, test sensitization, and timing of measurement (Kazdin, 2003c). Controlling these influences allows the researchers to more confidently generalize the results of the study to other circumstances and populations (Kazdin; Rosnow & Rosenthal, 2002).

Sample Characteristics
This threat to external validity refers to a phenomenon whereby the results of a study apply only to a particular sample. Accordingly, it is unclear whether the results can be applied to other samples that vary on characteristics such as age, gender, education, and socioeconomic status (Kazdin, 2003c).

An example of sample characteristics can be found in our earlier discussion about external validity. In that example, we noted that the sample consisted of college freshmen enrolled in an introductory-level psychology class. As we noted, we cannot assume that the findings of that study would necessarily hold true for a different sample, such as high school students or elementary school children. In addition, we cannot even assume that the findings would hold true for college freshmen generally. Through further research, we might discover that the intervention was effectively only for psychology students and did not generalize to freshmen taking introductory-level business or science classes. In other words, even this subtle difference in sample characteristics can have a significant effect on the generalizability of a study's results. Clearly, it would not be possible or practical to include every possible population characteristic in our sample, so we are always faced with the possibility that sample characteristics are a confound to the external validity of any study. Accordingly, conclusions

DON'T FORGET

Diversity Characteristics

Sample characteristics can encompass a wide variety of traits and demographic characteristics, with some of the most common being age, gender, education, and socioeconomic status. Commentators have noted that some diversity-related characteristics are not well represented in most forms of research (Kazdin, 2003c). The primary concern in this area is that there is an overrepresentation of some groups, such as college students; and a related, limited inclusion of underrepresented and minority groups, such as Hispanic Americans and women. Diversity characteristics are an important issue in terms of external validity, and they can have important and far-reaching consequences for all strata of society. For example, the results of a medication effectiveness study conducted only on White males might not hold true for a different racial group. The possible ramifications should be obvious. Similarly, a study designed to provide information needed to make an important public policy decision should include a sample diverse enough to accurately capture the particular group that will be directly impacted by the decision. Although these are only two examples, diversity factors should be considered in all types of research.

drawn from the results of a study tend to be limited to the characteristics represented by the sample used in the study.

Stimulus Characteristics and Settings

This threat to external validity refers to an environmental phenomenon in which particular features or conditions of the study limit the generalizability of the findings (Brunswik, 1955; Pedhazur & Schmelkin, 1991). Every study operates under a unique set of conditions and circumstances related to the experimental arrangement. The most commonly cited examples include the research setting and the researchers involved in the study. The major concern with this threat to external validity is that the findings from one study are influenced by a set of unique conditions, and thus may not necessarily generalize to another study, even if the other study uses a similar sample.

Let's return again to our previous example involving the intervention for test anxiety. That study found that the intervention was effective for test anxiety with college freshmen enrolled in an introductory-level psychology class at a major East Coast university. A colleague at a West Coast university decides to replicate the study using a sample of college freshmen enrolled in an introductory-level psychology class. Despite following our East Coast procedures to the letter, our colleague does not find that the intervention was effective. Although there could be a number of explanations for this, it is possible that a stimulus-characteristics-and-settings confound is present. The setting where the intervention is delivered is no doubt different at our West Coast colleague's university—for example, it could be less comfortable than our East Coast setting. Similarly, a different individual is delivering the intervention to the college freshmen on the West Coast, and this individual might be less competent or less approachable than his or her East Coast counterpart. Each of these is an example of potential sources of stimulus characteristics and settings.

Reactivity of the Experimental Arrangements

This threat to external validity refers to a potentially confounding variable that is a result of the influence produced by knowing that one is participating in a research study (Christensen, 1988). In other words, the participants' awareness that they are taking part in a study can have an impact on their attitudes and behavior during the course of the study. This, in turn, can have a significant impact on any results obtained from the study and is especially problematic when participants know the purpose or hypotheses of the study. We discussed strategies for limiting participants' knowledge about a study's hypotheses in Chapter 3. As a threat to external validity, the issue becomes whether the same results would have been obtained had the participants been unaware that they were being studied (Kazdin, 2003c). This threat to external validity is a very common one. The primary reason for this is that ethical standards require that participants provide informed consent before participating in most research studies.

For example, let's consider a study designed to evaluate the effectiveness of a 10-week behavior modification program devised to reduce recidivism in adolescent offenders. The experimental group receives the intervention (i.e., the independent variable) and the control group does not. The researchers find that the experimental group shows lower levels of recidivism (i.e., the dependent variable) when compared to the control group. The researchers might be tempted to say that the intervention was responsible for the findings; however, it might be that the behavior in question improved because the participants had assumed a compliant attitude toward the intervention. Alternatively, if the participants in the treatment group had adopted a more negativistic attitude toward the intervention, the results of the study might have suggested that the intervention was not successful. In any event, either outcome might be the result of reactivity to the experimental arrangements and not the intervention itself.

Multiple-Treatment Interference

This threat to external validity refers to research situations in which (1) participants are administered more than one experimental intervention (or independent variable) within the same study or (2) the same individuals participate in more than one study (Pedhazur & Schmelkin, 1991). Although it is most common in treatment-outcome studies, it is also prevalent in any study that has more than one experimental condition or independent variable. The major implication of this threat is that the research results may be due to the context or series of conditions in which the research presented (Kazdin, 2003c).

In the first research situation, independent variables administered simultaneously or sequentially may produce an interaction effect. In general, multiple independent variables administered in the same study act as a confound that makes it difficult to determine which one is responsible for the observed results. The second situation refers to the relative experience and sophistication of the participants. Familiarity with research can affect the behavior and responses of participants, which again makes it difficult to accurately interpret the results of the study.

For example, let's consider a common situation in which multiple-treatment interference can occur. A 12-week treatment study is designed to assess the effectiveness of a combined approach to treating depression that encompasses elements of both psychodynamic and cognitive therapy. The participants are randomly divided into a control group and an experimental group. Both groups are assessed to determine symptom severity. The experimental group then receives 6 weeks of psychodynamic therapy followed by 6 weeks of cognitive therapy. At the end of 12 weeks, both the control and experimental groups are reassessed for symptom severity. The results of the assessment suggest that the experimental group experienced significant symptom reduction while the control group did not. The researchers conclude that a combined psychodynamic–cognitive therapy model is an effective approach to treating depression.

Although this may indeed be the case, it is far from a certainty and there are many unanswered questions. For example, would the treatment have been as effective if the cognitive therapy had been administered first? Would 6 weeks of psychodynamic or cognitive therapy alone have produced similar results? Did the presence of both treatment modalities actually reduce the effectiveness of the overall intervention? Although the study produced significant symptom improvements, it might have produced even better results if both forms of therapy had not been used. These are aspects of multiple-treatment effects that are best controlled for through specific research designs that were discussed in Chapter 5.

Novelty Effects

This threat to external validity refers to the possibility that the effects of the independent variable may be due in part to the uniqueness or novelty of the stimulus or situation and not to the intervention itself. It is similar to the Hawthorne effect (discussed in Chapter 3; see also Rapid Reference 6.3) in that new or unusual treatments or experimental interventions might produce results that disappear once the novelty of the situation or condition wears off. In other words, the novelty of the intervention or situation acts as a confounding variable, and it is that novelty (and not the independent variable) that is the real explanation for the results. This threat to external validity is common across a wide variety of settings and experimental designs.

=== *Rapid Reference 6.3*

The Hawthorne Effect

Reactivity of the experimental arrangements is also referred to as the *Hawthorne effect*, which occurs when an individual's performance in a study is affected by the individual's knowledge that he or she is participating in a study. For example, some participants might be more attentive, compliant, or diligent, while others might be intentionally difficult or noncooperative despite having volunteered for the study (Bracht & Glass, 1968).

Take, for example, a situation in which researchers are trying to determine the effectiveness of a new therapy intervention for individuals with a history of chronic depression. They have decided to call this new intervention "smile therapy" because the therapist is trained to smile at the client on a regular schedule in the hope of encouraging a positive mood and outlook on life. Symptoms of depression are assessed, and then the participants are randomly assigned to either a control group or one of three experimental conditions. The three experimental conditions include smile therapy, cognitive-behavioral therapy, and interpersonal therapy. All of the participants undergo their respective treatments for 4 weeks and are then reassessed for severity of depression. The researchers find that smile therapy is more effective than both cognitive-behavioral and interpersonal therapy on symptoms of chronic depression.

By now, you have likely figured out that there might be a problem here because a novelty effect could also account for the results. Our population in this fictitious study consists of individuals with chronic depression, so it is likely that they have tried many treatment modalities or at least been in treatment in one modality for a significant period of time. Although these modalities are somewhat distinct, none of them involves the therapist smiling at the participant as the intervention. The smile therapy is therefore unique, or novel, and this alone might account for the improvements in depression. The other issue here is that the intervention took place over the course of 4 weeks. If these findings were the result of a novelty, then we would expect the treatment effect to disappear over time as the novelty of the smile therapy diminished. Four weeks might not be a sufficient amount of time for the novelty to diminish, and the results of the study at 12 weeks might not have demonstrated a significant finding for this new form of therapy. The presence of a novelty effect would limit the researcher's ability to generalize the results of this study to situations or context in which the same effect does not exist.

This effect can also be seen outside the treatment-intervention arena. Suppose you wanted to determine the effectiveness of an intervention designed to increase teamwork and related productivity for top-level managers in two distinct organizational settings. Putting aside the obvious threats to internal validity created by conducting your study without randomization in two separate environments, let's further explore the implications of the novelty effect. The researchers identify the top managers in both organizations and administer the intervention. One organization is a manufacturing company and the other is a large financial management firm. The researchers find that the intervention increases productivity and teamwork, but only in the financial management firm. The researchers therefore conclude that the intervention is effective, but only in the one environment.

It is also possible, however, that the finding is due to a novelty effect and not to the intervention itself. Let's add some additional relevant information. What if you knew that the manufacturing company was engaged in a total quality improvement program? These programs tend to involve a high level of teamwork and group interaction on a daily basis. You also discover that the financial management firm has never addressed the issue of teamwork or group productivity in the past. Therefore, the significant finding might be due to the novelty of introducing teamwork into a setting where it had never previously been considered, and not to the teamwork intervention itself. Conversely, the intervention might not have been effective in the manufacturing company because the organization had already incorporated the model into their corporate culture. What if we tried the intervention in a financial management firm that had already implemented a team approach? Again, we might find that the intervention is not effective. If that were indeed the case, then in terms of generalizability, the more accurate statement might be that the intervention is effective in financial management companies that have never been exposed to team-building interventions.

Reactivity of Assessment

This threat to external validity refers to a phenomenon whereby participants' awareness that their performance is being measured can alter their performance from what it would otherwise have been (Christensen, 1988; Kazdin, 2003c). Reactivity is a threat to external validity when this awareness leads study participants to respond differently than they normally would in the face of experimental conditions.

Reactivity is another common threat to external validity that can occur across a wide variety of environments and circumstances, and it is a substantial threat whenever formal or informal assessment is a necessary component of the study. For example, consider a psychotherapy outcome study where participants are assessed for number and severity of symptoms of emotional distress. The very fact that an assessment is taking place might cause the participants to distort their responses for a variety of reasons. For example, participants might feel uncomfortable or self-conscious and underreport their symptoms. Conversely, participants might overreport their symptom levels if they suspect that doing so might lead to more intensive treatment. Rapid Reference 6.4 discusses the obtrusiveness of the measurement process with regard to participant reactivity.

Rapid Reference 6.4

....

Obtrusive vs. Unobtrusive Measurement

As mentioned previously, *reactivity* becomes a threat to external validity when participants in a study respond differently than they normally would in the face of experimental conditions. Although a wide variety of stimuli can cause reactivity, the most common example occurs during formal measurement or assessment. If participants are aware that they are being assessed, then that assessment measure is said to be *obtrusive* and therefore likely to affect behavior. Conversely, the term *unobtrusive measurement* refers to assessment in which the participants are unaware that the measurement is taking place (Rosnow & Rosenthal, 2002).

Although reactivity is common in all forms of medical and psychological treatment intervention studies, it is prevalent in other settings as well. For example, directly asking employees about their attitudes toward management might lead to more favorable responses than might otherwise be expected if they filled out an anonymous questionnaire.

Pretest and Posttest Sensitization

These related threats to external validity refer to the effects that pretesting and posttesting might have on the behavior and responses of the participants in a study (Bracht & Glass, 1968; Lana, 1969; Pedhazur & Schmelkin, 1991). In many forms of research, participants are *pretested* to quantify the presence of some variable of interest and to provide a baseline of behavior against which the effects of the experimental intervention (independent variable) can be evaluated. For example, a pretest for symptoms of anxiety would be given to determine participant symptomology in a treatment study investigating the effectiveness of a new therapy for anxiety disorders. The pretest information would be used as a baseline measure and compared to a posttest measure of symptoms at the conclusion of the study to determine the intervention's effectiveness at reducing symptoms of anxiety. Generally, pretest sensitization is a possibility whenever participants are measured prior to the administration of the experimental intervention and the researchers are interested in measuring the effects of the independent variable on the dependent variable.

As a threat to external validity, the concern is that exposure to the pretest may contribute to, or be the sole cause of, the observed changes in the dependent variable. In other words, would the results of the study have been the same if the pretest had not been administered? This has obvious implications for external validity because pretest sensitization might render the results irrelevant in situations in which the same pretest was not administered. For example, in our previously mentioned anxiety study the same treatment effects might not be found in the absence of the pretest for current level of anxiety.

Whereas pretesting is focused on assessing the level of a variable before application of the experimental intervention (or independent variable), *posttesting* is conducted to assess the effectiveness of the independent variable. A posttest measurement can have a similar effect on external validity as a pretest assessment. Would the same results have been found if the posttest had not been administered? If not, then it can be said that posttest sensitization might account for the results either alone or in combination with the experimental intervention.

In both pre- and postassessment, the concern is whether participants were sensitized by either measure. If so, the findings might be less generalizable than if future research and actual interventions were conducted without the same procedure and assessment measures. In other words, the presence of pre- and posttesting becomes an integral part of the intervention itself. Therefore, the effects of the independent variable might be less prominent or even nonexistent in the absence of pretest or posttest sensitization.

Timing of Assessment and Measurement

This threat to external validity is particularly common in longitudinal forms of research, and it refers to the question of whether the same results would have been obtained if measurement had occurred at a different point in time (Kazdin, 2003c).

Although this threat to external validity can occur in most types of research design, it is most common in longitudinal research. (See Chapter 5 for a more detailed discussion of longitudinal research.) Longitudinal research occurs over time and is characterized by multiple assessments over the duration of the study. For example, a longitudinal therapy outcome study might find significant results after assessment of symptoms at 2 months, but not at 4 or 6 months. If the study concluded at the end of 2 months, the researchers might come to the general conclusion that the treatment is effective for a particular disorder. This might be an overgeneralization because if the study had continued for a longer period of time, the same treatment effect would not have been observed. Thus, the more appropriate conclusion about our 2-month study might be that the treatment produces symptom relief for up to or after 2 months. The more specific conclusion is supported by the study, while the more general conclusion about effectiveness might not be accurate due to the timing of measurement. Bear in mind that the reverse might also be true: A lack of significant findings after measurement at 2 months does not eliminate the possibility of significant results if the intervention and measurement occurred over a longer period of time.

Rapid Reference 6.5 summarizes the threats to external validity we have discussed in this section, and Rapid Reference 6.6 provides further discussion.

CONSTRUCT VALIDITY

In the context of research design and methodology, the term *construct validity* relates to interpreting the basis of the causal relationship, and it refers to the congruence between the study's results and the theoretical underpinnings guiding the research (Kazdin, 2003c). The focus of construct validity is usually on the study's independent variable. In essence, construct validity asks the question of whether the theory supported by the findings provides the best available explanation of the results. In other words, is the reason for the relationship between the experimental intervention (independent variable) and the observed phenomenon (dependent variable) due to the underlying construct or explanation offered by the researchers

Rapid Reference 6.5

Threats to External Validity

- **Sample characteristics:** The extent to which the results of a study apply only to a particular sample. The key question is whether the study's results can be applied to other samples that vary on a variety of demographic and descriptive characteristics, such as age, gender, sexual orientation, education, and socioeconomic status.

- **Stimulus characteristics and settings:** An environmental phenomenon whereby particular features or conditions of the study limit the generalizability of the findings so that the findings from one study do not necessarily apply to another study, even if the other study is using a similar sample.

- **Reactivity of experimental arrangements:** A potentially confounding variable that results from the influence produced by knowing that one is participating in a research study.

- **Multiple-treatment interference:** This threat refers to research situations in which (1) participants are administered more than one experimental intervention within the same study or (2) the same individuals participate in more than one study.

- **Novelty effects:** This refers to the possibility that the effects of the independent variable may be due in part to the uniqueness or novelty of the stimulus or situation and not to the intervention itself.

- **Reactivity of assessment:** A phenomenon whereby participants' awareness that their performance is being measured can alter their performance from what it otherwise would have been.

- **Pretest and posttest sensitization:** These threats refer to the effects that pretesting and posttesting might have on the behavior and responses of study participants.

- **Timing of assessment and measurement:** This threat refers to whether the same results would have been obtained if measurement had occurred at a different point in time.

≡Rapid Reference 6.6

....

Importance of Interaction Effects in Relation to External Validity

External validity can best be understood as an interaction between participant attributes and experimental settings and their related characteristics.
Generalization of results from any study is hampered when the independent variable interacts with participant attributes or characteristics of the
experimental setting to produce the observed results. Therefore, the
types of threats to external validity discussed in this chapter are far from
exhaustive. Depending on the experimental design and the research question, each study can create unique threats to external validity that should
be controlled for. If experimental control is not possible, the limitations of
the study's findings should be discussed in sufficient detail to clarify the
relevance and generalizability of the findings.

(Campbell & Stanley, 1966; Cook & Campbell, 1979; Christensen, 1988; Graziano & Raulin, 2004; Kazdin, 2003c)?

There are two primary methods for improving the construct validity of a study. First, strong construct validity is based on clearly stated and accu-rate operational definitions of a study's variables. Second, the underlying theory of the study should have a strong conceptual basis and be based on well-validated constructs (Graziano & Raulin, 2004). Cook and Campbell (1979) suggest several ways to improve construct validity; these are listed in Rapid Reference 6.7.

Let's consider a straightforward example to illustrate the importance of construct validity in a study. A team of researchers is interested in study-ing the factors that contribute to mortality rates in a number of different countries. The scope of the study prohibits the use of actual participants, so the researchers decide to conduct a correlational study in which they analyze the statistical relationships between different countries and avail-able demographic data. The researchers hypothesize that education level and family income will be significantly related to mortality rate. The spe-cific hypothesis is that mortality rate will drop as education level and family income rise. In other words, the researchers are hypothesizing that

≡ Rapid Reference 6.7

Improving Construct Validity

Cook and Campbell (1979) make the following suggestions for improving construct validity:

- Provide a clear operational definition of the abstract concept or independent variable.
- Collect data to demonstrate that the empirical representation of the independent variable produces the expected outcome.
- Collect data to show that the empirical representation of the independent variable does not vary with measures of related but different conceptual variables.
- Conduct manipulation checks of the independent variable.

there is a negative relationship between mortality and education level and family income. The underlying construct being tested in the study is that these two factors—education level and family income—are negatively related to mortality. The researchers conduct their analyses and discover that their hypothesis is confirmed—that is, that mortality rates are negatively related to education level and family income. The researchers conclude that educational level and family income are protective factors that reduce the likelihood of mortality.

Is this the most likely explanation for the results, or is there perhaps a better explanation that might function as a threat to the study's hypothesis regarding causation (or construct validity)? What might be a better causal explanation for the results of the study? One possible alternative explanation of the results might be that higher educational levels and family income reduce mortality rates because they are related to another factor that was not considered in the study. Considering that educational level is usually positively related to income level, higher levels of education tend to lead to higher levels of income. A higher level of income usually provides access to a wider variety of privileges and services, such as access to higher-quality health care. Access to health care is therefore related to education level and family income, and it is a plausible causal explanation for

the results obtained in the study
(other than those espoused by the
researchers).

There are phenomena that occur within the context of research
that can act as threats to construct
validity. As with internal and external validity, the number and
types of threats are related to the
unique aspects and design of the

study itself. Generally, these threats are features of a study that interfere
with the researcher's ability to draw causal inferences from the study's results (Kazdin, 2003c). In our previous discussions of internal and external
validity, we were able to identify and categorize specific and well-defined
threats. The threats to construct validity are more difficult to classify because they can be anything that relates to the design of the study and the
underlying theoretical construct under consideration. Despite this, the
most common sources of threats to construct validity closely parallel
some of the threats to external validity discussed earlier in this chapter
such as conditions surrounding the experimental situation, experimenter
expectancies, and characteristics of the participants.

STATISTICAL VALIDITY

The final type of validity that we will discuss in this chapter is the critically
important yet often-overlooked concept of statistical validity. As its name
implies, *statistical validity* (also referred to as *statistical conclusion validity*) refers
to aspects of quantitative evaluation that affect the accuracy of the conclusions drawn from the results of a study (Campbell & Stanley, 1966;
Cook & Campbell, 1979). Statistical procedures are typically used to test
the relationship between two or more variables and determine whether an
observed statistical effect is due to chance or is a true reflection of a causal
relationship (Rosnow & Rosenthal, 2002). At its simplest level, statistical
validity addresses the question of whether the statistical conclusions

drawn from the results of a study are reasonable (Graziano & Raulin, 2004).

The concepts of hypothesis testing and statistical evaluation are interrelated, and they provide the foundation for evaluating statistical validity. *Statistical evaluation* refers to the theoretical basis, rationale, and computational aspects of the actual statistics used to evaluate the nature of the relationship between the independent and dependent variables. Among other things, the choice of statistical techniques often depends on the nature of the hypotheses being tested in the study. This is where the concept of *hypothesis testing* enters our discussion of statistical validity. Put simply, every study is driven by one or more hypotheses that guide the methodological design of the study, the statistical analyses, and the resulting conclusions.

As discussed in Chapter 2, there are two main types of hypotheses in research: the null hypothesis (usually designated as H_0) and the experimental hypothesis (usually designated as H_1, H_2, H_3, etc., depending on the number of hypotheses). The *experimental hypothesis* represents the predicted relationship among the variables being examined in the study. Conversely, the *null hypothesis* represents a statement of no relationship among the variables being examined (Christensen, 1988).

At this point, we should review an important convention in research methodology as it relates to statistical analyses and hypotheses testing. Rejecting the null hypothesis is a necessary first step in evaluating the impact of the independent variable (Graziano & Raulin, 2004). Therefore, in terms of statistical analyses, the focus is always on the null hypothesis, and not on the experimental hypotheses. Researchers reject the null hypothesis if a statistically significant difference is found between the experimental and control conditions (Kazdin, 2003c). By contrast, researchers retain (or fail to reject) the null hypothesis if no statistically significant difference is found between the experimental and control conditions.

As with the other forms of validity discussed throughout this chapter, there are numerous threats to statistical validity. The most common include low statistical power, variability in the experimental procedures and participant characteristics, unreliability of measures, and multiple comparisons and error rates. Each of these threats can have a significant impact on the study's ability to delineate causal relationships and rule out plausible rival hypotheses.

Low Statistical Power

Low statistical power is the most common threat to statistical validity (Keppel, 1991; Kirk, 1995). The presence of this threat produces a low probability of detecting a difference between experimental and control conditions even when a difference truly exists. Low statistical power is directly related to small effect and sample sizes, with the presence of each increasing the likelihood that low statistical power is an issue in the research design. Accordingly, low statistical power can cause a researcher to conclude that there are no significant results even when significant results actually exist (Rosnow & Rosenthal, 2002). The concept of power will be discussed further in Chapter 7.

Variability

Variability is another threat to statistical validity that applies to both the participants and procedures used in a study. First, let's consider *variability in methodological procedures.* This concept includes a wide array of differences and questions that relate to the actual design aspects of the study. These differences can be found in the delivery of the independent variable, the procedures related to the execution of the study, variability in performance measures over time, and a host of other examples that are directly dependent on the unique design of a particular study. A related threat to statistical validity is *variability in participant characteristics.* Participants in a research study can vary along a variety of characteristics and dimensions, such as age, education, socioeconomic status, and race. As the diversity of participant characteristics increases, there is less likelihood that a difference between the control and experimental conditions can be detected. When variability across these two broad sources is minimized, the likelihood of detecting a true difference between the control and experimental conditions increases. This threat to statistical validity must be considered at the planning stage of the study, and it is usually controlled through the use of homogeneous samples, strict and well-defined procedural protocols, and statistical controls at the data analysis stage.

Unreliability of Measures

Unreliability of measures used in a study is another source of variability that is a threat to statistical validity. This threat refers to whether the measures used in the study assess the characteristics of interest in a consistent—or reliable—fashion (Kazdin, 2003c). If the research study's measures are unreliable, then more random variability is introduced into the experimental design. As with participant and procedural variability, this type of variability decreases statistical power and makes it less likely that the statistical analyses will detect a true difference between the control and experimental conditions when a difference actually exists.

Multiple Comparisons

The final threat to statistical validity that we will consider is often referred to as *multiple statistical comparisons* and the resulting error rates (Kazdin, 2003c; Rosnow & Rosenthal, 2002). This threat to statistical validity pertains to the number of statistical analyses used to analyze the data obtained in a study. Generally, as the number of statistical analyses increases, so does the likelihood of finding a significant difference between the experimental and control conditions purely by mathematical chance. In other words, the significant finding is a mathematical artifact and does not reflect a true difference between conditions. Accordingly, researchers should define their hypotheses before the study begins so as to conduct the minimum number of statistical analyses to address each of the hypotheses.

Rapid Reference 6.8 summarizes the threats to statistical validity that we have discussed in this section.

═Rapid Reference 6.8

Threats to Statistical Validity

- **Low statistical power:** Low probability of detecting a difference between experimental and control conditions even if a difference truly exists.

- **Procedural and participant variability:** Variability in methodological procedures and a host of participant characteristics, which decreases the likelihood of detecting a difference between the control and experimental conditions.

- **Unreliability of measures:** Whether the measures used in a study assess the characteristics of interest in a consistent manner. Unreliable measures introduce more random variability into the research design, which reduces statistical power.

- **Multiple comparisons and error rates:** The concept that, as the number of statistical analyses increases, so does the likelihood of finding a significant difference between the experimental and control conditions purely by chance.

SUMMARY

In this chapter, we have discussed the four types of validity that are critical to sound research methodology. In addition, we discussed the major threats to each type of validity. Although each type of validity and its related threats were presented independently, it is important to note that all types of validity are interdependent, and addressing one type may compromise the other types. As was discussed, all of the broad threats to validity should be considered at the design stage of the study if possible. In terms of priority, ensuring strong internal validity is regarded as more important than external validity, because we must control for rival hypotheses before we can even begin to think about generalizing the results of a study.

✍ TEST YOURSELF ✍

1. _____ is an important concept in research that refers to the conceptual and scientific soundness of a research study.

2. History, maturation, testing, statistical regression, and selection biases are threats to _____ _____.

3. External validity is concerned with the _____ of research results.

4. _____ _____ refers to aspects of quantitative evaluation that affect the accuracy of the conclusions drawn from the results of a study.

5. _____ _____ refers to the congruence between the study's results and the theoretical underpinnings guiding the research.

Answers: 1. Validity; 2. internal validity; 3. generalizability; 4. Statistical conclusion; 5. Construct validity

Seven

DATA PREPARATION, ANALYSES, AND INTERPRETATION

As we have discussed in previous chapters, in most research studies, the researcher begins by generating a research question, framing it into a testable (i.e., falsifiable) hypothesis, selecting an appropriate research design, choosing a suitable sample of research participants, and selecting valid and reliable methods of measurement. If all of these tasks have been carried out properly, then the process of data analysis should be a fairly straightforward process. Still, a variety of important steps must be taken to ensure the integrity and validity of research findings and their interpretation.

In most types of research studies, the process of data analysis involves the following three steps: (1) preparing the data for analysis, (2) analyzing the data, and (3) interpreting the data (i.e., testing the research hypotheses and drawing valid inferences). Therefore, we will begin this chapter with a brief discussion of data cleaning and organization, followed by a nontechnical overview of the most widely used descriptive and inferential statistics. We will conclude this chapter with a discussion of several important concepts that should be understood when interpreting and drawing inferences from research findings. Because a comprehensive discussion of statistical techniques is well beyond the scope of this book, researchers seeking a more detailed review of statistical analyses should consult one of the statistical textbooks contained in the reference list.

DATA PREPARATION

Virtually all studies, from surveys to randomized experimental trials, require some form of data collection and entry. Data represent the fruit of researchers' labor because they provide the information that will ultimately allow them to describe phenomena, predict events, identify and quantify differences between conditions, and establish the effectiveness of interventions. Because of their critical nature, data should be treated with the utmost respect and care. In addition to ensuring the confidentiality and security of personal data (as discussed in Chapter 8), the researcher should carefully plan how the data will be logged, entered, transformed (as necessary), and organized into a database that will facilitate accurate and efficient statistical analysis.

Logging and Tracking Data

Any study that involves data collection will require some procedure to log the information as it comes in and track it until it is ready to be analyzed. Research data can come from any number of sources (e.g., personal records, participant interviews, observations, laboratory reports, and pretest and posttest measures). Without a well-established procedure, data can easily become disorganized, uninterpretable, and ultimately unusable.

Although there is no one definitive method for logging and tracking data collection and entry, in this age of computers it might be considered inefficient and impractical not to take advantage of one of the many available computer applications to facilitate the process. Taking the time to set up a recruitment and tracking system on a computer database (e.g., Microsoft Access, Microsoft Excel, Claris FileMaker, SPSS, SAS) will provide researchers with up-to-date information throughout the study, and it will save substantial time and effort when they are ready to analyze their data and report the findings.

One of the key elements of the data tracking system is the recruitment log. The *recruitment log* is a comprehensive record of all individuals approached about participation in a study. The log can also serve to record the dates and times that potential participants were approached, whether they met eligibility criteria, and whether they agreed and provided informed consent to participate in the study. Importantly, for ethical reasons, no identifying information should be recorded for individuals who do not consent to participate in the research study. The primary purpose of the recruitment log is to keep track of participant enrollment and to determine how representative the resulting cohort of study participants is of the population that the researcher is attempting to examine.

In some study settings, where records are maintained on all potential participants (e.g., treatment programs, schools, organizations), it may be possible for the researcher to obtain aggregate information on eligible individuals who were not recruited into the study, either because they chose not to participate or because they were not approached by the researcher. Importantly, because these individuals did not provide informed consent, these data can only be obtained in aggregate, and they must be void of any identifying information. Given this type of aggregate information, the researcher would be able to determine whether the study sample is representative of the population.

In addition to logging client recruitment, a well-designed tracking sys-

DON'T FORGET

Record-Keeping Responsibilities

The lead researcher (referred to as principal investigator in grant-funded research) is ultimately responsible for maintaining the validity and quality of all research data, including the proper training of all research staff and developing and enforcing policies for recording, maintaining, and storing data. The researcher should ensure that

- research data are collected and recorded according to policy;
- research data are stored in a way that will ensure security and confidentiality; and
- research data are audited on a regular basis to maintain quality control and identify potential problems as they occur.

tem can provide the researcher with up-to-date information on the general status of the study, including client participation, data collection, and data entry.

Data Screening

Immediately following data collection, but prior to data entry, the researcher should carefully screen all data for accuracy. The promptness of these procedures is very important because research staff may still be able to recontact study participants to address any omissions, errors, or inaccuracies. In some cases, the research staff may inadvertently have failed to record certain information (e.g., assessment date, study site) or perhaps recorded a response illegibly. In such instances, the research staff may be able to correct the data themselves, if too much time has not elapsed. Because data collection and data entry are often done by different research staff, it may be more difficult and time consuming to make such clarifications once the information is passed on to data entry staff.

One way to simplify the data screening process and make it more time efficient is to collect data using computerized assessment instruments. Computerized assessments can be programmed to accept only responses within certain ranges, to check for blank fields or skipped items, and even to conduct cross-checks between certain items to identify potential inconsistencies between responses. Another major benefit of these programs is that the entered data can usually be electronically transferred into a permanent database, thereby automating the data entry procedure. Although this type of computerization may, at first glance, appear to be an impossible budgetary expense, it might be more economical than it seems when one considers the savings in staff time spent on data screening and entry.

Whether it is done manually or electronically, data screening is an essential process in ensuring that data are accurate and complete. Generally, the researcher should plan to screen the data to make certain that (1) responses are legible and understandable, (2) responses are within an acceptable range, (3) responses are complete, and (4) all of the necessary information has been included.

Constructing a Database

Once data are screened and all corrections are made, the data should be entered into a well-structured database. When planning a study, the researcher should carefully consider the structure of the database and how it will be used. In many cases, it may be helpful to think backward and to begin by anticipating how the data will be analyzed. This will help the researcher to figure out exactly which variables need to be entered, how they should be ordered, and how they should be formatted. Moreover, the statistical analysis may also dictate what type of program you choose for your database. For example, certain advanced statistical analyses may require the use of specific statistical programs.

While designing the general structure of the database, the researcher must carefully consider all of the variables that will need to be entered. Forgetting to enter one or more variables, although not as problematic as failing to collect certain data elements, will add substantial effort and expense because the researcher must then go back to the hard data to find the missing data elements.

DON'T FORGET

Retaining Data Records

Researchers should retain study data for a minimum period of 5 years after publication of their data in the event that questions or concerns arise regarding the findings. The advancement of science relies on the scientific community's overall confidence in disseminated findings, and the existence of the primary data serves to instill such confidence.

The Data Codebook

In addition to developing a well-structured database, researchers should take the time to develop a data codebook. A *data codebook* is a written or computerized list that provides a clear and comprehensive description of the variables that will be included in the database. A detailed codebook is essential when the researcher begins to analyze the data. Moreover, it serves as a permanent database guide, so that the researcher, when attempting to reanalyze certain data, will not be stuck trying to remember what certain variable names mean or what data were used for a certain analysis. Ultimately, the lack of a well-defined data codebook may render a database uninterpretable and useless. At a bare minimum, a data codebook should contain the following elements for each variable:

- Variable name
- Variable description
- Variable format (number, data, text)
- Instrument or method of collection
- Date collected
- Respondent or group
- Variable location (in database)
- Notes

Data Entry

After the data have been screened for completeness and accuracy, and the researcher has developed a well-structured database and a detailed code-

DON'T FORGET

Defining Variables Within a Database

Certain databases, particularly statistical programs (e.g., SPSS) allow the researcher to enter a wide range of descriptive information about each variable, including the variable name, the type of data (e.g., numeric, text, currency, date), label (how it will be referred to in data printouts), how missing data are coded or treated, and measurement scale (e.g., nominal, ordinal, interval, or ratio). Although these databases are extremely helpful and should be used whenever possible, they do not substitute for a comprehensive codebook, which includes separate information about the different databases themselves (e.g., which databases were used for each set of analyses).

book, data entry should be fairly straightforward. Nevertheless, many errors can occur at this stage. Therefore, it is critical that all data-entry staff are properly trained and maintain the highest level of accuracy when inputting data. One way of ensuring the accuracy of data entry is through double entry. In the *double-entry* procedure, data are entered into the database twice and then compared to determine whether there are any discrepancies. The researcher or data entry staff can then examine the discrepancies and determine whether they can be resolved and corrected or if they should simply be treated as missing data. Although the double-entry process is a very effective way to identify entry errors, it may be difficult to manage and may not be time or cost effective.

As an alternative to double entry, the researcher may design a standard procedure for checking the data for inaccuracies. Such procedures typically entail a careful review of the inputted data for out-of-range values, missing data, and incorrect formatting. Much of this work can be accomplished by running descriptive analyses and frequencies on each variable. In addition, many database programs (e.g., Microsoft Excel, Microsoft Access, SPSS) allow the researcher to define the ranges, formats, and types of data that will be accepted into certain data fields. These databases will make it impossible to enter information that does not meet the preset criteria. Defining data entry criteria in this manner can prevent many errors and it may substantially reduce the time spent on data cleaning.

Transforming Data

After the data have been entered and checked for inaccuracies, the researcher or data entry staff will undoubtedly be required to make certain transformations before the data can be analyzed. These transformations typically involve the following:

- Identifying and coding missing values
- Computing totals and new variables
- Reversing scale items
- Recoding and categorization

Identifying and Coding Missing Values

Inevitably, all databases and most variables will have some number of missing values. This is a result of either study participants' failing to respond to certain questions, missed observations, or inaccurate data that were rejected from the database. Researchers and data analysts often do not want to include certain cases with missing data because they may potentially skew the results. Therefore, most statistical packages (e.g., SPSS, SAS) will provide the option of ignoring cases in which certain variables are considered missing, or they will automatically treat blank values as missing. These programs also typically allow the researcher to designate specific values to represent missing data (e.g., –99). A small sample of the many techniques used for imputing missing data values are discussed in Rapid Reference 7.1.

Missing Value Imputation

Virtually all databases have some number of missing values. Unfortunately, statistical analysis of data sets with missing values can result in biased results and incorrect inferences. Although numerous techniques have been offered to impute missing values, there is an ongoing debate in contemporary statistics as to which technique is the most appropriate. A few of the more widely used imputation techniques include the following:

Hot deck imputation: In this imputation technique, the researcher matches participants on certain variables to identify potential donors. Missing values are then replaced with values taken from matching respondents (i.e., respondents who are matched on a set of relevant factors).

Predicted mean imputation: Imputed values are predicted using certain statistical procedures (i.e., linear regression for continuous data and discriminant function for dichotomous or categorical data).

Last value carried forward: Imputed values are based on previously observed values. This method can be used only for longitudinal variables, for which participants have values from previous data collection points.

Group means: Imputed variables are determined by calculating the variable's group mean (or mode, in the case of categorical data).

Computing Totals and New Variables

In certain instances, the researcher may want to create new variables based on values from other variables. For example, suppose a researcher has data on the total number of times clients in two different treatments attended their treatments each month. The researcher would have a total of four variables, each representing the number of sessions attended each week during the first month of treatment. Let's call them q1, q2, q3, and q4. If the researcher wanted to analyze monthly attendance by the different treatments, he or she would have to compute a new variable. This could be done with the following transformation:

$$total = q1 + q2 + q3 + q4$$

Still another reason for transforming variables is that the variable may not be normally distributed (see Rapid Reference 7.2). This can substantially alter the results of the data analysis. In such instances, certain data transformations (see Rapid Reference 7.3) may serve to normalize the distribution and improve the accuracy of outcomes.

Reversing Scale Items

Many instruments and measures use items with reversed scales to decrease the likelihood of participants' falling into what is referred to as a "response set." A *response set* occurs when a participant begins to respond in a patterned manner to questions or statements on a test or assessment measure, regardless of the content of each query or statement. For example, an individual may answer *false* to all test items, or may provide a 1 for all items requesting a response from 1 to 5. Here's an example of how reverse scale items work: Let's say that participants in a survey are asked to indicate their levels of agreement,

Rapid Reference 7.2

Normal Distributions

A *normal distribution* is a distribution of the values of a variable that, when plotted, produces a symmetrical, bell-shaped curve that rises smoothly from a small number of cases at each extreme to a large number of cases in the middle.

≡ Rapid Reference 7.3

Data Transformations

Most statistical procedures assume that the variables being analyzed are normally distributed. Analyzing variables that are not normally distributed can lead to serious overestimation (Type I error) or underestimation (Type II error). Therefore, before analyzing their data, researchers should carefully examine variable distributions. Although this is often done by simply looking over the frequency distributions, there are many, more-objective methods of determining whether variables are normally distributed. Typically, these involve examining each variable's *skewness*, which measures the overall lack of symmetry of the distribution, and whether it looks the same to the left and right of the center point; and its *kurtosis*, which measures whether the data are peaked or flat relative to a normal distribution. Unfortunately, many variables in the social sciences and within particular sample populations are not normally distributed. Therefore, researchers often rely on one of several transformations to potentially improve the normality of certain variables. The most frequently used transformations are the square root transformation, the log transformation, and the inverse transformation.

Square root transformation: Described simply, this type of transformation involves taking the square root of each value within a certain variable. The one caveat is that you cannot take a square root of a negative number. Fortunately, this can be easily remedied by adding a constant, such as 1, to each item before computing the square root.

Log transformation: There is a wide variety of log transformations. In general, however, a *logarithm* is the power (also known as the exponent) to which a base number has to be raised to get the original number. As with square root transformation, if a variable contains values less than 1, a constant must be added to move the minimum value of the distribution.

Inverse transformation: This type of transformation involves taking the inverse of each value by dividing it into 1. For example, the inverse of 3 would be computed as 1/3. Essentially, this procedure makes very small values very large, and very large values very small, and it has the effect of reversing the order of a variable's scores. Therefore, researchers using this transformation procedure should be careful not to misinterpret the scores following their analysis.

from 1 to 5, with a series of statements. In this survey, 1 corresponds with *completely disagree* and 5 corresponds with *completely agree*. The researcher may decide, however, to reverse-scale some of the items on the survey, so that 1 corresponds with *completely agree* and 5 corresponds with *completely disagree*. This may reduce the likelihood that participants will fall into a response set. Before data can be analyzed, it is important that all reversed items are recoded so that all of the responses fall in the same direction.

Recoding Variables

Some variables may be more easily analyzed if they are recoded into categories. For example, a researcher may wish to collapse income estimates or ages into specific ranges. This is an example of turning a continuous variable into a categorical variable (as was discussed in Chapter 2). Although categorizing continuous variables may ultimately reduce their specificity, in some cases it may be warranted to simplify data analysis and interpretation. In other instances, it may be necessary to recategorize or recode categorical variables by combining them into fewer categories. This is often the case when variables have so many categories that certain categories are sparsely populated, which may violate the assumptions of certain statistical analyses. To resolve this issue, researchers may choose to combine or collapse certain categories.

Once the data have been screened, entered, cleaned, and transformed, they should be ready to be analyzed. It is possible, of course, that the data will need to be recoded or transformed again during the analyses. In fact, the need for many of the transformations discussed previously will not be identified until the analyses have begun. Still, taking the time to carefully prepare the data first should make data analysis more efficient and improve the overall validity of the study's findings.

DATA ANALYSIS

As mentioned earlier, research data can be seen as the fruit of researchers' labor. If a study has been conducted in a scientifically rigorous manner, the data will hold the clues necessary to answer the researchers' questions. To unlock these clues, researchers typically rely on a variety of statistical procedures. These statistical procedures allow researchers to describe groups of individuals and events, examine the relationships between different variables, measure differences between groups and conditions, and examine and generalize results obtained from a sample back to the population from which the sample was drawn. Knowledge about data analysis can help a researcher interpret data for the purpose of providing meaningful insights about the problem being examined.

Although a comprehensive review of statistical procedures is beyond the scope of this text, in general, they can be broken down into two major areas: descriptive and inferential. *Descriptive statistics* allow the researcher to describe the data and examine relationships between variables, while *inferential statistics* allow the researcher to examine causal relationships. In many cases, inferential statistics allow researchers to go beyond the parameters of their study sample and draw conclusions about the population from which the sample was drawn. This section will provide a brief overview of some of the more commonly used descriptive and inferential statistics.

Descriptive Statistics

As their name implies, descriptive statistics are used to describe the data collected in research studies and to accurately characterize the variables under observation within a specific sample. Descriptive analyses are frequently used to summarize a study sample prior to analyzing a study's primary hypotheses. This provides information about the overall representativeness of the sample, as well as the information necessary for other researchers to replicate the study, if they so desire. In other research efforts (i.e., purely descriptive studies), precise and comprehensive descriptions may be the primary focus of the study. In either case, the principal objective of descriptive statistics is to accurately describe distributions of certain variables within a specific data set.

There is a variety of methods for examining the distribution of a variable. Perhaps the most basic method, and the starting point and foundation of virtually all statistical analyses, is the frequency distribution. A *frequency distribution* is simply a complete list of all possible values or scores for a particular variable, along with the number of times (frequency) that each value or score appears in the data set. For example, teachers and instructors who want to know how their classes perform on certain exams will need to examine the overall distribution of the test scores. The teacher would begin by sorting the scores so that they go from the lowest to the highest and then count the number of times that each score occurred. This information can be delineated in what is known as a *frequency table*, which is illustrated in Table 7.1.

To make the distribution of scores even more informative, the teacher could group the test scores together in some manner. For example, the

Table 7.1 Frequency Distribution of Test Scores

Value	Frequency	Cumulative Frequency
71	1	1
76	1	2
78	2	4
81	2	6
82	1	7
83	1	8
84	2	10
85	2	12
86	2	14
87	1	15
89	1	16
90	2	18
94	3	21
98	1	22
100	1	23

Table 7.2   Grouped Frequency Distribution of Test Scores

Value	Frequency	Cumulative Frequency
71–75	1	1
76–80	3	4
81–85	8	12
86–90	6	18
91–95	3	21
96–100	2	23

teacher may decide to group the test scores from 71 to 75, 76 to 80, 81 to 85, 86 to 90, 91 to 95, and 96 to 100. This type of grouping would result in the frequency distribution shown in Table 7.2.

Still another way that this distribution may be depicted is in what is known as a histogram. A *histogram* (see Figure 7.1) is nothing more than a graphic display of the same information contained in the frequency tables shown in Tables 7.1 and 7.2.

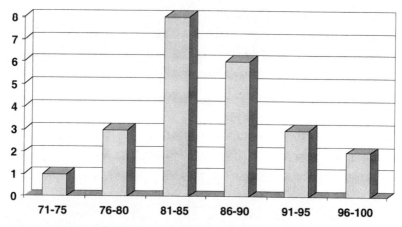

Figure 7.1   Grouped frequency histogram of test scores.

Although frequency tables and histograms provide researchers with a general overview of the distribution, there are more precise ways of describing the shape of the distribution of values for a specific variable. These include measures of central tendency and dispersion.

Central Tendency

The *central tendency* of a distribution is a number that represents the typical or most representative value in the distribution. Measures of central tendency provide researchers with a way of characterizing a data set with a single value. The most widely used measures of central tendency are the mean, median, and mode.

The *mean,* except in statistics courses and scientific journals, is more commonly known as the average. The mean is perhaps the most widely used and reported measure of central tendency. The mean is quite simple to calculate: Simply add all the numbers in the data set and then divide by the total number of entries. The result is the mean of the distribution. For example, let's say that we are trying to describe the mean age of a group of 10 study participants with the following ages:

$$34 \quad 27 \quad 23 \quad 23 \quad 26 \quad 27 \quad \mathbf{28} \quad 23 \quad 32 \quad 41$$

The summed ages for the 10 participants is 284. Therefore, the mean age of the sample is $284/10 = \mathbf{28.40.}$

The mean is quite accurate when the data set is normally distributed. Unfortunately, the mean is strongly influenced by extreme values or outliers. Therefore, it may be misleading in data sets in which the values are not normally distributed, or where there are extreme values at one end of the data set (skewed distributions).

For example, consider a situation in which study participants report annual earnings of between $25,000 and $40,000. The mean annual income for the sample might wind up being around $35,000. Now consider what would happen if one or two of the participants reported earnings of $100,000 or more. Their substantially higher salaries (outliers) would disproportionately increase the mean income for the entire sample. In such instances, a median or mode may provide much more meaningful summary information.

The *median,* as implied by its name, is the middle value in a distribution of values. To calculate the median, simply sort all of the values from lowest to highest and then identify the middle value. The middle value is the median. For example, sorting the set of ages in the previous example would result in the following:

23   23   23   26   **27**   **27**   28   32   34   41

In this instance, the median is **27,** because the two middle values are both 27, with four values on either side. If the two values were different, you would simply split the difference to get the median. For example, if the two middle values were 27 and 28, the median would be 27.5. Calculation of the median is even simpler when the data set has an odd number of values. In these cases, the median is simply the value that falls exactly in the middle.

The mode is yet another useful measure of central tendency. The *mode* is the value that occurs most frequently in a set of values. To find the mode, simply count the number of times (frequency) that each value appears in a data set. The value that occurs most frequently is the mode. For example, by examining the sorted distribution of ages listed below, we could easily see that the most prevalent age in the sample is **23,** which is therefore the mode.

23   **23**   **23**   26   27   27   28   32   34   41

With larger data sets, the mode is more easily identified by examining a frequency table, as described earlier. The mode is very useful with nominal and ordinal data or when the data are not normally distributed, because it is not influenced by extreme values or outliers. Therefore, the mode is a good summary statistic even in cases when distributions are skewed. Also note that a distribution can have more than one mode. Two modes would make the distribution *bimodal,* while a distribution having three modes would be referred to as *trimodal.*

Interestingly, although the three measures of central tendency resulted in different values in the previous examples, in a perfectly normal distribution, the mean, median, and mode would all be the same.

Dispersion

Measures of central tendency, like the mean, describe the most likely value, but they do not tell us anything about how the values vary. For example, two sets of data can have the same mean, but they may vary greatly in the way that their values are spread out. Another way of describing the shape of a distribution is to examine this spread. The spread, more technically referred to as the *dispersion,* of a distribution provides us with information about how tightly grouped the values are around the center of the distribution (e.g., around the mean, median, and/or mode). The most widely used measures of dispersion are range, variance, and standard deviation.

The *range* of a distribution tells us the smallest possible interval in which all the data in a certain sample will fall. Quite simply, the range is the difference between the highest and lowest values in a distribution. Therefore, the range is easily calculated by subtracting the lowest value from the highest value. Using our previous example, the range of ages for the study sample would be:

$$41 - 23 = \mathbf{18}$$

Because it depends on only two values in the distribution, it is usually a poor measure of dispersion, except when the sample size is particularly large.

A more precise measure of dispersion, or spread around the mean of a distribution, is the variance. The *variance* gives us a sense of how closely concentrated a set of values is around its average value, and is calculated in the following manner:

1. Subtract the mean of the distribution from each of the values.
2. Square each result.
3. Add all of the squared results.
4. Divide the result by the number of values minus 1.

The variance of the set of 10 participant ages would therefore be calculated in the following manner:

$$\text{Variance} = [(23 - 28.40)^2 + (23 - 28.40)^2 + (23 - 28.40)^2 + (26 - 28.40)^2$$

$$+ (27 - 28.40)^2 + (27 - 28.40)^2 + (28 - 28.40)^2 + (32 - 28.40)^2$$

$$+ (34 - 28.40)^2 + (41 - 28.40)^2] \div 9 = \mathbf{33.37}$$

The variance of a distribution gives us an average of how far, in squared units, the values in a distribution are from the mean, which allows us to see how closely concentrated the scores in a distribution are.

Another measure of the spread of values around the mean of a distribution is the standard deviation. The *standard deviation* is simply the square root of the variance. Therefore, the standard deviation for the set of participant ages is:

$$\sqrt{33.37} = \mathbf{5.78}$$

By taking the square root of the variance, we can avoid having to think in terms of squared units. The variance and the standard deviation of distributions are the basis for calculating many other statistics that estimate associations and differences between variables. In addition, they provide us with important information about the values in a distribution. For example, if the distribution of values is normal, or close to normal, one can conclude the following with reasonable certainty:

1. Approximately 68% of the values fall within 1 standard deviation of the mean.
2. Approximately 95% of the values fall within 2 standard deviations of the mean.
3. Approximately 99% of the values fall within 3 standard deviations of the mean.

Therefore, assuming that the distribution is normal, we can estimate that because the mean age of participants was 28.40 and the standard deviation was 5.78, approximately 68% of the participants are within ±5.78 years (1 standard deviation) of the mean age of 28.40. Similarly, we can estimate that 95% of the participants are within ±11.56 years (2 standard deviations) of the mean age of 28.40. This information has several important applications. First, like the measures of central tendency, it allows the researcher to describe the overall characteristics of a sample. Second, it allows researchers to compare individual participants on a given variable (e.g., age). Third, it provides a way for researchers to compare an individual participant's performance on one variable (e.g., IQ score) with his or her performance on another (e.g., SAT score), even when the variables are measured on entirely different scales.

Measures of Association

In addition to describing the shape of variable distributions, another important task of descriptive statistics is to examine and describe the relationships or associations between variables.

Correlations are perhaps the most basic and most useful measure of association between two or more variables. Expressed in a single number called a *correlation coefficient (r),* correlations provide information about the direction of the relationship (either positive or negative) and the intensity of the relationship (-1.0 to $+1.0$). Furthermore, tests of correlations will provide information on whether the correlation is statistically significant. There is a wide variety of correlations that, for the most part, are determined by the type of variable (e.g., categorical, continuous) being analyzed.

With regard to the direction of a correlation, if two variables tend to move in the same direction (e.g., height and weight), they would be considered to have a *positive* or *direct relationship.* Alternatively, if two variables move in opposite directions (e.g., cigarette smoking and lung capacity), they are considered to have a *negative* or *inverse relationship.* Figure 7.2 gives examples of both types.

Correlation coefficients range from -1.0 to $+1.0$. The sign of the coefficient represents the direction of the relationship. For example, a correlation of .78 would indicate a positive or direct correlation, while a correlation of $-.78$ would indicate a negative or inverse correlation. The

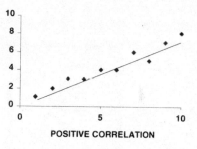
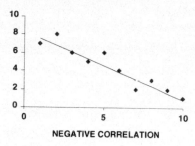

POSITIVE CORRELATION   NEGATIVE CORRELATION

Figure 7.2 Positive and negative correlation directions.

coefficient (value) itself indicates the strength of the relationship. The closer it gets to 1.0 (whether it is negative or positive), the stronger the relationship. In general, correlations of .01 to .30 are considered small, correlations of .30 to .70 are considered moderate, correlations of .70 to .90 are considered large, and correlations of .90 to 1.00 are considered very large. Importantly, these are only rough guidelines. A number of other factors, such as sample size, need to be considered when interpreting correlations.

In addition to the direction and strength of a correlation, the coefficient can be used to determine the proportion of variance accounted for by the association. This is known as the *coefficient of determination* (r^2). The coefficient of determination is calculated quite easily by squaring the correlation coefficient. For example, if we found a correlation of .70 between cigarette smoking and use of cocaine, we could calculate the coefficient of determination in the following manner:

$$.70 \times .70 = .49$$

The coefficient of determination is then transformed into a percentage. Therefore, a correlation of .70, as indicated in the equation, explains approximately 49% of the variance. In this example, we could conclude that 49% of the variance in cocaine use is accounted for by cigarette smoking. Alternatively, a correlation of .20 would have a coefficient of determination of .04 (.20 × .20 = .04), strongly indicating that other variables are likely involved. Importantly, as the reader might remember, correlation is not causation. Therefore, we cannot infer from this correlation that cigarette smoking causes or influences cocaine use. It is equally as likely that cocaine use causes cigarette smoking, or that both unhealthy behaviors are caused by a third unknown variable.

Although correlations are typically regarded as descriptive in nature, they can—unlike measures of central tendency and dispersion—be tested for *statistical significance*. Tests of significance allow us to estimate the likelihood that a relationship between variables in a sample actually exists in the population and is not simply the result of chance. In very general terms, the significance of a relationship is determined by comparing the results or findings with what would occur if the variables were totally unrelated (independent) and if the distributions of each dependent variable were identical. The primary index of statistical significance is the *p*-value. The *p*-value represents the probability of chance error in determining whether a finding is valid and thus representative of the population. For example, if we were examining the correlation between two variables, a *p*-value of .05 would indicate that there was a 5% probability that the finding might have been a fluke. Therefore, assuming that there was no such relationship between those variables whatsoever, we could expect to find a similar result, by chance, about 5 times out of 100. In other words, significance levels inform us about the degree of confidence that we can have in our findings.

There is a wide selection of correlations that, for the most part, are determined by the type of scale (i.e., nominal, ordinal, interval, or ratio) on which the variables are measured. One of the most widely used correlations is the Pearson product-moment correlation, often referred to as the Pearson *r*. The *Pearson* r is used to examine associations between two variables that are measured on either ratio or interval scales. For example, the Pearson *r* could be used to examine the correlation between days of exercise and pounds of weight loss.

Other types of correlations include the following:

- *Point-biserial* (r_{pbi}): This is used to examine the relationship between a variable measured on a naturally occurring dichotomous nominal scale and a variable measured on an interval (or ratio) scale (e.g., a correlation between gender [dichotomous] and SAT scores [interval]).

- *Spearman rank-order* (r_s): This is used to examine the relationship between two variables measured on ordinal scales (e.g., a correlation of class rank [ordinal] and socioeconomic status [ordinal]).
- *Phi* (Φ): This is used to examine the relationship between two variables that are naturally dichotomous (nominal-dichotomous; e.g., a correlation of gender [nominal] and marital status [nominal-dichotomous]).
- *Gamma* (γ): This is used to examine the relationship between one nominal variable and one variable measured on an ordinal scale (e.g., a correlation of ethnicity [nominal] and socioeconomic status [ordinal]).

Inferential Statistics

In the previous section, we provided a general overview of the most widely used descriptive statistics, including measures of central tendency, dispersion, and correlation. In addition to describing and examining associations of variables within our data sets, we often conduct research to answer questions about the greater population. Because it would not be feasible to collect data from the entire population, researchers conduct research with representative samples (see Chapters 2 and 3) in an attempt to draw inferences about the populations from which the samples were drawn. The analyses used to examine these inferences are appropriately referred to as *inferential statistics.*

Inferential statistics help us to draw conclusions beyond our immediate samples and data. For example, inferential statistics could be used to infer, from a relatively small sample of employees, what the job satisfaction is likely to be for a company's entire work force. Similarly, inferential statistics could be used to infer, from between-group differences in a particular study sample, how effective a new treatment or medication may be for a larger population. In other words, inferential statistics help us to draw general conclusions about the population on the basis of the findings identified in a sample. However, as with any generalization, there is some degree of uncertainty or error that must be considered. Fortunately, inferential statistics provide us with not only the means to make inferences, but the means to specify the amount of probable error as well.

Inferential statistics typically require random sampling. As discussed in Chapters 2 and 3, this increases the likelihood that a sample, and the data that it generates, are representative of the population. Although there are other techniques for acquiring a representative sample (e.g., selecting individuals that match the population on the most important characteristics), random sampling is considered to be the best method, because it works to ensure representativeness on all characteristics of the population—even those that the researcher may not have considered.

Inferences begin with the formulation of specific hypotheses about what we expect to be true in the population. However, as discussed in Chapter 2, we can never actually *prove* a hypothesis with complete certainty. Therefore, we must test the null hypothesis, and determine whether it should be retained or rejected. For example, in a randomized controlled trial (see Chapter 5), we may expect, based on prior research, that a group receiving a certain treatment would have better outcomes than a group receiving a standard treatment. In this case, the null hypothesis would predict no between-group differences. Similarly, in the case of correlation, the null hypothesis would predict that the variables in question would not be related.

There are numerous inferential statistics for researchers to choose from. The selection of the appropriate statistics is largely determined by the nature of the research question being asked and the types of variables being analyzed. Because a comprehensive review of inferential statistics could fill many volumes of text, we will simply provide a basic overview of several of the most widely used inferential statistical procedures, including the *t*-test, analysis of variance (ANOVA), chi-square, and regression.

T-Test

T-tests are used to test mean differences between two groups. In general, they require a single dichotomous independent variable (e.g., an experimental and a control group) and a single continuous dependent variable. For example, *t*-tests can be used to test for mean differences between experimental and control groups in a randomized experiment, or to test for mean differences between two groups in a nonexperimental context (such as whether cocaine and heroin users report more criminal activity). When a researcher wishes to compare the average (mean) performance between two groups on a continuous variable, he or she should consider the *t*-test.

Analysis of Variance (ANOVA)

Often characterized as an *omnibus* t-*test*, an ANOVA is also a test of mean comparisons. In fact, one of the only differences between a *t*-test and an ANOVA is that the ANOVA can compare means across more than two groups or conditions. Therefore, a *t*-test is just a special case of ANOVA. If you analyze the means of two groups by ANOVA, you get the same results as doing it with a *t*-test. Although a researcher could use a series of *t*-tests to examine the differences between more than two groups, this would not only be less efficient, but it would add experiment-wise error (see Rapid Reference 7.4), thereby increasing the chances of spurious results (i.e., Type I errors; see Chapter 1) and compromising statistical conclusion validity.

Interestingly, despite its name, the ANOVA works by comparing the differences between group means rather than the differences between group variances. The name "analysis of variance" comes from the way the procedure uses variances to decide whether the means are different.

There are numerous different variations of the ANOVA procedure to choose from, depending on the study hypothesis and research design. For example, a *one-way ANOVA* is used to compare the means of two or more levels of a single independent variable. So, we may use an ANOVA to examine the differential effects of three types of treatment on level of depression.

Treatment for Depression		
Treatment 1	Treatment 2	Treatment 3

≡Rapid Reference 7.4

Multiple Comparisons and Experiment-wise Error

Most research studies perform many tests of their hypotheses. For example, a researcher testing a new educational technique may choose to examine the technique's effectiveness by measuring students' test scores, satisfaction ratings, class grades, and SAT scores. If there is a 5% chance (with a p-value of .05) of finding a significant result on one outcome measure, there is a 20% chance (.05 × 4) of finding a significant result when using four outcome measures. This inflated likelihood of achieving a significant result is referred to as *experiment-wise error*. This can be corrected for either by using a statistical test that takes this error into account (e.g., multiple ANOVA, or MANOVA; see text) or by lowering the p-value to account for the number of comparisons being performed. The simplest and the most conservative method of controlling for experiment-wise error is the *Bonferroni correction*. Using this correction, the researcher simply divides the set p-value by the number of statistical comparisons being made (e.g., .05/4 = .0125). The resulting p-value is then the new criterion that must be obtained to reach statistical significance.

Alternatively, *multifactor ANOVAs* can be used when a study involves two or more independent variables. For example, a researcher might employ a 2 × 3 factorial design (see Chapter 5) to examine the effectiveness of the different treatments (Factor 1) and high or low levels of physical exercise (Factor 2) in reducing symptoms of depression.

		Treatment for Depression		
		Treatment 1	Treatment 2	Treatment 3
Exercise	Low			
	High			

Because the study involves two factors (or independent variables), the researcher would conduct a two-way ANOVA. Similarly, if the study had three factors, a three-way ANOVA would be used, and so forth. A multi-factor ANOVA allows a researcher to examine not only the main effects of each independent variable (the different treatments and high or low levels of exercise) on depression, but also the potential interaction of the two independent variables in combination.

Still another variant of the ANOVA is the *multiple analysis of variance*, or *MANOVA*. The MANOVA is used when there are two or more dependent variables that are generally related in some way. Using the previous example, let's say that we were measuring the effect of the different treatments, with or without exercise, on depression measured in several different ways. Although we could conduct separate ANOVAs for each of these outcomes, the MANOVA provides a more efficient and more informative way of analyzing the data.

Chi-Square (χ^2)

The inferential statistics that we have discussed so far (i.e., *t*-tests, ANOVA) are appropriate only when the dependent variables being measured are continuous (interval or ratio). In contrast, the *chi-square statistic* allows us to test hypotheses using nominal or ordinal data. It does this by testing whether one set of proportions is higher or lower than you would expect by chance. Chi-square summarizes the discrepancy between observed and expected frequencies. The smaller the overall discrepancy is between the observed and expected scores, the smaller the value of the chi-square will be. Conversely, the larger the discrepancy is between the observed and expected scores, the larger the value of the chi-square will be.

For example, in a study of employment skills, a researcher may randomly assign consenting individuals to an experimental or a standard skills-training intervention. The researcher might hypothesize that a higher percentage of participants who attended the experimental intervention would be employed at 1 year follow-up. Because the outcome being measured is dichotomous (employed or not employed), the researcher could use a chi-square to test the null hypothesis that employment at the 1 year follow-up is not related to the skills training.

Similarly, chi-square analysis is often used to examine between-group differences on categorical variables, such as gender, marital status, or grade level. The main thing to remember is that the data must be nominal or ordinal because chi-square is a test of proportions. Also, because it compares the tallies of categorical responses between two or more groups, the chi square statistic can be conducted only on actual numbers and not on precalculated percentages or proportions.

Regression

Linear regression is a method of estimating or predicting a value on some dependent variable given the values of one or more independent variables. Like correlations, statistical regression examines the association or relationship between variables. Unlike with correlations, however, the primary purpose of regression is prediction. For example, insurance adjusters may be able to predict or come close to predicting a person's life span from his or her current age, body weight, medical history, history of tobacco use, marital status, and current behavioral patterns.

There are two basic types of regression analysis: simple regression and multiple regression. In *simple regression,* we attempt to predict the dependent variable with a single independent variable. In *multiple regression,* as in the case of the insurance adjuster, we may use any number of independent variables to predict the dependent variable.

Logistic regression, unlike its linear counterpart, is unique in its ability to predict dichotomous variables, such as the presence or absence of a specific outcome, based on a specific set of independent or predictor variables. Like correlation, logistic regression provides information about the strength and direction of the association between the variables. In addition, logistic regression coefficients can be used to estimate odds ratios for each of the independent variables in the model. These *odds ratios* can tell us how likely a dichotomous outcome is to occur given a particular set of independent variables.

A common application of logistic regression is to determine whether and to what degree a set of hypothesized risk factors might predict the onset of a certain condition. For example, a drug abuse researcher may wish to determine whether certain lifestyle and behavioral patterns place former drug abusers at risk for relapse. The researcher may hypothesize that three specific factors—living with a drug or alcohol user, psychiatric status, and employment status—will predict whether a former drug abuser will relapse within 1 month of completing drug treatment. By measuring these variables in a sample of successful drug-treatment clients, the researcher could build a model to predict whether they will have relapsed by the 1-month follow-up assessment. The model could also be used to estimate the odds ratios for each variable. For example, the odds ratios could provide information on how much more likely unemployed individuals are to relapse than employed individuals.

INTERPRETING DATA AND DRAWING INFERENCES

Even researchers who carefully planned their studies and collected, managed, and analyzed their data with the highest integrity might still make mistakes when interpreting their data. Unfortunately, although all of the previous steps are necessary, they are far from sufficient to ensure that the moral of the story is accurately understood and disseminated. This section will highlight some of the most critical issues to consider when interpreting data and drawing inferences from your findings.

Are You Fully Powered?

One of the ways that study findings can be misinterpreted is through insufficient statistical power. Until fairly recently, most research studies were conducted without any consideration of this concept. In simple terms, *statistical power* is a measure of the probability that a statistical test will reject a false null hypothesis, or in other words, the probability of finding a significant result when there really is one. The higher the power of a statistical test, the more likely one is to find statistical significance if the null hypothesis is actually false (i.e., if there really is an effect).

For example, to test the null hypothesis that Republicans are as intelligent as Democrats, a researcher might recruit a random bipartisan sample, have them complete certain measures of intelligence, and compare their mean scores using a *t*-test or ANOVA. If Republicans and Democrats do indeed differ on intelligence in the population, but the sample data indicate that they do not, a Type II error has been made (see Chapter 1 for a discussion of Type I and Type II errors). A potential reason that the study reached such a faulty conclusion may be that it lacked sufficient statistical power to detect the actual differences between Republicans and Democrats.

According to Cohen (1988), studies should strive for statistical power of .80 or greater to avoid Type II errors. Statistical power is largely determined by three factors: (1) the significance criterion (e.g., .05, .01); (2) the *effect size* (i.e., the magnitude of the differences between group means or other test statistics); and (3) the size of the sample. Researchers should calculate the statistical power of each of their planned analyses prior to beginning a study. This will allow them to determine the sample size necessary to obtain sufficient power ($\geq$ .80) based on the set significance criterion and the anticipated effect size.

Unfortunately, determining that there is enough power at the outset of a study does not always ensure that sufficient power will be available at the time of the analysis. Many changes may occur in the interim. For example, the sample size may be reduced, due to lower than expected recruitment rates or attrition; or the effect sizes may be different than expected. In any case, the take-home message for researchers is that they must always consider how much power is available to detect differences between groups. This is particularly important when interpreting the results of a study in which no significant differences were found, because it may be that significant differences existed, but there was insufficient power to detect them.

Are Your Distributions in Good Shape?

Another factor that can lead to faulty interpretations of statistical findings is the failure to consider the characteristics of the distribution. Virtually all statistical tests have certain basic assumptions. For example, *parametric tests* (e.g., *t*-tests, ANOVA, linear regression) require that the distribution of data meet certain requirements (i.e., normality and independence). Failure to meet these assumptions may cause the results of an analysis to be inaccurate. Although statistics such as the *t*-test and ANOVA are considered relatively robust (see Rapid Reference 7.5) in terms of their sensitivity to normality, this is less true for the assumption of independence. For example, if a researcher were comparing the effect of two different teachers' methods on students' final grades, the researcher would have to make certain that none of the students had classes with both teachers. If certain students had classes with both teachers, and were therefore exposed to both teaching methods, the assumption of independence would have been violated. Because of this, probability statements regarding Type I and Type II errors may be seriously affected.

Robustness of Statistical Tests

Robustness of a statistical test refers to the degree to which it is resistant to violations of certain assumptions. The robustness of certain statistical techniques does not mean they are totally immune to such violations, but merely that they are less sensitive to them.

Another aspect of the distribution that should be considered when interpreting study findings is data outliers. As discussed earlier, extreme values in the distribution can substantially skew the shape of the distribution and alter the sample mean. Researchers should carefully examine the distributions of their data to identify potential outliers. Once identified, outliers can be either replaced with missing values or transformed through one of several available procedures (discussed previously in this chapter).

Still another aspect of the distribution that should be considered when analyzing and interpreting data is the range of values. Researchers often fail to find significant relationships because of the restricted range or variance of a dependent variable. For example, suppose you were examining the relationship between IQ and SAT scores, but everyone in the sample scored between 1100 and 1200 on their SATs. In this case, because of the restricted range, you would be unlikely to find a significant relationship, even if one did exist in the population.

Are You Fishing?

Although we covered the issue of multiple comparisons and experiment-wise error earlier in this chapter, it deserves additional mention here because it can seriously impact the interpretation of your findings. In general, *experiment-wise error* refers to the probability of committing Type I errors for a set of statistical tests in the same experiment. When you make many comparisons involving the same data, the probability that one of the comparisons will be statistically significant increases. Thus, experiment-wise error may exceed a chosen significance level. If you make enough comparisons, one or some of the results will undoubtedly be significant. Colloquially, this is often referred to as "fishing," because if you cast out your line enough times you are bound to catch something. Although this may be a good strategy for anglers, in research it is just bad science. This issue is most likely to occur when examining complex hypotheses that require many different comparisons. Failing to correct for these multiple comparisons can lead to substantial Type I error and to faulty interpretations of your findings.

How Reliable and Valid Are Your Measures?

Another major factor that can affect a study's findings is measurement error. Although most statistical analyses, and many of the researchers who conduct them, assume that assessment instruments are error free, this is usually far from the truth. In fact, assessment instruments are rarely, if ever, perfect (see Chapter 4 for a detailed discussion of this topic). This is particularly true when using unstandardized measures that may vary in their administration procedures, or when using instruments that have little if any demonstrated validity or reliability (see Chapter 6). For these reasons, it is essential that researchers, whenever possible, use psychometrically sound instruments in their studies. Using error-laden instruments may substantially reduce the sensitivity of your analyses and obscure otherwise significant findings.

Statistical Significance vs. Clinical Significance

Because of the technical and detailed nature of the research enterprise, it is often easy to miss the forest for the trees. Researchers can get so caught up in the rigor of data collection, management, and analysis that they may wind up believing that the final value of a research study lies in its p-value. This is, of course, far from the truth. The real value of a research finding lies in its *clinical significance,* not in its statistical significance. In other words, will the researching findings affect how things are done in the real world?

This is not to say that statistical significance is irrelevant. On the contrary, statistical significance is essential in determining how likely a result is to be true or due to chance. Before we can decide on the clinical significance of a finding, we must be somewhat certain that the finding is indeed valid. The misperception instead lies in the belief that statistical significance itself is meaningful. In fact, study results can be statistically significant, but clinically meaningless.

To interpret the clinical significance of their findings, researchers might examine a number of other indices, such as the effect size or the percentage of participants who moved from outside a normal range to within a normal range. For example, a study may reveal that two different studying methods lead to significantly different test scores, but that neither method results in passing scores. When interpreting research findings, researchers should consider not only the statistical significance, but its clinical, or real-world, importance.

Are There Alternative Explanations?

As we discussed in Chapter 5, the key element in true experimental research is scientific control and the ability to rule out alternative explanations. In Chapter 5, we noted that randomization is the best way to achieve this type of control. This point cannot be overemphasized. Unless you can be relatively certain that there are no systematic differences between the experimental groups or conditions, and that the only thing that varies is the independent variable that you are manipulating, you simply cannot rule out other potential explanations for your findings.

Even in randomized trials, there is a chance, however small, that there are between-group differences on variables other than the one that you are manipulating. The wise researcher should always view his or her findings with some degree of suspicion and always consider alternative explanations for those findings. It is this critical analysis and inability to be easily convinced that distinguishes true scientific endeavors from lesser pursuits.

AreYou Confusing Correlation With Causation?

We know that we already apologized for saying this too often, but here we go again: Correlation is *not* causation, period. Significant or not, hypothesized or not, large-magnitude associations or not, simple measures of association should never be interpreted as demonstrating causal relationships. Where would we be if we accepted such faulty logic? We would probably be in a society that believes cold temperatures cause colds, or that rock music leads to drug abuse. Okay, so maybe we are not always so literal. However, the thing that sets scientists apart from laypeople (other than our low incomes) is our knowledge of the scientific method and our ability to discriminate between assumption and fact (see Chapter 1 for a discussion of the scientific method).

The bottom line about causality is that it cannot be inferred without random assignment. In other words, the researcher must be the one who selects and manipulates the independent variables, and this must be done prospectively. If this is not the case, you may find a significant association between variables, but you simply cannot infer causation. Importantly, this is true regardless of the statistical tests that are used. It does not matter whether you used a linear regression, an ANOVA, or an even more sophisticated statistical technique. Unless randomization and control are employed, causation cannot be inferred.

How Significant Is Your Nonsignificance?

The last point that we want to cover with regard to the interpretation of study results is the issue of nonsignificance. As a general guideline, researchers should not be overly invested in finding a specific outcome. That is, even though they may have strong rationales for hypothesizing particular results, they should not place all their hopes on having their studies turn out as they may have expected. Not only could such an approach precipitate bias, but it could lead to a common misperception among research scientists—namely, that nonsignificant results are not useful. On the contrary, nonsignificant findings can be as important, if not more important, than significant ones.

The furtherance of science depends on the empirical evaluation of widely held assumptions and what many consider to be common sense. The furtherance of science also depends on attempts to replicate research findings and to determine whether findings found in one population generalize to other populations. In any of these cases, nonsignificant findings can have some very significant (important) implications. Therefore, it is strongly recommended that researchers be as neutral and objective as possible when analyzing and interpreting their results. In many cases, less may, in fact, be more.

SUMMARY

In this chapter, we have reviewed some of the major objectives and techniques involved in the preparation, analysis, and interpretation of study data. In the first section, we discussed the importance of properly logging and screening data, designing a well-structured database and codebook, and transforming variables into an ef-

CAUTION

Publication Bias

A number of studies (e.g., Ioannidis, 1998; Sterns & Simes, 1997) have found a connection between the significance of a study's findings and its publishability. Specifically, these researchers have found that a greater percentage of studies that report significant findings wind up being published and that there are also greater publication delays for such studies.

ficient and analyzable form. In the second section, we covered the two primary categories of statistical analyses—descriptive and inferential—and provided a brief overview of several of the most widely used analytic techniques. In the last section, we presented a wide range of issues that researchers should consider when interpreting their research findings. Specifically, we sought to express the potential influence that issues such as power, statistical assumptions, multiple comparisons, measurement error, clinical significance, alternative explanations, and inferences about causality can have on the way that you interpret your data.

TEST YOURSELF

1. A written or computerized record that provides a clear and comprehensive description of all variables entered into a database is known as a
_____ _____.

2. _____ statistics are generally used to accurately characterize the data collected from a study sample.

3. A graph that illustrates the frequency of observations by groups is known as a _____.

4. A measure of the spread of values around the mean of a distribution is known as the _____ _____.

5. Analysis of variance (ANOVA) is used to measure differences in group _____.

Answers: 1. data codebook; 2. Descriptive; 3. histogram; 4. standard deviation; 5. means

Eight

ETHICAL CONSIDERATIONS IN RESEARCH

In the previous chapters, we reviewed many of the methodological issues that should be considered when conducting research. We discussed how researchers should begin their research endeavors by generating relevant questions, formulating clear and testable hypotheses, and selecting appropriate and practical research designs. By adhering to the scientific method, researchers can, in due course, obtain valid and reliable findings that may advance scientific knowledge.

Unavoidably, however, to advance knowledge in this manner it is often necessary to impinge upon the rights of individuals. Virtually all studies with human participants involve some degree of risk. These risks may range from minor discomfort or embarrassment caused by somewhat intrusive or provocative questions (e.g., questions about sexual practices, drug and alcohol use) to much more severe effects on participants' physical or emotional well-being. These risks present researchers with an ethical dilemma regarding the degree to which participants should be placed at risk in the name of scientific progress.

A number of ethical codes have been developed to provide guidance and establish principles to address such ethical dilemmas. These codes include federally mandated regulations promulgated by the U.S. Department of Health and Human Services (Title 45, Part 46 of the *Code of Federal Regulations*), as well as those developed for specific fields of study, such as the APA's *Ethical Principles of Psychologists and Code of Conduct* (2002). These codified principles are intended to ensure that researchers consider all potential risks and ethical conflicts when designing and conducting research. Moreover, these principles are intended to protect research participants from harm (Sieber & Stanley, 1988).

To help the reader better contextualize and appreciate the importance of the protection of research participants, this chapter will begin by reviewing the historical evolution of research ethics. We will then discuss the fundamental ethical principles of respect for persons, beneficence, and justice, which serve as the foundation for the formal protection of research participants. Finally, we will review two of the most essential processes in the protection of research participants: informed consent and the institutional review board. The purpose of this chapter is to familiarize the reader with some of the most common ethical issues in research with human participants, and it should not be considered a comprehensive review of all ethical principles and regulatory and legal guidelines and requirements. Before researchers undertake any study involving human participants, they should consult the specific rules of their institutions, the requirements of their institutional review boards, and applicable federal regulations, including Title 45, Part 46 of the *Code of Federal Regulations.*

HISTORICAL BACKGROUND

Many of the most significant medical and behavioral advancements of the 20th century, including vaccines for diseases such as smallpox and polio, required years of research and testing, much of which was done with human participants. Regrettably, however, many of these well-known advancements have somewhat sinister histories, as they were made at the expense of vulnerable populations such as inpatient psychiatric patients and prisoners, as well as noninstitutionalized minorities. In fact, a large proportion of these study participants were involved in clinical research without ever being informed. Revelations about Nazi medical experiments and unethical studies conducted within the United States (e.g., the Tuskegee Syphilis Study—see Rapid Reference 8.1; Milgram's Obedience and Individual Responsibility Study [Milgram, 1974]; human radiation experiments) heightened public awareness about the potential for and often tragic consequences of research misconduct.

≡ Rapid Reference 8.1

The Tuskegee Syphilis Study

In 1932, the U.S. Public Health Service began a 40-year longitudinal study to examine the natural course of untreated syphilis. Four hundred Black men living in Tuskegee, Alabama, who had syphilis were compared to 200 uninfected men. Participants were recruited with the promise that they would receive "special treatment" for their "bad blood." Horrifyingly, government officials went to extreme lengths to ensure that the participants in fact received no therapy from any source. The "special treatment" that was promised was actually very painful spinal taps, performed without anesthesia—not as a treatment, but merely to evaluate the neurological effects of syphilis. Moreover, even though penicillin was identified as an effective treatment for syphilis as early as the 1940s, the 400 infected men were never informed about or treated with the medication. By 1972, when public revelations and outcry forced the government to end the study, only 74 of the original 400 infected participants were still alive. Further examination revealed that somewhere between 28 and 100 of these participants had died as a direct result of their infections.

Over the past half-century, the international and U.S. medical communities have taken a number of steps to protect individuals who participate in research studies. Developed in response to the Nuremberg Trials of Nazi doctors who performed unethical experimentation during World War II, the Nuremberg Code (see Rapid Reference 8.2) was the first major international document to provide guidelines on research ethics. It made voluntary consent a requirement in clinical research studies, emphasizing that consent can be voluntary only under the following conditions:

1. Participants are able to consent.
2. They are free from coercion (i.e., outside pressure).
3. They comprehend the risks and benefits involved.

The Nuremberg Code also clearly requires that researchers should minimize risk and harm, ensure that risks do not significantly outweigh potential benefits, use appropriate study designs, and guarantee participants'

The Nuremberg Code

1. The voluntary consent of the human subject is absolutely essential.

2. The experiment should be such as to yield fruitful results for the good of society, unprocurable by other methods or means of study, and not random and unnecessary in nature.

3. The experiment should be so designed and based on the results of animal experimentation and a knowledge of the natural history of the disease or other problem under study, that the anticipated results will justify the performance of the experiment.

4. The experiment should be so conducted as to avoid all unnecessary physical and mental suffering and injury.

5. No experiment should be conducted, where there is an a priori reason to believe that death or disabling injury will occur; except, perhaps, in those experiments where the experimental physicians also serve as subjects.

6. The degree of risk to be taken should never exceed that determined by the humanitarian importance of the problem to be solved by the experiment.

7. Proper preparations should be made and adequate facilities provided to protect the experimental subject against even remote possibilities of injury, disability, or death.

8. The experiment should be conducted only by scientifically qualified persons. The highest degree of skill and care should be required through all stages of the experiment of those who conduct or engage in the experiment.

9. During the course of the experiment, the human subject should be at liberty to bring the experiment to an end, if he has reached the physical or mental state, where continuation of the experiment seemed to him to be impossible.

10. During the course of the experiment, the scientist in charge must be prepared to terminate the experiment at any stage, if he has probable cause to believe, in the exercise of the good faith, superior skill and careful judgment required of him, that a continuation of the experiment is likely to result in injury, disability, or death to the experimental subject.

Source: *Trials of War Criminals Before the Nuremberg Military Tribunals Under Control Council Law No. 10.* (1949). Vol. 2, pp. 181–182. Washington, D.C.: U.S. Government Printing Office.

freedom to withdraw at any time. The Nuremberg Code was adopted by the United Nations General Assembly in 1948.

The next major development in the protection of research participants came in 1964 at the 18th World Medical Assembly in Helsinki, Finland. With the establishment of the Helsinki Declaration, the World Medical Association adopted 12 principles to guide physicians on ethical considerations related to biomedical research. Among its many contributions, the declaration helped to clarify the very important distinction between *medical treatment,* which is provided to directly benefit the patient, and *medical research,* which may or may not provide a direct benefit. The declaration also recommended that human biomedical research adhere to accepted scientific principles and be based on scientifically valid and rigorous laboratory and animal experimentation, as well as on a thorough knowledge of scientific literature. These guidelines were revised at subsequent meetings in 1975, 1983, and 1989.

In 1974, largely in response to the Tuskegee Syphilis Study, the U.S. Congress passed the National Research Act, creating the National Commission for the Protection of Human Subjects of Biomedical and Behavioral Research. The National Research Act led to the development of *institutional review boards (IRBs).* These review boards, which we will describe in detail later, are specific human-subjects committees that review and determine the ethicality of research. The National Research Act required IRB review and approval of all federally funded research involving human participants. The Commission was responsible for (1) identifying the ethical principles that should govern research involving human participants and (2) recommending steps to improve the Regulations for the Protection of Human Subjects.

In 1979, the National Commission for the Protection of Human Subjects of Biomedical and Behavioral Research issued "The Belmont Report: Ethical Principles and Guidelines for the Protection of Human Subjects of Research." The Belmont Report established three principles that underlie the ethical conduct of all research conducted with human participants: (1) respect for persons, (2) beneficence, and (3) justice (see Rapid Reference 8.3).

The Belmont Report: Summary of Basic Principles

1. Respect for Persons

Respect for persons incorporates at least two ethical convictions: first, that individuals should be treated as autonomous agents, and second, that persons with diminished autonomy are entitled to protection. The principle of respect for persons thus divides into two separate moral requirements: the requirement to acknowledge autonomy, and the requirement to protect those with diminished autonomy.

2. Beneficence

Persons are treated in an ethical manner, not only by respecting their decisions and protecting them from harm, but also by making efforts to secure their well-being. Such treatment falls under the principle of beneficence. The term "beneficence" is often understood to cover acts of kindness or charity that go beyond strict obligation. In this document, beneficence is understood in a stronger sense, as an obligation. Two general rules have been formulated as complementary expressions of beneficent actions in this sense: (1) do not harm, and (2) maximize possible benefits, and minimize possible harms.

3. Justice

Who ought to receive the benefits of research and bear its burdens? This is a question of justice, in the sense of "fairness in distribution" or "what is deserved." An injustice occurs when some benefit to which a person is entitled is denied without good reason, or when some burden is imposed unduly. Another way of conceiving the principle of justice is that equals ought to be treated equally. However, this statement requires explication. Who is equal and who is unequal? What considerations justify departure from equal distribution? Almost all commentators allow that distinctions based on experience, age, deprivation, competence, merit, and position do sometimes constitute criteria justifying differential treatment for certain purposes. It is necessary, then, to explain in what respects people should be treated equally. There are several widely accepted formulations of just ways to distribute burdens and benefits. Each formulation mentions some relevant property, on the basis of which burdens and benefits should be distributed. These formulations are (1) to each person an equal share, (2) to each person according to individual need, (3) to each person according to individual effort, (4) to each person according to societal contribution, and (5) to each person according to merit.

The Belmont Report explains how these principles apply to research practices. For example, it identifies informed consent as a process that is essential to the principle of respect. In response to the Belmont Report, both the U.S. Department of Health and Human Services and the U.S. Food and Drug Administration revised their regulations on research studies that involve human participants.

In 1994, largely in response to information about 1940s experiments involving the injection of research participants with plutonium as well as other radiation experiments conducted on indigent patients and children with mental retardation (see Rapid Reference 8.4), President Clinton created the National Bioethics Advisory Commission (NBAC). Since its in-

≡Rapid Reference 8.4

Human Radiation Experiments

President William J. Clinton formed the Advisory Committee on Human Radiation Experiments in 1994 to uncover the history of human radiation experiments. According to the committee's final report, several agencies of the United States government, including the Atomic Energy Commission, and several branches of the military services, conducted or sponsored thousands of human radiation experiments and several hundred intentional releases of radiation between the years of 1946 and 1974. Among the committee's harshest criticisms was that physicians used patients without their consent in experiments in which the patients could not possibly benefit medically. The principal purpose of these experiments was ostensibly to help atomic scientists understand the potential dangers of nuclear war and radiation fallout. These experiments were conducted in "secret" with the belief that this was necessary to protect national security. The committee concluded that the government was responsible for failing to implement many of its own protection policies. The committee further concluded that individual researchers failed to comply with the accepted standards of professional ethics. In October 1995, after receiving the committee's final report, President Clinton offered a public apology to the experimental subjects, and in March 1997, he agreed to provide financial compensation to all of the individuals who were injured.

ception, NBAC has generated a total of 10 reports. These reports have served to provide advice and make recommendations to the National Science and Technology Council and to other government entities, and to identify broad principles to govern the ethical conduct of research.

FUNDAMENTAL ETHICAL PRINCIPLES

The many post-Nuremberg efforts just reviewed have largely defined the philosophical and administrative basis for most existing codes of research ethics. Although these codes may differ slightly across jurisdictions and disciplines, they all emphasize the protection of human participants and, as outlined in the Belmont Report, have been established to ensure autonomy, beneficence, and justice.

Respect for Persons

As described in the Belmont Report, "Respect for persons incorporates at least two ethical mandates: first, that individuals be treated as autonomous agents, and second, that individuals with diminished autonomy are entitled to protection" (1979, p. 4). The concept of *autonomy*, which is clearly integral to this principle, means that human beings have the right to decide what they want to do and to make their own decisions about the kinds of research experiences they want to be involved in, if any. In cases in which one's autonomy is diminished due to cognitive impairment, illness, or age, the researcher has an obligation to protect the individual's rights. Respect for persons therefore serves as the underlying basis for what might be considered the most fundamental ethical safeguard underlying research with human participants: the requirement that researchers obtain informed consent from individuals who freely volunteer to participate in their research.

Coercion, or forcing someone to participate in research, is antithetical to the idea of respect for persons and is clearly unethical. Although there are many safeguards in place to ensure that explicit coercion to research, such as the research practiced in Nazi concentration camps, is no longer likely, there are still many situations in which more subtle or implicit coercion may take place. For example, consider a population of prison inmates or individuals who have just been arrested. If they are asked to participate in a study, is it coercive? It may be, if the prison administrators, judge, or other criminal justice staff are who ask them to participate, or if the distinction between researchers and criminal justice staff is unclear. In such instances, the participants may feel unduly pressured or coerced to participate in the study, fearing negative repercussions if they choose to decline. This type of implicit coercion might also occur in any situation in which the participant is in a vulnerable position or in which the study recruiter or perceived recruiter is in a position of power or authority (e.g., teacher-student, employer-employee).

Importantly, the principle of respect for persons does not mean that potentially vulnerable or coercible populations should be prevented from participating in research. On the contrary, respect for persons means that these individuals should have every right to participate in research if they so choose. The main point is that these individuals should be able to make this decision autonomously. For these reasons, it is probably good practice for researchers to maintain clear boundaries between themselves and persons who have authority over prospective research participants.

Beneficence

Beneficence means being kind, or a charitable act or gift. In the research context, the ethical principle of beneficence has its origins in the famous edict of the Hippocratic Oath, which has been taken by physicians since ancient times: "First, do no harm." Above all, researchers should not harm their participants and, ultimately, the benefits to their participants should be maximized and potential harms and discomforts should be minimized. In conducting research, the progress of science should not come at the price of harm to research participants. For example, even if the Tuskegee experiments had resulted in important information on the course of syphilis (which remains unclear), the government did not have the right to place individuals at risk of harm and death to obtain this information.

Importantly, the edict "do no harm" is probably more easily adhered to in clinical practice in which clinicians employ well-established and well-validated procedures. The potential risks and benefits are typically less predictable in the context of research in which new procedures are being tested. This poses an important ethical dilemma for researchers. On the one hand, the researcher may have a firm basis for believing and hypothesizing that a specific treatment will be helpful and beneficial. On the other hand, because it has not yet been tested, he or she can only speculate about the potential harm and side effects that may be associated with the treatment or intervention.

To determine whether a research protocol has an acceptable risk/benefit ratio, the protocol describing all aspects of the research and potential alternatives must be reviewed. According to the Belmont Report, there should also be close communication between the IRB and the researcher. The IRB should (1) determine the validity of the assumptions on which the research is based, (2) distinguish the nature of the risk, and (3) determine whether the researcher's estimates of the probability of harm or benefits are reasonable.

The Belmont Report delineates five rules that should be followed in determining the risk/benefit ratio of a specific research endeavor (National Commission for the Protection of Human Subjects of Biomedical and Behavioral Research, 1979, p. 8):

1. Brutal or inhumane treatment of human subjects is never morally justified.

2. Risks should be reduced to those necessary to achieve the research objective. It should be determined whether it is in fact necessary to use human subjects at all. Risk can perhaps never be entirely eliminated, but it can often be reduced by careful attention to alternative procedures.

3. When research involves significant risk of serious impairment, review committees should be extraordinarily insistent on the justification of the risk (looking usually to the likelihood of benefit to the subject or, in some rare cases, to the manifest voluntariness of the participation).

4. When vulnerable populations are involved in research, the appropriateness of involving them should itself be demonstrated. A number of variables go into such judgments, including the nature and degree of risk, the condition of the particular population involved, and the nature and level of the anticipated benefits.

5. Relevant risks and benefits must be thoroughly arrayed in documents and procedures used in the informed consent process.

Justice

The principle of justice relates most directly to the researcher's selection of research participants. According to the Belmont Report, the selection of research participants must be the result of fair selection procedures and must also result in fair selection outcomes. The justness of participant selection relates both to the participant as an individual and to the participant as a member of social, racial, sexual, or ethnic groups. Importantly, there should be no bias or discrimination in the selection and recruitment of research participants. In other words, they should not be selected because they are viewed positively or negatively by the researcher (e.g., involving so-called undesirable persons in risky research).

In addition to the selection of research participants, the principle of justice is also relevant to how research participants are treated, or not treated. As we discussed in Chapter 5, the use of control conditions is essential to randomized, controlled studies, which is the only true method to confidently evaluate the effectiveness of a specific treatment or intervention. The dilemma here is whether it is ethical or just to assign some participants to receive a potentially helpful intervention, and others to not receive it. Although this may be less an issue in certain types of research, it is a critical issue in medical studies involving treatment for debilitating conditions, or in criminal justice or social policy research involving potentially life-changing opportunities. One might ask why the researcher could not simply ask for volunteers for the control condition. The answer to this question is that participants' awareness of being in a control condition may alter the results. It is therefore necessary to blind the participants (i.e., to keep participants unaware of their experimental assignments), which raises yet another potential ethical dilemma.

Fortunately, there are several ways to address these ethical concerns. First, the research participants must be clearly informed that they will be randomly assigned to either an experimental condition or a control condition, and they should also be informed of the likelihood (e.g., one in two, one in three) of being assigned to one condition or the other. Second, the researcher should assure participants that they will receive full disclosure regarding their assignment following the completion of the study, and the researcher should provide the opportunity to those who had been assigned to the control condition to receive the experimental treatment if it is shown to be effective.

DON'T FORGET

Confidentiality

The right to confidentiality is embodied in the principles of respect for persons, beneficence, and justice. Generally, *confidentiality* involves both an individual's right to have control over the use or access of his or her personal information as well as the right to have the information that he or she shares with the research team kept private. The researcher is responsible not only for maintaining the confidentiality of all information protected by law, but also for information that might affect the privacy and dignity of research participants. During the consent process, the researcher must clearly explain all issues related to confidentiality, including who will have access to their information, the limits of confidentiality, risks related to potential breaches of confidentiality, and safeguards designed to protect their confidentiality (e.g., plans for data transfer, data storage, and recoding and purging data of client identifiers). Researchers should be aware of the serious effects that breaches in confidentiality could have on the research participants, and employ every safeguard to prevent such violations, including careful planning and training of research staff. Researchers should also familiarize themselves with all applicable institutional, local, state, and federal regulations governing their research.

≡ Rapid Reference 8.5

Federal Research Protections

There are two primary categories of federal research protections for human participants. The first is provided in the Federal Policy for the Protection of Human Subjects, also known as the *Common Rule*. The Common Rule is a set of regulations adopted independently by 17 federal agencies that support or conduct research with human research participants. The 17 agencies adopted regulations based on the language set forth in Title 45, Part 46, Subpart A, of the *Code of Federal Regulations (CFR)*. Thus, the Common Rule is, for most intents and purposes, Subpart A of the Department of Health and Human Services' regulations. The second category of federal protections that relates to human research participants is the set of rules governing drug, device, and biologics research. These rules are administered by the U.S. Food and Drug Administration (FDA). Specifically, the FDA regulates research involving products regulated by the FDA, including research and marketing permits for drugs, biological products, and medical devices for human use, regardless of whether federal funds are used.

To ensure that the basic tenets of the Belmont Report were adhered to, the federal government, through the Department of Health and Human Services, codified a set of research-related regulations. Known as 45 CFR 46, indicating the specific Title 45 and Part 46 of the *Code of Federal Regulations,* the document details the regulations that must be observed when conducting research with human participants (see Rapid Reference 8.5). In general, the federal regulations focus on two main areas that are integral to the protection of human participants: informed consent and institutional review boards.

INFORMED CONSENT

The principle mechanism for describing the research study to potential participants and providing them with the opportunity to make autonomous and informed decisions regarding whether to participate is *in-*

formed consent. For this reason, informed consent has been characterized as the cornerstone of human rights protections. The three basic elements of informed consent are that it must be (1) competent, (2) knowing, and (3) voluntary. Notably, each of these three prongs may be conceptualized as having its own unique source of vulnerability. In the context of research, these potential vulnerabilities may be conceptualized as stemming from sources that may be intrinsic, extrinsic, or relational (Roberts & Roberts, 1999):

1. *Intrinsic* vulnerabilities are *personal characteristics* that may limit an individual's capacities or freedoms. For instance, an individual who is under the influence of a psychoactive substance or is actively psychotic might have difficulty comprehending or attending to consent information. Such vulnerabilities relate to the first prong of informed consent, that of competence (also referred to in the literature as "decisional capacity"). Many theorists have broadly conceptualized *competence* to include such functions as understanding, appreciation, reasoning, and expressing a choice (Appelbaum & Grisso, 2001). However, these functions are directly related to the legal and ethical concept of competence only insofar as they refer to an individual's intrinsic capability to engage in these functions.

2. *Extrinsic* vulnerabilities are *situational factors* that may limit the capacities or freedoms of the individual. For example, an individual who has just been arrested or who is facing sentencing may be too anxious or confused, or may be subject to implicit or explicit coercion to provide voluntary and informed consent. Such extrinsic vulnerabilities may relate either to knowingness or to voluntariness to the degree that the situation, not the individual's capacity, prevents him or her from making an informed and autonomous decision.

3. *Relational* vulnerabilities occur as a result of a *relationship* with another individual or set of individuals. For example, a prisoner who is asked by the warden to participate in research is unlikely

to feel free to decline. Similarly, a terminally ill person recruited into a study by a caregiver may confuse the caregiving and research roles. Relational vulnerabilities typically relate to the third prong of the informed consent process, voluntariness. Certain relationships may be implicitly coercive or manipulative because they may unduly influence the individual's decision.

Competence

The presence of cognitive impairment or limited understanding does not automatically disqualify individuals from consenting or assenting to research studies. As discussed, the principle of respect for persons asserts that these individuals should have every right to participate in research if they so choose. According to federal regulations (45 CFR § 46.111[b]), "When some or all of the subjects are likely to be vulnerable to coercion or undue influence, such as children, prisoners, pregnant women, mentally disabled persons, or economically or educationally disadvantaged persons, additional safeguards have been included in the study to protect the rights and welfare of these subjects." Therefore, the critical issue is not whether they should be allowed to participate, but whether their condition leads to an impaired decisional capacity.

To our knowledge, there has been only one instrument developed specifically for this purpose, the MacArthur Competence Assessment Tool for Clinical Research (Appelbaum & Grisso, 2001). Developed by two of the leading authorities in consent and research ethics, the instrument provides a semistructured interview format that can be tailored to specific research protocols and used to assess and rate the abilities of potential research participants in four areas that represent part of the standard of competence to consent in many jurisdictions. The instrument helps to determine the degree to which potential participants (1) understand the nature of the research and its procedures; (2) appreciate the consequences of participation; (3) show the ability to consider alternatives, including the option not to participate; and (4) show the ability to make a reasoned choice. Although this instrument appears to be appropriate for assessing competence, researchers should make certain to carefully consult local and institutional regulations before relying solely on this type of instrument. Depending on the specific condition of the potential participants, researchers may want to engage the services of a specialist (e.g., a neurologist, child psychologist) when making competence determinations.

Importantly, researchers should not mistakenly interpret potential participants' attentiveness and agreeable comments or behavior as evidence of their competence because many cognitively impaired persons retain attentiveness and social skills. Similarly, performance on brief mental status exams should not be considered sufficient to determine competence, although such information may be helpful in combination with other competence measures.

If the potential research participant is determined to be competent to provide consent, the researcher should obtain the participant's informed consent. If the potential participant is not sufficiently competent, informed consent should be obtained from his or her caregiver or surrogate and assent should be obtained from the participant.

Knowingness

It is still not clear whether many research participants actually participate knowledgeably in decision making about their research involvement. In fact, evidence suggests that participants in clinical research often fail to understand or remember much of the information provided in consent documents, including information relevant to their autonomy, such as the voluntary nature of participation and their right to withdraw from the study at any time without negative repercussions.

Problems with the understanding of both research and treatment protocols have been widely reported (e.g., Dunn & Jeste, 2001). Studies indicate that research participants often lack awareness of being participants in a research study, have poor recall of study information, have inadequate recall of important risks of the procedures or treatments, lack understanding of randomization procedures and placebo treatments, lack

CAUTION

···

The Therapeutic Misconception

The *therapeutic misconception* occurs when research participants confuse general intentions of research with those of treatment, or the role of researchers with the role of clinicians. This misconception refers specifically to the mistaken belief that the principle of personal care applies even in research settings. This may also be seen as a sort of "white-coat phenomenon," in which, as a result of their learning history, individuals may hold on to the mistaken belief that any doctor or professional has only their best interests in mind. This may compromise their ability to accurately weigh the potential risks and benefits of participating in a particular study.

awareness of the ability to withdraw from the research study at any time, and are often confused about the dual roles of clinician versus researcher (Appelbaum, Roth, & Lidz, 1982; Cassileth, Zupkis, Sutton-Smith, & March, 1980; Sugarman, McCrory, & Hubal, 1998).

A number of client variables are associated with the understanding of consent information. Several studies (e.g., Aaronson et al., 1996; Agre, Kurtz, & Krauss, 1994; Bjorn & Holm, 1999) found educational and vocabulary levels to be significantly and positively correlated with measures of understanding of consent information. Although age alone has *not* been consistently associated with diminished performance on consent quizzes, it does appear to interact with education in that older individuals with less education display decreased understanding of consent information (Taub, Baker, Kline, & Sturr, 1987).

Drug and alcohol abusers may present a unique set of difficulties in terms of their comprehension and retention of consent information, not only because of the mental and physical reactions to the psychoactive substances, but also because of the variety of conditions that are comorbid with substance abuse (McCrady & Bux, 1999). Acute drug intoxication or withdrawal can impair attention, cognition, or retention of important information (e.g., Tapert & Brown, 2000). Limited educational opportunities, chronic brain changes resulting from long-term drug or alcohol use, prior head trauma, poor nutrition, and comorbid health problems (e.g., AIDS-related dementia) are common in individuals with substance abuse or dependence diagnoses and may also reduce concentration and limit understanding during the informed consent process (McCrady & Bux).

Although the number of articles published on informed consent has increased steadily over the past 30 years (Kaufmann, 1983; Sugarman et al., 1999), the number of studies that have actually tested methods for improving the informed consent process is quite limited. In their 2001 article, Dunn and Jeste reviewed a total of 34 experimental studies that had examined the effects of interventions designed to increase understanding of informed consent information. Of the 34 studies reviewed, 25 found that participants' understanding or recall showed improvement using a limited array of interventions. The strategies that have proven most successful fall into two broad categories: (1) those focusing on the *structure* of the consent document, and (2) those focusing on the *process* of presenting consent information. Successful strategies directed toward the structure of the consent form involved the use of forms that were more highly structured, better organized, shorter, and more readable, and that used simplified and illustrated formats. Successful strategies involving the consent process included corrected feedback and multiple learning trials, and the use of summaries of consent information. Other efforts that were generally not successful or that showed mixed results included the use of videotape methodologies and the use of highly detailed consent information, which were not associated with improved understanding in either a research or clinical context.

Other strategies have been shown to help individuals remember consent information beyond the initial testing period. This has specific importance in that it speaks to the ability of research participants to retain information related to (1) their right to withdraw from the research study at any time with no negative consequences, (2) procedures for contacting designated individuals in the occasion of an adverse event, and (3) procedures for obtaining compensation for harm or injury incurred as a result of study participation. Successful strategies for improving recall of consent information have included making postconsent telephone contacts, using simplified and illustrated presentations, and providing corrected feedback and multiple learning trials. Still, there is much room for improvement and research should continue to explore methods of improving participants' comprehension and retention of consent information.

Voluntariness

The issue of whether consent is voluntary is of particular importance when conducting research with disenfranchised and vulnerable populations, such as individuals involved with the criminal justice system. These populations are regularly exposed to implicit and explicit threats of coercion, deceit, and other kinds of overreaching that may jeopardize the element of voluntariness. In particular, there is a substantial risk that, as a result of their current situation, they may become convinced, rightly or wrongly, that their future depends on cooperating with authorities. This source of vulnerability is very different from knowingness or competence, because even the most informed and capable individual may not be able to make a truly autonomous decision if he or she is exposed to a potentially coercive or compromising situation.

Despite the obvious importance of this central element of informed consent, virtually *no* studies have examined potential methods for decreasing coercion in research. McGrady and Bux (1999) surveyed a sample of researchers funded by the National Institutes of Health who were currently recruiting participants from settings considered to be implicitly coercible (e.g., inpatient units, detoxification facilities, prisons). The researchers were surveyed about the types of procedures they used to ensure that participants were free from coercion. Among the most commonly reported protections were (1) discussing with participants the possibility of feeling coerced, (2) obtaining consent from the individuals responsible for the participants, (3) changing the compensation to prevent the coercive effects of monetary incentives, (4) making clear that treatment is not influenced by participation in research, (5) reminding participants that participation is voluntary, (6) having participants delay consent to think about participation, and (7) providing a clear list of treatment options as an alternative to research.

Developing a Consent Form

Given the importance of informed consent and the many problems regarding its comprehension and retention, researchers should be careful to provide consent information to potential research participants or their representatives in language that is understandable and clear. Typically, informed consent must be documented by the use of a written consent form approved by the IRB and signed by the participant or the participant's legally authorized representative, as well as a witness. One copy should then be given to the individual signing the form and another copy should be kept by the researcher. The basic elements of a consent form include each of the following:

1. An explanation of the purpose of the study, the number of participants that will be recruited, the reason that they were selected, the amount of time that they will be involved, their responsibilities, and all experimental procedures.
2. A description of any potential risks to the participant.
3. A description of any potential benefits to the participant or to others that may reasonably be expected from the research.
4. A description of alternative procedures or interventions, if any, that are available and that may be advantageous to the participant.
5. A statement describing the extent, if any, to which confidentiality of records identifying the participant will be maintained.
6. For research involving more than minimal risk, an explanation as to whether any compensation will be provided and whether any medical treatments are available if injury occurs and, if so, what they consist of, or where further information may be obtained.
7. Information about who can be contacted in the event that par-

ticipants require additional information about their rights or specific study procedures, or in the event of a research-related injury or adverse event. The document should provide the names and contact information for specific individuals who should be contacted for each of these concerns. Many IRBs require that a consent form include a contact person not directly affiliated with the research project, for questions or concerns related to research rights and potential harm or injury.

8. A clear statement explaining that participation is completely voluntary and that refusal to participate will involve no penalty or loss of benefits to which the participant is otherwise entitled.

9. A description of circumstances under which the study may be terminated (e.g., loss of funding).

10. A statement that any new findings discovered during the course of the research that may relate to the participant's willingness to continue participation will be provided to the participant.

Under federal regulations contained in 45 CFR § 46.116(d), an IRB may approve a *waiver* or *alteration* of informed consent requirements whenever it finds and documents all of the following:

1. The research involves *no more than minimal risk* to participants.

2. The waiver or alteration *will not adversely affect the rights and welfare* of participants.

3. The research *could not practicably be carried out* without the waiver or alteration.

4. Where appropriate, the participants will be provided with additional pertinent information after participation.

The IRB may also approve a waiver of the requirement for written documentation of informed consent under limited circumstances described at 45 CFR § 46.117(c).

INSTITUTIONAL REVIEW BOARDS

All research with human participants in the United States is regulated by institutional review boards (IRBs). As mentioned earlier, before any research study can be conducted, the researcher must have the procedures approved by an IRB.

IRBs are formed by academic, research, and other institutions to protect the rights of research participants who are participating in studies being conducted under the jurisdiction of the IRBs. IRBs have the authority to approve, require modifications of, or disapprove all research activities that fall within their jurisdiction as specified by both the federal regulations and local institutional policy. Researchers are responsible for complying with all IRB decisions, conditions, and requirements.

Researchers planning to conduct research studies must begin by preparing written research protocols that provide complete descriptions of the proposed research (see Rapid Reference 8.6). The protocol should include detailed plans for the protection of the rights and welfare of prospective research participants and make certain that all relevant laws and regulations are observed. Once the written protocol is completed, it is sent to the appropriate IRB along with a copy of the consent form and any additional materials (e.g., test materials, questionnaires). The IRB will then review the protocol and related materials.

According to 45 CFR § 46.107, IRBs must have at least five members, including the IRB chairperson, although most have far more. IRBs should be made up of individuals of varying disciplines and backgrounds. This heterogeneity is necessary to ensure that research protocols are reviewed from many different perspectives. This includes having researchers, laypeople, individuals from different disciplines, and so on. For example, an IRB may include scientists and/or methodologists who are familiar with research and statistical issues; social workers who are familiar with social, familial, and support issues; physicians and psychologists who are familiar with physical and emotional concerns; lawyers who can address legal issues; and clergy who can address spiritual and community issues. And when protocols involve vulnerable populations, such as children, prisoners, pregnant

≡ Rapid Reference 8.6

....

IRB Review: Protocol Submission Overview

1. Introduction and rationale for study.
2. Specific aim(s).
3. Outcomes to be measured.
4. Number of participants to be enrolled per year and in total.
5. Considerations of statistical power in relation to enrollment.
6. Study procedures.
7. Identification of the sources of research material obtained from individually identifiable living human participants in the form of specimens, records, or data.
8. Sample characteristics (i.e., anticipated number, ages, gender, ethnic background, and health status). Inclusion and exclusion criteria. Rationale for use of vulnerable populations (i.e., prisoners, pregnant women, disabled persons, drug users, children) as research participants.
9. Recruitment procedures, nature of information to be provided to prospective participants, and the methods of documenting consent.
10. Potential risks and benefits of participation. (Are the risks to participants reasonable in relation to the anticipated benefits to participants and in relation to the importance of the knowledge that may reasonably be expected to result from the research?)
11. Procedures for protecting against or minimizing potential risks. Plans for data safety monitoring and addressing adverse events if they occur. Alternative interventions and procedures that might be advantageous to the participants.
12. Inclusion of or rationale for excluding children (rationale to be based on specific regulations outlined in 45 CFR § 46).

women, or handicapped or mentally disabled persons, the IRB must consider the inclusion of one or more individuals who are knowledgeable about and experienced in working with these potential participants.

In addition to their diversity and professional competence, IRBs must have a clear understanding of federal and institutional regulations so that they can determine whether the proposed research is in line with institutional regulations, applicable law, and standards of professional conduct and practice. Importantly, IRBs are required to have at least one member who has no affiliation with the institution (even through an immediate family member). Finally, the IRB must make every effort to ensure that it does not consist entirely of men or entirely of women, although selections cannot be made on the basis of gender.

One of the initial questions an IRB must ask when reviewing a research protocol is whether that IRB has jurisdiction over the research. That is, the IRB must ask, "Is the research subject to IRB review?" To answer this question, the IRB must determine (1) whether the activity involves *research* and (2) whether it involves *human participants.* *Research* is defined by the federal regulations as "a systematic investigation, including research development, testing and evaluation, designed to develop or contribute to generalizable knowledge" (45 CFR § 46.102[d]). *Human participants* are defined by the regulations as "living individual(s) about whom an investigator (whether professional or student) conducting research obtains (1) data through intervention or interaction with the individual, or (2) identifiable private information" (45 CFR § 46.107[f]).

Some types of research involving human participants may be exempt from IRB review (45 CFR § 46.101[b]). These include certain types of educational testing and surveys for which no identifying information is collected or recorded. In such instances, the participants would not be at risk of any breach of confidentiality.

If the study is not deemed to be exempt from IRB review, the IRB must determine whether the protocol needs to undergo expedited review or full review. To meet the requirements for *expedited review,* a study must involve no more than minimal risk, or otherwise fall into one of several specific categories, such as survey research or research on nonsensitive topics. *Minimal risk* is defined by federal regulations as the fact that the "probability and magnitude of harm or discomfort anticipated in the research are no greater in and of themselves from those ordinarily encountered in daily life or during the performance of routine physical or psychological examination or tests" (45 CFR § 46.110[b]). Expedited review can also be obtained for minor changes in previously approved research protocols during the period (of one year or less) for which the original protocol was authorized. Expedited reviews can be handled by a single IRB member (often the chair) and therefore are much more expeditious (as the name suggests).

Protocols that do not meet the criteria for expedited review must receive a full review by all members of the IRB. Under *full review*, all members of the IRB receive and review the protocol, consent, and any additional materials prior to their scheduled meeting. Depending on the particular IRB and the number of protocols that they normally review, an IRB may meet anywhere from biweekly to quarterly. Following a thorough review and discussion of issues and concerns within the committee, many IRBs invite the researchers in to answer specific questions from the IRB members. Questions may address any or all aspects of the research procedures. After all of the IRB's questions have been answered and the researchers leave the room, the committee votes to either grant approval or not. In most cases, the committee will vote to withhold approval pending certain modifications or changes to the protocol or the consent procedures. Once the modifications are made, the protocol must be resubmitted. If the IRB is satisfied that the necessary modifications were made, they will typically grant approval and provide the researcher with a copy of the study consent form bearing the IRB's stamped, dated approval. Only copies of this stamped consent form may be used to obtain informed consent from study participants. Although IRB approval can be granted for one full year, certain studies (often those involving a less clear risk/benefit ratio) may receive approval for 6 months or less. In any case, researchers must make certain to keep approvals and consent forms current. If the study is approved, the researcher is then responsible for reporting the progress of the research to the IRB and/or appropriate institutional officials as often as (and in the manner) prescribed by the IRB, but no less than once per year (45 CFR § 46.109[e]).

DATA SAFETY MONITORING

Concerns about respect, beneficence, and justice are not entirely put to rest by institutional review and informed consent. Although these processes ensure the appropriateness of the research protocol and allow potential participants to make autonomous informed decisions, they do not provide for ongoing oversight that may be necessary to maintain the safety and ethical protections of participants as they proceed through the research experience. To accomplish this may require the development of a data safety monitoring plan (DSMP).

DSMPs set specific guidelines for the regular monitoring of study procedures, data integrity, and adverse events or reactions to certain study procedures. According to federal regulations (45 CFR § 46.111[a][6]), "[W]hen appropriate, the research plan makes adequate provision for monitoring the data collected to ensure the safety of subjects." The NIH, along with other public and private agencies, have developed specific criteria for their DSMPs. For example, for Phase I and Phase II NIH clinical trials (NIH, 1998), researchers are required to provide a DSMP as part of their grant applications. DSMPs are then reviewed by the scientific review groups, who provide the researchers with feedback. Subsequently, researchers are required to submit more detailed monitoring plans as part of their protocols when they apply for IRB approval.

In addition to the DSMP, researchers may be required by their funding agencies or IRBs to establish a data safety monitoring board (DSMB). The DSMB serves as an external oversight committee charged with protecting the safety of participants and ensuring the integrity of the study. The DSMBs, which must be very familiar with the research protocols, are responsible for periodically reviewing outcome data to determine whether participants in one condition or another are facing undue harm as a result of certain experimental interventions. The DSMBs may also monitor study procedures such as enrollment, completion of forms, record keeping, data integrity, and the researchers' adherence to the study protocol. Based on these data, the DSMB can make specific recommendations regarding appropriate modifications. In trials that are conducted across several programs or agencies (i.e., multicenter trials), DSMBs may act as overarching IRBs that are responsible for the ethical oversight of the entire project.

ADVERSE AND SERIOUS ADVERSE EVENTS

Researchers are required to report (to the governing IRBs) any untoward or adverse events involving research participants during the course of their research involvement. Although the specific reporting requirements differ by IRB and funding source, the definitions of adverse events (originating in the FDA's definitions of adverse events in medical trials) are generally the same.

An *adverse event* (AE) is defined as any untoward medical problem that occurs during a treatment or intervention, whether it is deemed to be related to the intervention or not. A *serious adverse event* (SAE) is defined as any occurrence that results in death; is life-threatening; requires inpatient hospitalization or prolongation of existing hospitalization; or creates persistent or significant disability/incapacity, or a congenital anomaly/birth defects.

SUMMARY

This chapter was intended to provide a general history and overview of some of the central ethical issues relating to the conduct of scientific research. Unfortunately, comprehensive coverage of many specific research ethics (e.g., publication credit, reporting research results, plagiarism) was beyond the scope of this chapter. Therefore, we strongly recommend that readers refer to specific ethical codes and federal, local, and institutional regulations when planning and engaging in research.

The many revelations of human rights violations and atrocities in the name of scientific research have led to a heightened public awareness about the need for regulations to protect the rights of human research participants. In response to this heightened awareness and call for protections, the federal government has established an extensive system of regulations and guiding principles to promote respect for persons, beneficence, and justice in research with human participants. These regulations have helped to delineate the specific types of information that must be conveyed to potential research participants in an effort to ensure that consent to research is voluntary, knowing, and intelligent. In addition, these regulations have generated mandatory ethical oversight of research studies. Despite these many developments, there is still a need for further research in the area of ethical protections in research studies. If anything has been learned in the years since Nuremberg and Tuskegee, it is that we must continue to be vigilant in protecting the rights and interests of our human research participants.

TEST YOURSELF

1. The three principles set forth by the Belmont Report are (1) respect for persons, (2) beneficence, and (3) _____.

2. Beneficence has its origins in the famous edict of the Hippocratic oath, which states, "First, do no _____.

3. In most cases, before an individual can participate in any research study, he or she must provide _____ _____.

4. Before any study can take place, it must first be approved by an _____ _____ _____.

5. The three basic elements of informed consent are that it must be (1) competent, (2) knowing, and (3) _____.

Answers: 1. justice; 2. harm; 3. informed consent; 4. institutional review board (or human subjects committee); 5. voluntary

Nine

DISSEMINATING RESEARCH RESULTS AND DISTILLING PRINCIPLES OF RESEARCH DESIGN AND METHODOLOGY

At this point in the book, you should have a fairly good conceptualization of the major considerations that are involved in conducting a research study. In the preceding chapters, we have covered each step in the process of conducting research, from the earliest stages—choosing a research idea, articulating hypotheses, and selecting an appropriate research design—to the final stages—analyzing the data and drawing valid conclusions. Along the way, we have also discussed several important research-related considerations, including several types of validity, methods of controlling artifact and bias, and the ethical issues involved in conducting research. Although you may not feel like an expert in research yet, you should take comfort in knowing that the concepts and strategies that you learned from this book will provide you with a solid foundation of research-related knowledge. As you gain additional research experience, these concepts and strategies will become second nature. We have certainly covered a good deal of information in this book, but we are not quite finished yet.

In this concluding chapter, we will discuss what is often considered the final step of conducting a research study: disseminating the results of the research. As will be discussed, there are numerous options available for those researchers who desire to share the results of their studies with others. From books to journals to the Internet, today's society offers many effective and efficient outlets for the dissemination of research study results. After discussing the dissemination of research results, the final part of this chapter will present a distillation of the major principles of research design and methodology. Finally, to assist the reader in designing a sound research design, this chapter will include a checklist of the major research-related concepts and considerations we have covered in this book.

DISSEMINATING THE RESULTS OF RESEARCH STUDIES

This book would certainly be incomplete if we did not discuss the dissemination of research results. This is an important topic that is occasionally overlooked in research design and methodology textbooks. As we will see, the dissemination of research study results plays a vital role in the advancement of science and, consequently, in the way we all live.

If you recall, at the beginning of this book, we discussed the role that research plays in science. Specifically, we stated that research is the primary vehicle by which science advances. Among other things, research has the capacity to answer questions, solve problems, and describe things, all of which may lead to an improvement in the way we live. But here is the essential point to remember: For a research study to change the way we live, or to have any effect at all, the researcher must share the results of the research with other people in the scientific community. Then, in turn, the information gleaned from the research study—regardless of whether it relates to technology, medicine, economics, or any other field of study—must ultimately be shared with the general public in one form or another.

We would all likely agree that it would certainly do little good if a researcher who discovered something important decided to keep those results quiet. Can you imagine how different the world would be if Thomas Edison had invented the light bulb, but then decided not to tell anyone about his invention? What if Albert Einstein had decided not to share his special and general theories of relativity? What if Bill Gates had decided to keep his computer technology all to himself? What if Jonas Salk decided that his cure for polio should not be shared with other people? Clearly, then, sharing the results of research studies is important, but let's take a closer look at *why* it is so important. After discussing the importance of sharing the results of research studies, we will briefly discuss the various outlets that are available to researchers who decide to share their results.

Sharing the Results of Research Studies

There are several benefits to sharing the results of research studies. First, it adds to the knowledge base in a particular scientific field. As you know, science is essentially an accumulation of knowledge, and sharing research results adds an incremental amount of knowledge to what is already known about a particular topic. Thus, the dissemination of research results helps to advance the progress of science.

Second, sharing the results of research ultimately improves the overall quality of the research being conducted. For example, when a researcher seeks to publish the results of his or her research in a professional journal, the manuscript describing the research is typically reviewed by several editors who have special expertise in the topic area of the research. As we will discuss in the next section, the editors evaluate the quality of the study and the manuscript, and then they make a recommendation regarding whether the manuscript should be published in the journal. This is referred to as the *peer-review process.* Presumably, only the most well-conducted studies and well-written manuscripts will make it through this peer-review process to publication. As a result, the publication process tends to weed out poorly conducted studies, which has the effect of improving the quality of the research being conducted. In summary, if researchers have an eye toward eventually publishing the results of their studies, those researchers will need to ensure

DON'T FORGET

Benefits of Sharing Research Results

1. Adds to the knowledge base in a particular scientific field.

2. Improves the overall quality of research being conducted.

3. Allows other researchers to replicate a study's results or extend the study's findings.

4. Improves the way we live.

that their studies are well designed and well conducted. We will talk more about the publication process in the next section.

Third, sharing the results of research allows other researchers to evaluate the study's results in the context of other research studies. For example, other researchers may attempt to replicate the original study's findings, which we already established is an important component of scientific research; or may even extend the original study's findings in perhaps unanticipated ways. In either case, the original study's results are being evaluated by other researchers in other contexts. This tends to function as a quality check on the original research.

Finally, for the results of a research study to have an effect on the way we all live, those results need to be shared with others. This is the point we addressed earlier in this section. To refresh your memory, we established that a ground-breaking research study would do little good if the researcher decided not to share the study's results with others. In fact, some would argue that the true test of a research study's value lies in its ability to improve some facet of the way we live. For that improvement to take place, a study's results need to be shared with other people. For example, when Bill Gates developed his revolutionary computer technology, that technology had to be shared with others (e.g., scientists, manufacturers, distributors, marketing firms), and then that technology had to be translated into something that would benefit the public at large—that is, personal computers for individual sale.

Now that we have addressed the importance of sharing the results of research studies, let's take a closer look at the various options that are available for researchers who desire to disseminate their research findings.

Presentation of Research Results

One option available to those researchers who decide to share the results of their research is to present their findings at professional conferences. Most scientific fields have guiding professional organizations that sponsor regularly held professional conferences. One of the primary functions of these conferences is to serve as outlets for the presentation of research results that are relevant to that particular scientific field. Because professional conferences are held so frequently, they provide for the dissemination of up-to-date research findings. By contrast, the lag time between completing a research study and the eventual publication of those results in a professional journal is typically much longer. As we will discuss in the next section, it can often take well over a year for a submitted manuscript to be published in a professional journal. By that time, the study's results may have been expanded upon, refuted, or made obsolete by other studies. For these reasons, professional conferences are a valuable and efficient outlet for research results.

Researchers have several options available to them in terms of presenting their results at professional conferences. Although the format for presentations differs from conference to conference, most conferences offer some combination of the following presentation formats: poster presentations, oral presentations, and symposiums. A *poster presentation,* as the name indicates, involves presenting the results of a research study in a poster format. At many conferences, this is a preferred presentation format for students and beginning researchers (probably because there are many available presentation slots, which makes it less competitive than other presentation formats). An *oral presentation* involves speaking about the research results for a specified amount of time (sometimes as short as 10 minutes). Finally, a *symposium* is a collection of related oral presentations that are presented as a group.

Getting to present the results of a research study at a professional conference is a competitive process. Typically, researchers submit short summaries of their research studies to the conference organizers who, in turn, ask reviewers to evaluate the research and determine whether the study is worthy of being presented at the conference. If accepted, it must be determined whether the research study will be presented as a poster or an oral presentation. At most conferences, it is generally considered more prestigious to have your study accepted as an oral presentation. Often, short summaries of the research—abstracts—are then published in a journal so that people who did not attend the conference can become familiar with the results of the studies.

Publication of Research Results

Publication of research results is, by far, the most common method of disseminating the results of a research study. There are several publication options, including books, book chapters, monographs, newsletters, working reports, technical reports, and Internet-based articles. However, publication in a peer-reviewed professional journal is generally considered the primary and most valued outlet for the dissemination of research results (see Kazdin, 1992, 2003b). Let's take a closer look at publishing a research study's results in a peer-reviewed journal.

Earlier in this chapter, we briefly discussed the peer-review process, which is the procedure used by most professional journals to determine which articles should be published. In this section, we will add a few comments to our previous discussion. Once a researcher completes a study, there are several decisions that need to be made (see Kazdin, 1992). The first is whether the study's findings merit publication. In other words, the researcher must determine, among other things, whether the study makes a valuable contribution to the field. If the researcher decides to seek publication of the study's findings, he or she must then determine what aspects of the study should be published. In large studies, it may not be practical to publish the entire study in one manuscript, so it may need to be subdivided in some rational manner. For example, if a research study has two distinct parts, the researcher may decide to publish each part of the study

DON'T FORGET

Publishing a Study's Results Begins in the Planning Stage

It is important to note that decisions made in the planning and design stages of a research study have a direct effect on whether that study will eventually be accepted for publication. Many of the decisions made in the early stages of a study, such as what topic to study, what sample to use, and which research design to implement, play an important role in determining the overall quality and impact of the study, which are two important considerations in whether it will later be published.

≡*Rapid Reference 9.1*

Least Publishable Units

Researchers must be careful to avoid breaking up a study into something referred to as *least publishable units*. Although it is certainly desirable to publish the results of a research study, most researchers agree that it is not advisable to pad your curriculum vitae with more publications by breaking up a study into the largest number of smallest publishable parts. A study should be divided into separate manuscripts only if the division is logically supported by the design of the study.

in a separate manuscript (but see Rapid Reference 9.1 for a word of caution about doing this).

Having decided to publish the study, the researcher must then decide to which journal he or she will submit a manuscript describing the study. There may literally be hundreds of journals in a given scientific field, and the researcher must carefully determine which journal would be the most appropriate outlet for his or her research. It is important to note that, in some fields of study, researchers can submit a manuscript to only one journal at a time. In these situations, the researcher must await a final publication decision from the journal before submitting the manuscript to another journal (if necessary). Given that it can take several months, or perhaps even longer, for a manuscript to be reviewed and for a publication decision to be made, researchers must decide carefully where they will send their manuscripts. If time is of the essence, as it often is with research, choosing an appropriate journal is an extremely important decision.

Once a researcher decides on a particular journal, he or she must prepare the manuscript in accordance with the style and formatting requirements of the journal. Different journals—and even different fields of study—have different formatting and style requirements, and it is very important that researchers strictly adhere to those specifications. For example, in psychology (and related disciplines), the style and format of manuscripts is specified by the APA (2001). The final manuscript consists of several different sections (see Rapid Reference 9.2) that describe

≡ Rapid Reference 9.2

Typical Sections of a Manuscript

For manuscripts that describe empirical studies, the following sections are typically included:

1. Title
2. Abstract (brief summary of the study)
3. Introduction (rationale and objectives for the study; hypotheses)
4. Method (description of research design, study sample, and research procedures)
5. Results (presentation of data, statistical analyses, and tests of hypotheses)
6. Discussion (major findings, interpretations of data, conclusions, limitations of study, and areas for future research)

all aspects of the research study, including the rationale for the study, related research, study procedures, statistical analyses, results, and implications.

After the manuscript is submitted to a journal, the editor of the journal sends the manuscript to several reviewers who are asked to review the manuscript and make a publication recommendation. There are generally two categories of reviewers for journals: (1) consulting editors (who review manuscripts for the journal on a regular basis) and (2) ad hoc editors (who review manuscripts for the journal less frequently, typically on an as-needed basis). The reviewers are usually selected because of their knowledge and expertise in the area of the study (Kazdin, 1992).

The reviewers evaluate each research study in terms of its substance, methodology, contribution to the field, and other considerations relating to the overall quality of the research study and the accompanying manuscript. It is also worth noting that, depending on the particular field of study, the editorial reviews may be either anonymous or signed. After all of the reviewers have completed their reviews and submitted their written comments to the journal editor, the journal editor makes a final publication decision based on his or her evaluation of the manuscript and the reviewers' written editorial comments.

Although journals differ with respect to how they handle manuscript submissions, most journals use some combination of the following publication decisions:

1. *Accepted:* The manuscript is accepted contingent on the author's making revisions specified by the journal reviewers. Almost no manuscript is accepted for publication as submitted (i.e., with no revisions), and some accepted manuscripts may require several rounds of revisions before finally being published.

2. *Rejected:* The manuscript is rejected, and the author will not be invited to revise and resubmit the manuscript for further publication consideration. Manuscripts can be rejected for many different reasons, including design flaws, an unimportant topic, and a poorly written manuscript.

3. *Rejected-resubmit:* The manuscript is rejected, but the author is invited to revise and resubmit the manuscript for future publication consideration. In this instance, the required revisions are typically extensive, and there is no guarantee that the manuscript will be published, even if all of the specified revisions are made.

Most researchers would likely agree that going through the peer-review publication process can be both time consuming and humbling. Two aspects of this process can be particularly difficult to handle for inexperienced and experienced researchers alike: First, the peer-review process is often excruciatingly slow. As previously noted, once a manuscript is submitted to a journal, it can take several months for a publication decision to be made. If extensive revisions are required as a condition of publication, then it can take significantly longer than that. Even after a journal decides to publish the manuscript, it can take many more months—sometimes well over a year—for the article to finally be published. The slow pace of the peer-review publication process is often a source of frustration for researchers. Moreover, it is possible for research results to become stale, or obsolete, by the time that the results are finally published.

Second, it is not easy to have your research evaluated, criticized, and (more often than not) rejected by journals. After putting a great deal of thought, energy, time, and money into a research study, it can be difficult to handle criticism and rejection. Yet rejection—and lots of it—is part of the business of conducting research. Some of the more prestigious professional journals have rejection rates of over 90%, which means that they are accepting for publication approximately 1 manuscript out of every 10 that are submitted. Even seasoned and well-published researchers experience their fair share of rejection. (At this point, it may seem that we should comfort the reader by indicating that the rejection aspect of publishing becomes easier over time, but we're not exactly sure that's true.) Despite the frustrations associated with the peer-review process—in fact, perhaps *because* of the frustrations associated with the peer-review process—getting a research study published is a very exciting and rewarding accomplishment.

PRINCIPLES OF RESEARCH DESIGN AND METHODOLOGY

To assist you in digesting the large amount of material presented in this book, we have distilled some overarching principles of research methodology that should be kept in mind when engaging in research. The following principles should serve as helpful guides as you engage in the process of designing and conducting a research study.

Keep Your Eyes Open

Perhaps the most basic lesson to guide your research is to keep your eyes open. As we discussed in Chapter 2, many ideas for research studies are discovered simply by observation of the environment in which we live. It is often through the simple act of observation that researchers formulate their research ideas and choose their research questions. A keen eye to your surroundings may reveal questions that need to be answered, problems that need to be solved, things that need to be improved, or phenomena that need to be described, all of which can be accomplished through well-designed and well-conducted research. Therefore, keeping your eyes open is often the first step in the research process.

Be An Empiricist

The hallmark of being a good researcher is being an empiricist. As you may recall from Chapter 1, empiricists rely on the scientific method to acquire new knowledge. The scientific method's heavy emphasis on direct and systematic observation and hypothesis testing in the acquisition of new knowledge effectively distinguishes science from pseudo-science and nonscience. Moreover, to be able to draw valid conclusions based on your research, which is the goal of all research, it is essential that you adhere to the empirical approach.

Be Creative

Throughout this book, we have emphasized the importance of using an appropriate research design and sound methodology. As you know, engaging in well-designed research studies is the only way of ensuring that researchers can draw valid conclusions based on the results of their studies. Clearly, then, basing your research design and methodology on accepted scientific principles is an important consideration.

It is also important, however, to be creative when conducting research. Creativity is particularly important in generating new research ideas, coming up with appropriate and perhaps novel research designs, and thinking about the implications of your research studies. Thinking outside the box has led to many great scientific discoveries. Good research is often as much art as it is science, so being creative is an important asset to the process.

Research Begets Research

This principle emphasizes the importance of following a logical progression when conducting research. In other words, to have a coherent body of research, each research study should be the next logical step in the overall line of research. As we have repeatedly noted throughout this book, science advances in small increments through well-conducted research studies. Therefore, it is important that research studies answer discrete questions that flow logically from prior research studies. Following this logical progression of research ensures that research studies, and the findings gleaned from them, are based on a solid theoretical and empirical foundation.

Adhere to Ethical Principles

The importance of adhering to applicable ethical principles was discussed in detail in Chapter 8, but it cannot be overemphasized. The rights of study participants are of paramount importance in the research context, and protecting those rights takes precedence over all other research-related considerations. Violating applicable ethical guidelines may hurt the study participants, the reputation of the researchers who conducted the study, and, in some ways, the entire field of scientific research. Thus, researchers have an obligation to be aware of the ethical guidelines that govern the research that they are conducting.

Have Fun

This almost seems axiomatic, but we'll state it anyway. Try to have fun while conducting research. Conducting research can certainly be an arduous endeavor, but it is important to have fun. As with anything else, if you are having fun while you do it, you will be more likely to become engaged in the process. Research can be exciting, so take pride in being part of something that will advance science and potentially improve the way we all live.

CHECKLIST OF RESEARCH-RELATED CONCEPTS AND CONSIDERATIONS

We have finally reached the concluding section of this book. In this section, we will present a convenient checklist of the major research-related concepts and considerations that we have covered. Although the following checklist could not possibly contain every conceivable consideration that researchers must take into account, it should serve to alert researchers to the major considerations that must be kept in mind when designing and conducting a research study.

1. *Follow the scientific method.* The scientific method is what separates science from nonscience. The scientific method, with its emphasis on observable results, assists researchers in reaching valid and scientifically defensible conclusions.

2. *Keep the goals of scientific research in mind.* The goals of scientific research are to describe, predict, and understand or explain. Keeping these goals in mind will assist you in achieving the broad goals of science—that is, answering questions and acquiring new knowledge.

3. *Choose a research topic carefully.* There are two considerations with respect to choosing a research topic. First, a research question must be answerable using available scientific methods. If a question cannot be answered, then it cannot be investigated using science. Second, it is important to make sure that the question you are asking has not already been definitively answered; this emphasizes the importance of conducting a thorough literature review.

4. *Use operational definitions.* Operational definitions clarify exactly what is being studied in the context of a particular research study. Among other things, this reduces confusion and permits replication of the results.

5. *Articulate hypotheses that are falsifiable and predictive.* As you may recall, each hypothesis must be capable of being refuted based on the results of the study. Furthermore, a hypothesis must make a prediction, which is subsequently tested empirically by gathering and analyzing data.

6. *Choose variables based on the research question and hypotheses.* The variables selected for a particular study should stem logically from the research question and the hypotheses.

7. *Use random selection whenever possible.* Use random selection when choosing a sample of research participants from the population of interest. This helps to ensure that the sample is representative of the population from which it was drawn.

8. *Use random assignment whenever possible.* Use random assignment when assigning participants to groups within a study. Random assignment is a reliable procedure for producing equivalent groups because it evenly distributes characteristics of the sample among all of the groups within the study. This helps the researcher isolate the effects of the independent variable by ensuring that nuisance variables do not interfere with the interpretation of the study's results.

9. *Be aware of multicultural considerations.* Be cognizant of the effects that cultural differences may have on the research question and design. For certain types of research, such as treatment-based research, it is important to determine whether the intervention being studied has similar effects on both genders and on diverse racial and ethnic groups.

10. *Eliminate sources of artifact and bias.* To the extent possible, eliminate sources of artifact and bias so that more confidence can be placed in the results of the study. The effects of most types of artifact and bias can be eliminated (or at least considerably reduced) by employing random selection when choosing research participants and random assignment when assigning those participants to groups within the study.

11. *Choose reliable and valid measurement strategies.* When selecting measurement strategies, let validity and reliability be your guides. Measurement strategies should measure what they purport to measure, and should do so in a consistent fashion.

12. *Use rigorous experimental designs.* Whenever possible, researchers should use a true experimental design. Only a true experimental design, one involving random assignment to experimental and control groups, permits researchers to draw valid causal infer-

ences about the relationship between variables. Because it may not always be possible or feasible to use a true experimental design, a good rule of thumb is that researchers should strive to use the most rigorous design possible in each situation.

13. *Attempt to increase the validity of a study.* A well-conducted research study will have strong internal validity, external validity, construct validity, and statistical validity. This maximizes the likelihood of drawing valid inferences from the study.

14. *Use care in analyzing and interpreting the data.* A crucial aspect of research studies is preparing the data for analysis, analyzing the data, and interpreting the data. The proper analysis of a study's data enhances the ability of researchers to draw valid inferences from the study.

15. *Become familiar with commonly encountered ethical considerations.* Researchers have an obligation to avoid violating ethical standards when conducting research. This means that researchers must be familiar with, among other things, the rights of study participants.

16. *Disseminate the results of research studies.* Science advances through the dissemination of research findings, so researchers should attempt to share the results of their research with the scientific community.

SUMMARY

We have covered quite a bit of research-related information in this book, and we hope that you have learned a great deal about the process and importance of conducting well-designed research studies. We are confident that the material covered in this book will serve you well in your research endeavors, and we believe that this book will provide you with a solid foundation of research-related knowledge and skills. As you continue to develop as a researcher, we hope that the lessons learned from this book will remain in the forefront of your mind.

🖎 TEST YOURSELF 🖎

1. The final step in a research study is _____ the results of the study.

2. The _____-_____ process is used by journals to determine which manuscripts should be accepted for publication.

3. Presentations and publications are two options available to researchers who desire to share the results of their studies. True or False?

4. What are the three possible editorial decisions following the peer review of a manuscript?

5. A _____ is a collection of related oral presentations that are presented as a group at a professional conference.

Answers: 1. disseminating (or sharing or publishing); 2. peer-review; 3. True; 4. Accepted, rejected, rejected-resubmit; 5. symposium

References

Aaronson, N. K., Visser-Pol, E., Leenhouts, G. H. M. W., Muller, M. J., van der Schot, S. C. M., van Dam, F. S. A. M., et al. (1996). Telephone-based nursing intervention improves the effectiveness of the informed consent process in cancer clinical trials. *Journal of Clinical Oncology, 14,* 984–996.

Adair, J. G. (1973). *The human subject: The social psychology of the psychological experiment.* Boston: Little, Brown.

Agre, P., Kurtz, R. C., & Krauss, B. J. (1994). A randomized trial using videotape to present consent information for colonoscopy. *Gastrointestinal Endoscopy, 40,* 271–276.

American Psychological Association. (2001). *Publication manual of the American Psychological Association* (5th ed.). Washington, DC: Author.

American Psychological Association. (2002). Ethical principles of psychologists and code of conduct. *American Psychologist, 57,* 1060–1073.

American Psychological Association. (2003). Guidelines on multicultural education, training, research, practice, and organizational change for psychologists. *American Psychologist, 58,* 377–402.

Anastasi, A., & Urbina, S. (1997). *Psychological testing* (7th ed.). Englewood Cliffs, NJ: Prentice Hall.

Anderson, N. H. (1961). Scales and statistics: Parametric and nonparametric. *Psychological Bulletin, 58,* 305–316.

Andrich, D. (1981). Stability of response, reliability, and accuracy of measurement. *Educational and Psychological Measurement, 41,* 253–262.

Appelbaum, P. S., & Grisso, T. (2001). *MacArthur Competence Assessment Tool for Clinical Research.* Sarasota, FL: Professional Resource Press.

Appelbaum, P. S., Roth, L. H., & Lidz, C. (1982). The therapeutic misconception: Informed consent in psychiatric research. *International Journal of Law and Psychiatry, 5,* 319–329.

Barber, T. X. (1976). *Pitfalls in human research: Ten pivotal points.* New York: Pergamon Press.

Barber, T. X., & Silver, M. J. (1968). Fact, fiction, and the experimenter bias effect. *Psychological Bulletin, 70,* 1–29.

Bechtold, H. P. (1959). Construct validity: A critique. *American Psychologist, 14,* 619–629.

Beck, A. T., Ward, C. H., Mendelson, M., Mock, J., & Erbaugh, J. (1961). An inventory for measuring depression. *Archives of General Psychiatry, 4,* 561–571.

Beins, B. C. (2004). *Research methods: A tool for life.* Boston: Allyn & Bacon.

Beutler, L. E., & Martin, M. A. (1999). Publishing and communicating research findings: Seeking scientific objectivity. In P. C. Kendall, J. N. Butcher, & G. N. Holmbeck (Eds.), *Handbook of research methods in clinical psychology* (pp. 107–121). New York: John Wiley & Sons.

Bjorn, E., Rossel, P., & Holm, S. (1999). Can the written information to research subjects be improved? An empirical study. *Journal of Medical Ethics, 25,* 263–267.

Bracht, G. H., & Glass, G. V. (1968). The external validity of experiments. *American Educational Research Journal, 5,* 437–474.

Brunswik, E. (1955). Representative design and probabilistic theory in a functional psychology. *Psychology Review, 62,* 193–217.

Campbell, A. A., & Katona, G. (1953). The sample survey: A technique for social science research. In L. Festinger & D. Katz (Eds.), *Research methods in the behavioral sciences* (pp. 14–55). New York: Dryden Press.

Campbell, D. T. (1957). Factors relevant to the validity of experiments in social settings. *Psychological Bulletin, 54,* 297–312.

Campbell, D. T. (1960). Recommendations for APA test standards regarding construct, trait, or discriminant validity. *American Psychologist, 15,* 546–553.

Campbell, D. T. (1969). Reforms as experiments. *American Psychologist, 24,* 409–429.

Campbell, D. T., & Fiske, D. W. (1959). Convergent and discriminant validation by the multitrait-multimethod matrix. *Psychological Bulletin, 56,* 81–105.

Campbell, D. T., & Stanley, J. C. (1963). Experimental and quasi-experimental designs for research on teaching. In N. L. Gage (Ed.), *Handbook of research on teaching* (pp. 171–246). Chicago: Rand McNally.

Cassileth, B. R., Zupkis, R. V., Sutton-Smith, K., & March, V. (1980). Informed consent: Why are its goals imperfectly realized? *New England Journal of Medicine, 302,* 869–900.

Christensen, L. B. (1988). *Experimental methodology* (4th ed.). Boston: Allyn & Bacon.

Christensen, L. B. (2001). *Experimental methodology* (8th ed.). Boston: Allyn & Bacon.

Christensen, L. B. (2004). *Experimental methodology* (9th ed.). Boston: Allyn & Bacon.

Cochran, W. G. (1977). *Sampling techniques.* New York: John Wiley & Sons.

Cohen, J. (1988). *Statistical power analysis for the behavioral sciences* (2nd ed.). Hillsdale, NJ: Lawrence Erlbaum.

Cook, T. D., & Campbell, D. T. (1979). *Quasi-experimentation: Design and analysis issues for field settings.* Chicago: Rand McNally.

Council of National Psychological Associations for the Advancement of Ethnic Minority Interests. (2000). *Guidelines for research in ethnic minority communities.* Washington, DC: American Psychological Association.

Cozby, P. C. (1993). *Methods in behavioral research* (5th ed.). Mountain View, CA: Mayfield Publishing Co.

Dunn, L. B., & Jeste, D. V. (2001). Enhancing informed consent for research and treatment. *Neuropsychopharmacology, 24,* 595–605.

Egharevba, I. (2001). Researching an-"other" minority ethnic community: Reflections of a Black female researcher on the intersections of race, gender and other power positions in the research process. *International Journal of Social Research Methodology: Theory and Practice, 4,* 225–241.

Fisher, R. A. (1953). *The design of experiments* (6th ed.). New York: Hafner Press.

Fitzpatrick, A. R. (1983). The meaning of content validity. *Applied Psychological Measurement, 7,* 3–13.

Graziano, A. M., & Raulin, M. L. (2004). *Research methods: A process of inquiry* (5th ed.). Boston: Allyn & Bacon.

Groth-Marnat, G. (2003). *Handbook of psychological assessment* (4th ed.). Hoboken, NJ: John Wiley & Sons.

Hair, J. F., Anderson, R. E., Tatham, R. L., & Black, W. C. (1995). *Multivariate data analysis* (4th ed.). Englewood Cliffs, NJ: Prentice-Hall.

Howell, D. C. (1992). *Statistical methods for psychology* (3rd ed.). Belmont, CA: Wadsworth.

Hoyle, R. H., Harris, M. J., & Judd, C. M. (2002). *Research methods in social relations* (7th ed.). Pacific Grove, CA: Wadsworth.

Huitema, E. (1980). *The analysis of covariance and alternatives.* New York: John Wiley & Sons.

Impara, J. C., & Plake, B. S. (Eds.). (1998). *The thirteenth mental measurements yearbook.* Lincoln, NE: Buros Institute of Mental Measures.

Ioannidis, J. P. A. (1998). Effect of the statistical significance of results on the time to completion and publication of randomized efficacy trials. *Journal of the American Medical Association, 279,* 281–286.

Isaac, S., & Michael, W. B. (1997). *Handbook in research and evaluation* (3rd ed.). San Diego, CA: Educational and Industrial Testing Services.

Kaplan, A. (1964). *The conduct of inquiry: Methodology for behavioral science.* San Francisco: Chandler.

Kaufmann, C. L. (1983). Informed consent and patient decision making: Two decades of research. *Social Science & Medicine, 17,* 1657–1664.

Kazdin, A. E. (1973). Methodological and assessment considerations in evaluating reinforcement programs in applied settings. *Journal of Applied Behavioral Analysis, 6,* 517–531.

Kazdin, A. E. (1982). *Single-case designs: Methods for clinical and applied settings.* New York: Oxford University Press.

Kazdin, A. E. (1992). *Research design in clinical psychology* (2nd ed.). Boston: Allyn & Bacon.

Kazdin, A. E. (2003a). Methodology: What it is and why it is so important. In A. E. Kazdin (Ed.), *Methodological issues and strategies in clinical research* (3rd ed., pp. 5–22). Washington, DC: American Psychological Association.

Kazdin, A. E. (2003b). Publication and communication of research. In A. E. Kazdin (Ed.), *Methodological issues and strategies in clinical research* (3rd ed., pp. 807–810). Washington, DC: American Psychological Association.

Kazdin, A. E. (2003c). *Research design in clinical psychology* (4th ed.). Boston: Allyn & Bacon.

Keppel, G. (1991). *Design and analysis: A researcher's handbook.* Englewood Cliffs, NJ: Prentice Hall.

Kerlinger, F. N. (1973). *Foundations of behavioral research.* New York: Holt, Rinehart & Winston.

Kerlinger, F. N. (1992). *Foundations of behavioral research* (3rd ed.). Fort Worth, TX: Harcourt Brace.

Kintz, B. L., Delprato, D. J., Mettee, D. R., Persons, C. E., & Shappe, R. H. (1965). The experimenter effect. *Psychological Bulletin, 63,* 223–232.

Kirk, R. E. (1995). *Experimental design: Procedures for the behavioral sciences.* Pacific Grove, CA: Brooks/Cole.

Kruglanski, A. W. (1975). The human subject in the psychology experiment: Fact and artifact. *Advances in Experimental Social Psychology, 8,* 101–147.

Lana, R. E. (1969). Pretest sensitization. In R. Rosenthal & R. L. Rosnow (Eds.), *Artifact in behavioral research* (pp. 119–141). New York: Academic Press.

Leary, M. R. (2004). *Introduction to behavioral research methods.* Boston: Allyn & Bacon.

McCrady, B. S., & Bux, D. A., Jr. (1999). Ethical issues in informed consent with substance abusers. *Journal of Consulting and Clinical Psychology, 67,* 186–193.

McGuigan, F. J. (1983). *Experimental psychology: Methods of research* (4th ed.). Englewood Cliffs, NJ: Prentice Hall.

Milgram, S. (1974). *Obedience to authority: An experimental view.* New York: Harper & Row.

Murphy, L. L., Impara, J. C., & Plake, B. S. (Eds.). (1999). *Tests in print.* Lincoln, NE: Buros Institute of Mental Measures.

National Bioethics Advisory Commission. (1999, August). *Research involving human biological materials: Ethical issues and policy guidance. Vol. I: Report and recommendations of the National Bioethics Advisory Commission.* Rockville, MD: Author.

National Commission for the Protection of Human Subjects of Biomedical and Behavioral Research. (1979). *The Belmont Report: Ethical principles and guidelines for the protection of human subjects of research.* Washington, DC: U.S. Government Publishing Office.

Neale, J. M., & Liebert, R. M. (1973). *Science and behavior: An introduction to methods of research.* Englewood Cliffs, NJ: Prentice Hall.

NIH policy for data and safety monitoring. (1998). Retrieved July 7, 2004, from http://grants.nih.gov/grants/guide/notice-files/not98-084.html

Nisbett, R. E., & Wilson, T. D. (1977). Telling more than we can know: Verbal reports on mental processes. *Psychological Review, 84,* 231–259.

O'Leary, K. D., Kent, R. N., & Kanowitz, J. (1975). Shaping data collection congruent with experimental hypotheses. *Journal of Applied Behavior Analysis, 8,* 43–51.

Orne, M. T. (1962). On the social psychology of the psychological experiment:

With particular reference to demand characteristics and their implications. *American Psychologist, 17,* 776–783.

Pedhazur, E. J., & Schmelkin, L. P. (1991). *Measurement, design, and analysis: An integrated approach.* Hillsdale, NJ: Lawrence Erlbaum.

Phillips, E. L. (1985). *Psychotherapy revised: New frontiers in research and practice.* Hillsdale, NJ: Lawrence Erlbaum.

Popper, K. (1963). *Conjectures and refutations.* London: Routledge & Kegan Paul.

Quintana, S. M., Troyano, N., & Taylor, G. (2001). Cultural validity and inherent challenges in quantitative methods for multicultural research. In J. G. Ponterotto, J. M. Casas, L. A. Suzuki, & C. M. Alexander (Eds.), *Handbook of multicultural counseling* (2nd ed., pp. 604–630). Thousand Oaks, CA: Sage.

Ray, W. J., & Ravizza, R. (1988). *Methods: Toward a science of behavior and experience* (3rd ed.). Belmont, CA: Wadsworth Publishing Company.

Reid, P. T. (2002). Multicultural psychology: Bringing together gender and ethnicity. *Cultural Diversity and Ethnic Minority Psychology, 8,* 103–114.

Roberts, L. W., & Roberts, B. (1999). Psychiatric research ethics: An overview of evolving guidelines and current ethical dilemmas in the study of mental illness. *Biology and Psychiatry, 46,* 1025–1038.

Rosen, N. A. (1970). Demand characteristics in the field experiment. *Journal of Applied Psychology, 54,* 163–168.

Rosenthal, R., Persinger, G. W., Vikan-Kline, L., & Mulry, R. C. (1963). The role of the research assistant in the mediation of experimenter bias. *Journal of Personality, 31,* 313–335.

Rosenthal, R., & Rosnow, R. L. (Eds.). (1969). *Artifact in behavioral research.* New York: Academic Press.

Rosnow, R. L. (1970). When he lends a helping hand, bite it. *Psychology Today, 4*(1), 26–30.

Rosnow, R. L., & Rosenthal, R. (2002). *Beginning behavioral research: A conceptual primer.* (4th ed.). Upper Saddle River, NJ: Prentice Hall.

Rosnow, R. L., Rosenthal, R., McConochie, R. M., & Arms, R. L. (1969). Volunteer effects on experimental outcomes. *Educational and Psychological Measurement, 29,* 825–846.

Serlin, R. C. (1987). Hypothesis testing, theory building, and the philosophy of science. *Journal of Counseling Psychology, 34,* 365–371.

Shaughnessy, J. J., & Zechmeister, E. B. (1997). *Research methods in psychology* (4th ed.). Boston: McGraw Hill.

Sieber, J. E., & Stanley, B. (1988). Ethical and professional dimensions of socially sensitive research. *American Psychologist, 43,* 49–55.

Sigall, H., Aronson, E., & Van Hoose, T. (1970). The cooperative subject: Myth or reality? *Journal of Experimental Social Psychology, 6,* 1–10.

Spinner, B., Adair, J. G., & Barnes, G. E. (1977). A reexamination of the faithful subject role. *Journal of Experimental Social Psychology, 13,* 543–551.

Stern, J. M., & Simes, R. J. (1997). Publication bias: Evidence of delayed publication in a cohort study of clinical research projects. *British Medical Journal, 315,* 640–645.

Stokes, G. S., Mumford, M. D., & Owens, W. A. (Eds.). (1994). *Biodata handbook: Theory, research, and the use of biographical information in selection and performance prediction.* Palo Alto, CA: Consulting Psychologists Press.

Sudman, S. (1976). *Applied sampling.* New York: Academic Press.

Sugarman, J., McCrory, D. C., & Hubal, R. C. (1998). Getting meaningful informed consent from older adults: A structured literature review of empirical research. *Journal of the American Geriatrics Society, 46,* 517–524.

Sugarman, J., McCrory, D. C., Powell, D., Krasny, A., Adam, B., Ball, E., et al. (1999). Empirical research on informed consent: An annotated bibliography. *The Hastings Center Report, Jan.–Feb.,* S1–S42.

Sullivan, J. L., & Feldman, S. (1979). *Multiple indicators: An introduction.* Beverly Hills, CA: Sage.

Tapert, S. F., & Brown, S. A. (2000). Substance dependence, family history of alcohol dependence and neuropsychological functioning in adolescence. *Addiction, 95,* 1043–1053.

Taub, H. A., Baker, M. T., Kline, G. E., & Sturr, J. F. (1987). Comprehension of informed consent information by young-old through old-old volunteers. *Experimental Aging Research, 13,* 173–178.

Trochim, W. M. K. (2001). *The research methods knowledge base* (2nd ed.). Cincinnati, OH: Atomic Dog Publishing.

Wampold, B. E., Davis, B., & Good, R. H., III. (2003). Hypothesis validity of clinical research. In A. E. Kazdin (Ed.), *Methodological issues and strategies in clinical research* (3rd ed., pp. 389–406). Washington, DC: American Psychological Association.

Weber, S. J., & Cook, T. D. (1972). Subject effects in laboratory research: An examination of subject roles, demand characteristics, and valid inference. *Psychological Bulletin, 77,* 273–295.

White, B. W., & Saltz, E. (1957). Measurement of reproducibility. *Psychological Bulletin, 54,* 81–99.

Winer, B. J. (1971). *Statistical principles in experimental design* (2nd ed.). New York: McGraw Hill.

Yin, R. K. (1994). *Case study research: Design and methods* (2nd ed.). Newbury Park, CA: Sage.

Index

CPSIA information can be obtained
at www.ICGtesting.com
Printed in the USA
BVOW01n1148160317

478497BV00002BA/8/P

9 780471 470533